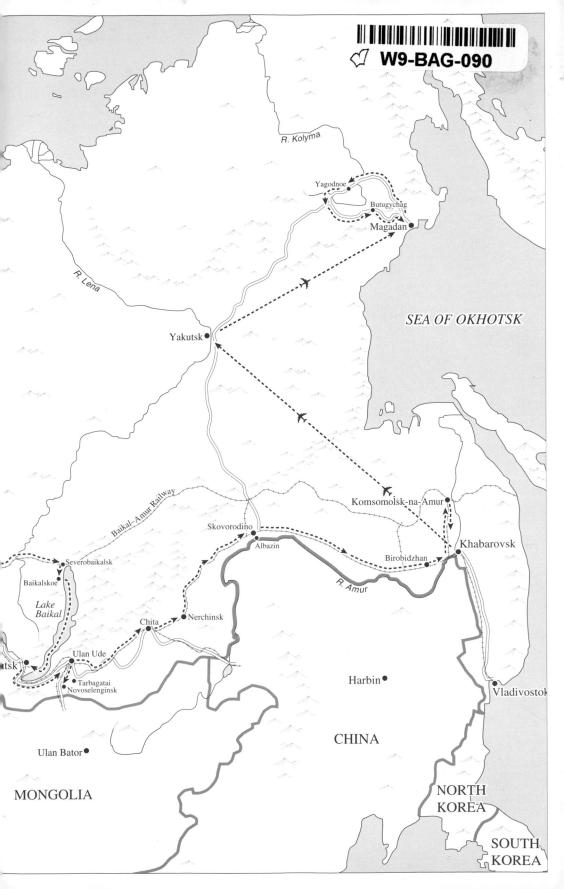

213
−246
−249

IN
SIBERIA

BY THE SAME AUTHOR

IN SIBERIA

COLIN THUBRON

HarperCollins*Publishers*

HarperCollins books may be purchased for educational, business, or sales pro-
motional use. For information please write: Special Markets Department,
HarperCollins Publishers Inc., 10 East 53rd Street, New York, NY 10022.

FIRST U.S. EDITION

Library of Congress Cataloging-in-Publication Data

Thubron, Colin, 1939–
      In Siberia/Colin Thubron.—1st ed.
         p.   cm.
      Includes index.
      ISBN 0-06-019543-6
      1. Siberia (Russia)—Description and travel. 2. Thubron, Colin,
   1939– —Journeys—Russia (Federation)—Siberia. I. Title.
   DK756.2.T48 2000
   957—dc21   99-4136

00 01 02 03 04 ❖/RRD 10 9 8 7 6 5 4 3 2 1

For Margreta

CONTENTS

IN
SIBERIA

I

Hauntings

The ice-fields are crossed for ever by a man in chains. In the farther distance, perhaps, a herd of reindeer drifts, or a hunter makes a shadow on the snow. But that is all. Siberia: it fills one twelfth of the land-mass of the whole Earth, yet this is all it leaves for certain in the mind. A bleak beauty, and an indelible fear.

The emptiness becomes obsessive. Until a few years ago only five towns, scattered along the Trans-Siberian Railway, were open to foreigners under supervision, while Siberia itself receded into rumour. Even now the white spaces induce fantasies and apprehension. There is a place where white cranes dance on the permafrost, where a great city floats lost among the ice-floes, where mammoths sleep under glaciers. And there are places (you could fear) where the terrors of the Gulag secretly continue, and the rocket silos are rebuilding. . . .

Over the Urals the train-wheels putter pathetically, like old men running out of breath. The mountains look too shallow to form a frontier, let alone the divide between Europe and Asia: only a faint upheaval of pine-darkened slopes.

Beyond my window the palisades of conifer and birch part to disclose sleepy villages and little towns by weed-smeared pools. The summer railway banks are glazed with flowers. Beyond them the clearings shut on and off like lantern slides: wooden cottages and vegetable patches boxed in picket fences, and cattle asleep in the grass.

Dusk arrives suddenly, as if this were the frontier also between light and darkness. Siberia is only a few miles away. It sets up a tingle of alarm. I am sliding out of European Russia into somewhere which seems less a country than a region in people's minds, and even at this last moment, everything ahead – the violences of geography and time – feels a little thinned, too cold or vast to be precisely real. It impends through the darkness as the ultimate, unearthly Abroad. The place from which you will not return.

I chose it against my will. I was subverted by the sudden falling open of a vast area of the forbidden world. The immensity of Siberia had shadowed all my Asian journeys. So the casual beginnings – the furtive glance in an atlas – began to nag and deepen, until the wilderness seemed less to be empty than overlooked, or scrawled with invisible ink. Insidiously, it began to infect me.

The Azeri merchant who shares my carriage never looks out of the window. Siberia is dull, he says, and poor. He trades clothes between Moscow and Omsk, and taps continually on a pocket calculator. 'I wouldn't stay long out there,' he says. 'Everything's falling to bits. I'd try China, if I were you. China's the coming place.' He is big and hirsute, thirty-something, and going to seed. After dozing, he checks his face in his shaving-mirror and groans, as if he had expected someone else.

Suddenly in our window there springs up the ghostly obelisk raised by Czar Alexander I nearly two centuries ago. It stands on a low bank, whitened by the glimmer of our train. Here, geographically, Siberia begins. On its near side the plinth proclaims 'Europe', on its far side 'Asia'. It flickers past us, and the darkness comes down again. And nothing, of course, changes. Because the boundary between Europe and Asia is only an imagined one. Physically the continents are undivided. Ancient geographers in the West (itself an artificial concept) perhaps decided one day that here was Europe – the known – and over there was somewhere else, Asia.

So I wait for the change which I know will not happen. In the dark the railway cuttings seem to plunge deeper, and the trees to rush up more vertiginously above them. A few suffocated stars appear. Occasionally the land breaks into valleys slung with faint lights, and once, from the restaurant-car, I see a horizon blanched with the refracted glow of an invisible city.

I don't sleep. The Azeri's snores thunder a yard from my head. Instead, as I scrutinise my maps, I feel alternate waves of exhilaration and unease, so that my eye always returns consolingly to where I am. From here – the mountains west of Yekaterinburg – Siberia stretches eastward more than six thousand miles, and my journey reaches after it, unravelling across seven time-zones and one third of the northern hemisphere. The carriage rocks and murmurs. For the last time, the future looks shapely and whole. It lives in the simplicity of maps. Anything may change it, I know – the collapse of transport, the intrusion of the police or harassment by mafia. But for the moment my eye bathes in the mountains enchaining the south for three thousand miles, then travels along three of the world's greatest rivers – the Ob, Yenisei, Lena – which pour down from the borders of Mongolia to the Arctic Ocean. Each of their basins is bigger than western Europe. Then comes Lake Baikal, deepest and oldest of all inland waters; the Amur river abutting China; the snow-fields of Kolyma, where the temperature drops to a meaningless −97°F. . . . These prodigies flow in seductive and dangerous procession to the Pacific – and suddenly the distances seem hopeless, and I wonder where I'll have to stop.

For this is Russia's Elsewhere. Long before Communism located the future in an urban paradise, Siberia was a rural waste into which were cast the bacilli infecting the state body: the criminal, the sectarian, the politically dissident. Yet paradoxically, over the centuries, it was seen as a haven of primitive innocence and salvation, and peasants located their *Belovodye* here, their Promised Land. So sometimes the censure of Siberian savagery would be reversed into applause for its freedom, and its inhabitants praised as pioneering supermen, uncontaminated by the rot in the bones of Europe. Now, as Moscow succumbs to the contagion of the West, Siberia becomes a pole of purity and authentic 'Russianness'. I heard rumours that it might secede from western Russia altogether, or fracture into independent provinces. What, I wondered, had replaced its shattered Communist faith?

Across the lower part of my map, the Trans-Siberian Railway is slung like a hammock cradling something of pallid inconsequence. Perhaps it is the snail's-pace of the train – it moves at an unchanging 50 m.p.h. – that touches me with anxiety. Because now the region's statistics are staring me in the face, radiating from under my feet. Everything seems inaccessibly distant. If Siberia were detached from Russia, it would remain by far the largest country on earth. At almost five million square miles, it is bigger than the United States, including Alaska, and western Europe combined. As the sun is rising over the Urals, it is setting on the Bering Sea. My journey, I fear, will vanish in it.

It is perversely shocking, the calm and handsome Yekaterinburg. A seriousness, even an austerity, pervades it. But the city founded as a mining centre by Peter the Great in 1723, and named after the adulterous servant-girl he crowned his empress, is too ferocious in memory to feel serene. In 1918 the last Czar and his family were slaughtered in one of its cellars. During the Second World War, hundreds of dismantled factories from western Russia were reassembled here against the Germans, and its biological and weapons plants flourished (and leaked) until the Soviet collapse depleted them.

I walked here in apprehension. It was seventeen years since I'd travelled far in Russia (and never in Siberia) and now I gazed round as if with weak vision, waiting for the return of what I remembered. It was very quiet. The avenues opened under a soft, midsummer light. There were public buildings in the stuccoed fawn and white of St Petersburg, and double-jointed Hungarian buses wandered from one boulevard corner to another.

I felt light-headed. I kept expecting something to happen. I couldn't shake off a lingering disquiet, even guilt. It came, I knew, from another era: from the Brezhnev years, when I had been dogged through the western Soviet Union by the KGB. My footfalls sounded light and exposed to me. But now nothing disturbed or followed them. People were out walking their dogs – it was Sunday. A pair of boyish soldiers were sweeping leaves in their barracks, and some caparisoned droshkies were trotting up and down as they had in the nineteenth century. On Central Avenue (formerly Lenin Street) the crowds looked dreamy and anonymous: pale-eyed men in track-suits or jeans, women in loose-fitting dresses. Nobody stared at me. I felt as if I had disappeared under the membrane of the city, dressed with the same indifferent shabbiness as everyone else – black trousers, grey shirt – my head cropped into a proletarian hedgehog, my rucksack unnoticed among the knapsacks around me. Speaking bad Russian, I hoped to pass for an Estonian.

In the city centre half the street-names had been changed. Old Bolshevik favourites – Lunacharsky, Kuybyshev, Rosa Luxemburg – had gone; and in their place were poets and writers or bland safeguards such as Central and Siberia Prospect. But whenever I asked the way it was the old, Communist names that fluttered to people's lips. And in an island in ex-Lenin Street the statue of Yakov Sverdlov survived: he who organised the Czar's murder, and gave his name to the city for seventy years. He stood thin and young on an artificial rock. His body seemed wrenched by a fit of anger. Once his statue had enshrined the force of an impassioned idea; but now, with that power faded, it seemed to depict only a frenetic student. Someone had splashed over the legs a bucket of crimson paint which dribbled down the rock.

From time to time a surge of colour or dash of style mesmerised me. There was colour in the streetside kiosks and markets, and everywhere an intrusion of once-heretical names: Lancome, Levis, Proctor & Gamble.... People passed wearing US army forage caps, or baseball hats marked 'Montana' or 'Chicago Bulls'. Groups of young women in miniskirts, with sleepy, wide-set eyes, were clopping along the pavements on platform shoes and long, willowy legs. Where had their parents been in Brezhnev's time, I wondered. I remembered nobody like them. The rooftop slogans which once glorified the Party now advertised insurance companies ('Your dependable partner'). Trams went by blazoned 'Pepsi' or 'Enjoy Coca-Cola'. For this was a city which was holding its own in the New Russia, nested in a region rich in natural resources. Its governor was an ardent reformist. Its mafia chiefs, when they were murdered, were embalmed expensively in Moscow before returning for burial.

I wondered if I had imagined the blank public gaze of twenty years ago, when nobody in the street acknowledged you. My memories were slipping and eliding. Yet from the faces around me some veil, I was sure, had dropped away. They were placid, but no longer absent. Sometimes they argued or sang. And still others were openly dispossessed. They sat with heads bowed over their unfolded palms, motionless, and sometimes dangled placards explaining their homelessness, beginning: 'Dear People . . .' A man I had seen everywhere in the old Soviet Union – a drunk in seedy middle age – had lurched into sharper focus. I thought of him as Ivan. His eyes were smeared over, and the creases of his face trickled down into hopelessness. He looked both angrier and more futile than when I remembered him. Now he was out of work, and sometimes buttonholed me for money.

But my old unease was draining away. Once, half from habit, I stopped among parkland trees to check if anyone was following me. My breathing, I noticed, had quickened in the sultry quiet. After five minutes a pretty woman with a fat terrier went by. Then nobody. They don't care, I thought: they are engaged in industrial espionage, or they've joined the mafia. Or they've joined Ivan.

I went back into the confusing streets. I was looking for sign-posts, I knew. I couldn't imagine a Russia without destiny. So I was hunting for symptoms of a new faith or identity, but hunting impatiently, as people do on first arriving somewhere, hoping for talismans, for simple meanings. Hundreds of homemade advertise-ments and posters fluttered from walls or trees, and I read them like runic clues. They offered slimming courses, transcendental meditation, English lessons. Psychologists promised release from communication problems. Others offered work. 'Turn to us. . . . Take off thirty kilos. . . . Discover your future. . . . Master everything. . . .'

I wandered into a show called 'People of Moment': twenty waxworks which circled an exhibition hall. Socrates and Leonardo da Vinci were followed by Genghis Khan dressed as a Chinese mandarin, and by the gangling giant Peter the Great. But later came no Marx, no Lenin. Instead the ballerina Plisetskaya contemplated her ankle, while Elvis Presley elbowed Freddie Mercury, and Arnold Schwarzenegger flexed beside Dracula.

Now anything seemed possible. In my empty guest-house, once the haven of Party members, I asked about the region's vaunted independence from Moscow, as if I were enquiring after a hotel guest. Yekaterinburg had its own flag, after all – a white, green and black tricolour – and plans (I'd read) for its own currency, the Ural franc. But behind the reception desk three faces lifted towards mine in identical surprise. 'Oh that! Every province has its own flag now, that's nothing! Who's ever seen a Ural franc?' The faces crumpled and tittered. 'Independence is just a game of the governor's!'

And they burst into laughter.

But one place lies starkly empty. It is in an old quarter opposite the cream and turquoise tower of the Ascension Church, whose cross the imprisoned family could sometimes glimpse from their windows. The house of the merchant Ipatiev is nothing now but a sheet of crumpled tarmac and a tangled copse. In 1977, on Brezhnev's orders, it was bulldozed away by the local Party boss, Boris Yeltsin (who later called this a 'senseless decision'), for fear it become a place of pilgrimage.

A skeletal canopy now rises where a memorial church will be, and a white cross stands over the site where Czar Nicholas II, his empress, children and last servants were butchered in the merchant's cellar. Two weeks before, the boorish Bolshevik shock-troops who guarded them had been replaced by a secret police squad, and they began to be afraid. White forces were closing in on Yekaterinburg, and a letter had been smuggled in promising rescue by loyal officers. But the letter was forged. And at midnight on 16 July the family was awoken and ordered to dress and come downstairs. Nicholas carried his haemophiliac son, whose arms were clasped round his neck. Anastasia carried her dog.

Now a trickle of pilgrims was coming and going, and one or two lingered under the canopy, hysterical or obsessed. An old couple stood side by side, unfolded prayer-books and sang for over an hour, she in a whining plainsong, he in a tragic whisper, and crossed themselves with trembling fingers. A mournful Armenian returned here again and again, he said, thinking about his father. 'My father was sent to the Kolyma camps, and my mother too. The years in Kolyma killed him. Stalin killed him.' His eyes swam over the undulating ground – gravel and weeds sloping west where the cellar window had opened just above the earth. 'It was criminal, it was terrible what he suffered,' he cried. He had conflated his father's fate with the Czar's. He came here, he said, because he was sick at heart. 'I just feel ill here.' A purple rash was boiling over his neck. He wanted to feel ill, I think. He felt better feeling ill. 'My family were aristocrats, like the Romanovs, so they were destroyed. Now that Russia's thrown out Communism, she'll go back to what she was. That's the future. You see, everything returns. . . .'

The family waits, as if for a photograph. The empress, ill with sciatica, is seated beside her thirteen-year-old son. The rest are standing – the Czar in front, and the four princesses in the first row, the doctor and three servants behind. The cellar is less than 13 feet square. In the doorway the execution-squad is packed in three ranks with heavy revolvers, so close that the powder burns their wrists. The Czar is killed instantly, and the empress and her eldest daughter never complete the sign of the cross. The diamonds sewn secretly into the princesses' corsets send bullets ricocheting round the room. For a moment they seem endowed with a ghastly immortality. The panicking guards empty their revolvers into them, then club and stab everyone still moving. When the smoke clears, the Czarevitch is still clinging to his father's shirt; and as her body is being dragged away on a sheet, one of the princesses wakes and screams. Perhaps she imagines a nightmare. They bayonet her to death.

The quiet of this empty space is the quiet of enforced forgetting. In Communist propaganda the dead Czar declined from a blood-thirsty tyrant into a spineless simpleton. Then he disappeared from history. Now, in the void where the Ipatiev house stood, his fate seemed to shed its politics and become the personal tragedy of a gentle but stubborn man, his wilful wife and sheltered children.

I walked for a while in its sadness. A splash of colour came from three beds of marigolds and Michaelmas daisies. A sightseeing bus arrived, but the only person to dismount was a young woman. She tiptoed across the gravel, and handed me her camera. 'Will you shoot me?' I expected her to stand smiling, but instead she flushed her long hair out over her shoulders, then knelt down on the tarmac at the foot of the white cross. There, in profile, she remained praying and crossing herself for long minutes, while I wondered how many snapshots she wanted.

'Thank you, thank you.' She took the camera and then my hand. 'Olga.'

This was the name of the Czar's eldest daughter. Perhaps she had been praying for her. 'I'm Colin.'

'Colin, Nikolai!' – the Russians always linked the names, one a diminutive of the other. She sent me a disconnected smile, then stared round her. 'Look at this, look at this.'

'It's been destroyed.'

'And our ruler did this.' From fear or disgust, she would not say Yeltsin.

'But everything's changed now,' I said, for some reason comforting her. 'There'll be a church here, and they will be made saints.' Their canonisation, I thought, was only a matter of time.

She flared almost angrily. 'They are already saints! They head the saints in the cathedral of heaven!' She spoke with lilting, passionate certainty. 'It's only here, in Russia, that we've been slow to know this. The Russian Church abroad canonised them long ago. Abroad the Mother of God took them up to heaven!'

I nodded vaguely, wondering how she knew.

'And not only Nikolai and his Czarina, but his whole family, she took them up, Aleksei, Olga, Tatiana . . . and those others, Doctor Botkin and the servants who died because of compassion for them!'

'Your Patriarch in Moscow . . .'

'I don't know about our Patriarch. I don't know him. I've heard that someone has even verified their bones, but I don't know. . . .'

She lifted her eyes to the sky. She did not care for any mortal remains. The family was living in the heaven of her will. 'In the church where I worship, the Mother of God has told St John the Baptist that they are her ladies-in-waiting, her favourite children . . . Olga also, who protects and prays for me. . . .'

I thought doubtfully of the shy, capricious Olga, but the woman continued in a rush of celestial detail. John the Baptist, the Czar, Olga, the Virgin Mary . . . the throne-rooms and antechambers of heaven filled up like those of the Winter Palace, astir with favourites and intercessors. Her voice bustled and sang. Twice she called me Nikolai, and I felt flattered. 'Now they all live in the courtyard of the Mother of God, and send our prayers to her. *Direct*.'

On the edge of the desolation a tiny chapel had been raised to the Czarina's favourite sister, the pious Elizabeth, who was martyred when the Bolsheviks threw her alive down a mineshaft. Years before, she had enchanted the French ambassador by her beauty and innocent seriousness, and after her husband, the Grand Duke Sergei, was blown to bits in the abortive 1905 revolution, she founded an order of nuns to care for the dying and abandoned. Now she was a saint.

Under her chapel cupola, sheathed in wooden scales and topped by a high cross, we entered a sanctuary blazing with votive candle-flames, and Olga prayed to an icon of St Elizabeth floating in glory above her mineshaft.

'We'd lost all that history until now,' she said. 'For years we lived in a dark valley – twenty million gone in the last war, and forty million more taken by Stalin. And nothing in return! Only in 1991 the Mother of God gave back the truth which Communism had concealed for eighty years.'

Her eyes glittered over me unfocused as she replaced the Soviet myth with her own. The next moment we were standing, astonished, where a sheaf of flickering lights enshrined an icon of the imperial family, newly done: they had already been turned into saints. Olga set her taper before them with shaking hands, crying: 'There they are!' Her kisses fell softly on their painted hems and slippered feet. I examined them in fascination. In their icon they had acquired the elongated bodies and court robes of Byzantine saints, and their tapering hands held up white crosses. Crowned and haloed, they seemed to gaze out with a sad foreknowledge of their end. Their features echoed one another's, as in some inbred clan, and they were all washed in the same amber light. All the vitality of remembered photographs – the moods and stains of real life – was emptied and stilled. Sainthood did not allow for them. Even the emergent individuality of the princesses – the imperious beauty Tatiana, the plump tomboy Anastasia – was drowned in this mist of holiness.

Olga said: 'Soon, Nikolai, there will be a resurrection of the Church.'

'You mean a new czar?' It was barely conceivable. Two years before, a young Romanov claimant had travelled to Russia with his mother, and been received with bewilderment and official circumspection.

'No, not a czar.' Even Olga demurred. 'But a celestial union. The Church on earth will be united with the Church in Heaven! Soon, very soon!' Her voice started its hypnotic music again. 'Light for the future of humanity!'

I said dully: 'When?'

'At any moment! Because now the Mother of God wants to carry Russia upward. Quickly, quickly Russia is going to the light! Perhaps it will happen through grief. Then the heart of Russia will open! A new, holy Russia!'

It was an old Orthodox idea: that suffering would flower into purity. Out of the anguish of history – even of daily, Chekhovian frustration – a new world must be born. It made sense of sorrow, of tedium. It made suffering dangerously embraceable. It seemed to heal Time.

On the night of the murders the corpses were driven into woods twenty miles from the city. There they were stripped naked – the girls' corsets oozing jewels – and lowered into a flooded mine. But the next evening they were dredged up again and taken towards a remoter site. When the lorry that carried them broke down, two of the corpses were painstakingly burnt and the rest heaped into a shallow grave and doused with acid. Yekaterinburg fell to the White army a week later.

The Whites found the Czarevitch's spaniel wandering half-starved in the Ipatiev garden. But when they located the mine they discovered no bodies: little but the doctor's false teeth, a finger of the empress, and the medallions of Rasputin which the princesses had worn round their necks.

Only in 1991 was the impromptu grave fully excavated. Then a forensic scientist from Moscow's Ministry of Health reassembled the skeletons, and DNA testing on samples from living relatives proved whose bones these were. The missing two were Aleksei and the third daughter, Maria.

For a long time the rest lay in fragments on a tin table in a Yekaterinburg morgue. Then they were buried with small ceremony in the imperial mausoleum in St Petersburg. Their obsequies divided Church and State, even the Romanov heirs. At the service, their names were never mentioned, for the Church, pandering to the Russian Orthodox abroad, refused to acknowledge whom they were burying. Their canonisation has become a political and ecclesiastical minefield. It is the living, now, who will not rest in peace.

Behind the vanished Ipatiev house is a medley of trees and shrubs long ago gone wild. Here, under the eyes of their guards, Nicholas would carry the Czarevitch out to a chair, then walk for half an hour with his daughters in the garden. In these last weeks, he wrote, the scent from orchards all around was overpowering.

A path went through the trees – less a man-made track, it seemed, than the spoor of some animal. I followed it idly, and arrived where a broken ladder crossed to a rubbish-tip. My feet snagged on wires and bottles. For all I knew some fragments of the Ipatiev house were here, whose bulk had ended up on the municipal dump. But an eerie sense of habitation touched the place. Around me someone had festooned the trees with carrier-bags – twenty or thirty of them – all rotted and split. They drooped from the branches like dead bats. In the dump's crater, bits of debris had returned to their old use: a defunct stove set with dented kettles, a sodden sofa facing a broken chair, two shoes decomposing side by side. And a campfire was guttering.

At first I thought it the play-house of a child, but from above me a voice bellowed: 'Get the fuck out of here!'

He seemed very small, and bent, and old. Either through weakness or drink he half fell through the trees towards me, then recovered. His features were nested in white hair, and as he straightened, his eyes snapped open. 'Oh, it's you! I thought you were one of those officials. But' – and his voice turned quite tender, blurred by drink – 'it's you. You've come back.'

My words rang polite in the rubbish-dump: 'It's the first time we've met.'

But he didn't hear. 'Sit down! . . . not there, that's wet . . . find some rags.'

I perched on the chair, and he on the sofa. Already the damp was leaking through my trousers. It had thundered and poured all night, and his shelter of canvas and branches lay collapsed nearby. 'The water came in everywhere. It put out the fire after you left, and I didn't sleep. . . .' Then his black eyes refocused me, and he realised I was a stranger. He said: 'The bastard, I knew he wouldn't come back.' His shoulders hunched. 'In September I'll go away too. It's terrible here in winter. The frost clutches you. If you take my advice, you'll go south in the autumn.' He fingered the points of the compass in mid-air. 'I'll go to Rostov, to the Black Sea. . . .'

'Alone?'

'Yes,' he said. 'You too, alone?'

'Well, yes.'

'My wife and son are up in Archangel. We . . . well, she . . .' His words trailed into privacy. Then he asked ceremoniously: 'Would you like lunch?'

So we sat there, he on the sofa-springs, I on the three-legged chair, while a rusty pan of potatoes bubbled over the fire. Around us spread a sea of scrap-iron and rags, splintered furniture, gutted machinery and pots. We enquired about one another. He found a jar of green peas awash with rainwater and forked them fastidiously out. I passed him some English sweets. Once he plumped up a tattered cushion for me, then reached into a box of sodden magazines and offered me a ten-year-old copy of *The Orthodox Times*; and twice we toasted one another in vodka, rather formally.

I asked him about his family and work. He seemed so old, I thought, it must all be long ago. He answered in a code of hints and omissions. Locked in his rough quiet, an urban delicacy survived. From time to time he let out a long, guttural *Errrr*, which seemed to comfort and stabilise him. 'Maybe I committed crimes during my marriage, I suppose I did. Now God go with her . . . she lives alone.' He prodded the potatoes with a soft *Err, errr.* 'That's how it is. Both of us, alone.' His tone showed no regret or pleasure: solitude was simply a fact of life, perhaps its law.

I said: 'You're used to that?'

He looked vacantly round him. 'My father was killed in the war, I never knew him. And my mother died in the factory when I was thirteen. An electric cable fell on her. And then my sister brought me up, and I sat with her when she died just as I'm sitting with you now, for a long time. I was nineteen then, in 1958. . . . *Errr.*'

With a shock I realised that he was the same age as me. For a second I gaped at his features, then at his scarred hands, their nails black and worn to the quick, and up again at his face, and for a moment saw in that tangled froth of hair and beard my own mortality. Then I grew confused. Sometimes his face seemed a trembling wreck in its tempest of hair. But his voice was strong, and at other times the delta of lines radiating down his cheeks appeared to reverse its course and fill his eyes with mirth, or even contempt.

I said: 'How long have you been travelling then?'

He answered at once: 'Thirty-four years. I began in Khrushchev's day, in the hard times.'

'But those times were better than before.'

'No, not better. Stalin's time was better! I've seen his villa on the Black Sea, where he used to sit in battledress smoking his pipe!' He swelled back on the sofa and bent his cheap cigarette into an imaginary pipe. 'That was a man who didn't insult the people! It's a lie that he made Russian life a misery. In his day a man in prison was better off than a free man now. And today the prisons are still overflowing. You can get sentenced for nothing.' He jabbed a thumb back and forth between us. 'You steal my bag, and you go to prison! Five years! . . . *Errr* . . . I steal somebody else's bag, and – prison!'

I heard myself say: 'You did that?'

'Yes.' No change of tone interrupted him. 'I sneaked off with someone's carrier-bag. I got five years. And that's the minimum, I might have got ten.'

I glanced up involuntarily at the trees. A wind had sprung up and was swinging the rotted carrier-bags in the branches, and rustling papers over the waste-tip. I said: 'And now you have as many as you like?'

'Oh those, yes.' But he went silent, as if wondering himself why he had hung them there. Then he said: 'That prison was the cell system. I was in with rapists and murderers. . . . But others had done nothing.' He wiped a chipped plate with a rag, and speared me two potatoes. 'It was like home.'

'Home?'

'Somewhere to sleep and get food. It was better there.' He was suddenly depressed. 'You could watch television there. And here there's nothing. Here you have to find food.'

'You watched television in prison?'

'All night, sometimes, in the camp. I went on to a camp, where I worked at a lathe, then a metal press. After that I took to the road. I used to watch television through people's windows. Sometimes I did manual work to keep alive. But being on the move, that's the thing! Central Asia, Latvia, the Ukraine . . . I've been to all of them. But then the years came, and my legs swelled.'

I felt a naive surprise. So even in Brezhnev's time this gypsy life had continued, the life of people who moved beyond official sight, migrating with the seasons, by roads and systems of their own.

He poured me a tumbler of vodka. 'Somebody wrote that to walk our Russian countryside is to see a land of miracles. Just like in Turgenev's time! I've been in parts like that, without even tractors. Those were the good days, a century ago. People lived simply then, gathering mushrooms and berries. . . .'

The vodka was tipping him into paradise, a bucolic summer that had never been. He filled my tumbler again. 'To Turgenev!' Then he clambered to his feet and struggled over a ramp of garbage to hunt among the sticks and canvas of his fallen hut. At last he drew out a bunch of dahlias and handed them to me.

'Where on earth did you get these?'

His eyes avoided mine. 'Well, people grow them . . . then they . . . bring them.'

I knew he had pilfered them from the memorial cross. Pilgrims often left flowers there; on weekends, he said, wedding parties brought bouquets, and sometimes shared their vodka. Squatting like nemesis in the ruined garden, he stole the flowers overnight.

'Here,' he said, 'take them. Put them in your room.' He thrust them against my chest.

I said woodenly: 'They were meant for the Czar's family.'

He blinked at me. 'That family . . . they shot them all, didn't they?' He looked down at the dahlias as if they had turned to ash. He was very drunk. 'They shouldn't have done that, the bastards. Children are the flower of life!' He tossed the bouquet stubbornly into my lap. 'If people ask "Was the Czar a good man?" I always say "Yes! He gave the people food!" Wonderful man, the Czar was. . . .'

The vodka closed his eyes, and he grew grateful for everything. The Czar might not measure up to Stalin, but he had become the benefactor of the poor and vagrant, and his dahlias still served. By the time I got up to leave, the hermit had reeled back on to the sofa, his beard and cigarette jutting at the sky.

I wondered what to leave him. I had brought from England some souvenir key-rings and two solar calculators. But this man had nothing to add up, nothing to lock up. I laid some money near his head, and went back through the trees. After a while his voice echoed: 'You'll come back tomorrow? I'll make a proper campfire! You'll come?'

Back over the littered earth, his cries sounding after me – 'God give you health! Good health!' – I tried to find sense in his presence there, to believe it other than accident; but I heard instead the soulless twittering of sparrows in the branches among the carrier-bags, and somewhere in the thicket, from eighty years before, imagined other footsteps.

*　　*　　*

At the Paris Universal Exposition in 1900, visitors crowding into the Palace of Russian Arts could board a lavish replica of the half-completed Trans-Siberian Railway. Each compartment of the *wagons-lits* was served by a marble-lined washroom with a porcelain bath, and lounges done up in Louis XVI or Empire style adjoined Moorish or chinoiserie smoking-rooms. While multilingual waiters served caviar and bortsch in the restaurant-car, a diorama of Siberia, painted by scenic artists from the Paris Opera, was wound slowly past the windows in an illusion of snug villages and eternal forest.

Many of these luxuries never materialised. The hairdressing salon in white sycamore and the ice-box air-cooling system survived only in the Parisian memory, and travellers reported variously that poor food was doled out by clottish waiters, and that the only bath-tub was to be found in the baggage car, where it had been requisitioned for meat storage. Yet in general the de luxe wagons were ponderously palatial, and within fourteen years of the railway's foundation in 1891 they were rumbling along the Pacific. Reaching five and a half thousand miles from the Urals to Vladivostok, they travelled by far the longest railway in the world.

These vaunted trains, with their expensive cargo of merchants, diplomats and adventurers, were interspersed by others – more important – which went almost unrecorded. Chains of cattle-trucks, lugged by primitive, wood-burning engines, crawled over the Urals and far into the steppeland. Stacked on three tiers of shelves, or crammed into wagons labelled '40 people or 8 horses', went a horde of migrating peasantry. Some wagons became moving farmyards as three-generation families decamped wholesale with their cattle, fowl and angry dogs haunch-deep in excrement. The few foreigners who glimpsed them described a verminous, pale-faced multitude huddled in fetid sheepskins, and whole wagon-loads of single men, barefoot and half-savage.

This onset of migrants before the First World War was the climax of an eastward trickle which had been going on for three centuries and which had given Siberia its peculiar personality. In the wake of the sixteenth-century Cossack bands trading in the 'soft gold' of furs, came farmers and hunters, vagabonds and religious dissenters, whom European Russia either threatened or cramped. Sometimes encouraged, sometimes impeded, restless and ambitious peasants filtered into the limitless state lands to settle. Many were in flight from serfdom; others were in exile; but it was land-hunger, in the end, which drove most from the oppressive, sometimes famine-stricken central provinces in the west, and the abolition of serfdom in 1861 turned the trickle to a steady flow. For long months they laboured eastward beside horse-drawn carts heaped with household goods and sentimental treasures, and many died along the way. Only at the century's end did the railway ease their passage, and carried in such a tide of poorer peasantry that in less than twenty years Siberia's population had doubled to ten million.

So the region became Russia's Wild East. It was born out of optimism and dissent. The power of the landowning nobility and of the Church died over its huge distances, where the immigrant carved out all the estate he needed, sometimes subsidised by the Crown, and held it as his own. Serfdom was illegal here. The only landowner who tried to enforce it, wrote a traveller, was instantly murdered. 'God is high up and the Czar is far off', the Siberians said, and their native aristocracy comprised not the corrupt bureaucrats sent out from St Petersburg (whom they despised as 'ink-souls') but their own rustic, self-made, and sometimes vastly wealthy merchant-adventurers.

So the Siberians' solitude set them free. Like their American counterparts whose mythology they shared, they were hardy realists and egalitarians, self-reliant and open-handed. They were stupendous eaters and profligate drinkers, and if they came into money they might blow it all in a string of suicidal alcoholic debauches, ending in penury or murder. Society was more flexible than in the west, and dangerous. The country had always been a dumping-ground for criminals, and a vigorous exile culture permeated it, from urban socialites with shadowy beginnings to gangs of escapees who garrotted wayfarers.

By the start of the twentieth century this was the burgeoning Siberia which the swifter population shifts and mass deportations of the future were to dilute. Its rough democratic society, warned the prime minister Stolypin in 1910, might one day come west and crush them all.

The cheaper Trans-Siberian carriages – open dormitory-cars with bunk-lined corridors – bring to mind the untidy migrations of the past as I lumber east towards Tyumen. The railway moves along a gauge uniquely wide, and its wagons run high and tottering, like state rooms on the move. Instead of swaying, they gently, soporifically bounce, and lull the passengers into a slovenly torpor. The Siberians colonise wherever they are. Their clothes dangle from every strut and hook. Their picnics litter the cubicle tables in a jumble of bottled fruit, dried fish and tea.

I lie like an early migrant on a corridor bunk pressed close against the ceiling, and stare through its grimy window. The Urals are slipping behind us in forested shadows thrown low across the horizon, substanceless. Rain is falling like a mist. And slowly the West Siberian Plain surrounds us with the watery infinity that since the last Ice Age has slumbered here between the Arctic and Central Asia. Early Siberians imagined that in mid-creation this muddle of earth and water had been forgotten by God.

But beneath it lie the richest oil-fields in the world.

I sit above the Tura river, a distant tributary of the Ob, and think of Georg Steller, who died here. Behind me the wooden mansions and churches of the oldest town in Siberia, Tyumen, founded by Cossacks in 1586, nudge along the bank in a procession of rustic vanity. A few fishermen stand in silhouette under the bridge, and beneath me a glacis of unhewn stone shores up the curve of the river, where the current has bitten away the earth, and eaten Steller's grave.

Of all the prodigies nurtured by Siberia, this German naturalist, ignored in his lifetime, was one of the most brilliant. By the time he died – fanatical and friendless – after years of Arctic travel in the service of Russia, he had discovered and classified a host of new plants and shrubs, with an astonishing variety of hitherto unknown mammals, birds and fish. The spectacled cormorant which he annotated – an ungainly dumpling with useless wings – is now extinct, and Steller's White Raven has never been seen again. But Steller's Sea-Lion, Steller's Eider, the beautiful Steller's Jay and Steller's Greenling – an iridescent marine trout – still exist; and so, perhaps, does the white-headed Steller's Sea-Eagle, bigger than the Golden, although it has only twice been sighted since. But Steller's sea-monkey, which reared upright in the water and gazed at his ship's crew in the moonlight as they crossed the Bering Sea, was either a bachelor fur-seal or something still unknown.

In 1741, during Bering's Great Northern Expedition, Steller became the first white man to set foot on Alaska. Soon after the crew had been half decimated by scurvy, and Bering himself laid under the frozen soil, Steller was rigging up a driftwood shelter and notating in scrupulous Latin a colony of beasts now known as Steller's Sea-Cow. These giant manatees shared an ancient ancestry with the elephant, and were cousins to the dugong (and so to the mermaid). But they survive only in Steller's meticulous notes, for they were exterminated by hunters within thirty years. Wallowing among beds of weed, they grazed like cattle over the sea-bed, moving dreamily forward on hoofed forelegs, and gluttonously oblivous of danger, so that sometimes Steller could stroke them. They might measure up to 35 feet long, and weigh four tons, yet were touchingly anthropomorphic. In mating, he wrote, they embraced like humans, and whenever the starving crew harpooned one, the others would rush to its aid and try to snap the rope or dash out the hook with their tails.

But Steller never lived to see his name immortalised for the anatomical analyses he left behind. Hounded by a lawsuit from officials whom he had offended, haunted by the wild wife he had left in St Petersburg, and sick with alcoholism, he died in Tyumen at the age of thirty-seven, and was buried on a bluff above the river. But robbers dug him up, leaving the body a prey to wolves, and a few days later some natives reinterred him beneath a boulder. Over many years the river, gnawing at the bank beneath my feet, undermined the grave and swept it into the Arctic, where Steller's Sea-Cow was already extinct.

I hitch a lift to the village of Pokrovskoe, sixty miles to the northeast. The truck-driver had never seen an Englishman before, and bellowed genially about Big Ben and Sherlock Holmes. Pokrovskoe was the village where Rasputin was born, but it looked deserted. The main street was a rutted cart-track scarred wide between cottages plunged in unkempt gardens. It was typical, I guessed, of half the villages ahead of me: rambling hutments which the surrounding emptiness seems to have shaken loose over the steppes. The next wind, I felt, might dust it from the earth.

The truck-driver had known the place before, and swore that a relative of Rasputin survived here. But the only people in sight were some old women seated strategically on benches at street crossroads. At the mention of a man resembling Rasputin they waved us in varying directions, until we arrived outside a ramshackle house with closed shutters, and a voice inside cried out: 'Viktor!'

Perhaps he had been warned of our approach, because he was dressed for the part. As he loped towards us across his vegetable patch, even the truck-driver was taken aback. All the photographs of Rasputin that I had seen sprang to shocking life in his face. He was like a ghastly distillation. He wore the belted peasant smock of an earlier time, and the loose-fitting boots, and his black beard splayed down untrimmed. It was a conscious act of theatre. Greasy locks of hair dangled round his shoulders and divided across his forehead in two bands; and enshrined in this black halo, the remembered face with its heavy nose and pale eyes watched us with a kind of naive cunning.

The truck-driver said: 'Are you his grandson then?'

'There aren't any relatives left, officially. But my great-grandmother was Rasputin's maid. She helped in the house.' His voice was melodious and cynical. 'I think she sinned with him.' He touched his hair and beard. Rasputin's sin had become his glory. 'That is why I look like this.'

He took my arm with the same confusing intimacy reported of his notional great-grandfather, and asked what he could do for me. I answered automatically: 'I need a room for the night.' Mentally I divested Viktor's face of its props – the beard, the contrived slicks of hair – and still, I was sure, an extraordinary likeness remained. He emanated the dissoluteness and guile of his idol too, and perhaps cultivated them, together with the same intermittent tenderness. But there was no authority in him.

The villagers seemed to shun him. The truck-driver went away. Viktor was living with his sister and brother-in-law, because his own house was a wreck. When he asked them to accommodate me for the night, I glimpsed through the slats of the fence an angry-faced peasant kneeling waist-deep among his cabbages, and a bitter-looking wife, and soon above Viktor's pleas, suddenly whining, a harsh voice told him to fuck off.

He returned smiling, and petitioned three old women seated in the softening sunlight. I stood beside him as if I were being auctioned. They were the babushkas of cliche: matriarchs with a stout, vegetable calm, in flowery skirts and felt slippers. They looked me over with misgiving. One of them turned a creaseless, rather childlike face to mine, and said: 'I'm afraid of men!' But the others burst out laughing, and she took me in.

But Viktor would not let me go yet. He conducted me about his village, bathing in the prestige of a foreigner. The dirt road swept 20 yards wide beneath our feet – a great rutted void, too big for the scattering of cottages. Mud streets drifted in and out of it, and the Tura river snaked through meadows beyond. A few farmers had appeared in the quiet evening, or were working their vegetable patches. They looked desperately poor: ill-nourished men with grizzled heads, faces louche and exhausted, and heavy, enduring women. They acknowledged Viktor reluctantly or not at all. In his half-mocking theft of Rasputin's identity, he seemed to occupy the timeless role of the village *yurodivy*, who played with God and simulated foolishness. He made people uneasy. In

Rasputin's day the settlement had been busier than now, alive with summer water-traffic, and prosperous.

'It was full of Rasputins then,' said Viktor. 'Thirty-three families. But at the start of collectivisation in 1929 they disappeared – they were rich, you see, kulaks – so they were taken off in convoys to exile, or they died. There are still Rasputin families to the north somewhere . . . but the real relatives, they're gone.' From time to time he would clasp my arm and stop, his breath warm and close over my face. His silky smile said: *Only I am left.* 'And you see that mound? That's where the church was, the tallest building here. They destroyed it after the war. The masonry was so strong it took them over three months. That's where Rasputin wanted to sing.' His voice fell to a soft, transfigured bass:

> 'We have seen the true light
> And welcomed in the heavenly spirit. . . .

But the clergy hated him.'

I asked: 'Is there anyone left who remembers him?'

'There was an old woman who used to cut the grass in his garden, but she died last year. She always said he was kind. And that's the memory he's left here. Whenever he came back from St Petersburg there was a village holiday. He usually came in the spring, when the corn was being sown, and in the autumn for the harvest.' Viktor's voice liquefied as he drifted closer to daydream. 'He gave out presents – sweets for the children, and little cakes, and promissory notes for people to buy things in the store. They say he gave away everything. . . .'

So he had left behind a memory of the emigrant made good, visiting to scatter benevolence and receive applause, and perhaps to feel at peace. Yet he belonged nowhere. He had arrived in St Petersburg as an itinerant holy man, at a court susceptible to rural mysticism and the occult, and because some hypnotic authority in him calmed (it seemed) the internal bleeding of the Czar's haemophiliac son, he gained an ascendancy over the imperial couple which barely slackened until his murder in 1916.

Who was he? He slips away as you observe him. He enacts the

old Russian intimacy between holiness and sin. He was a lecher and drunkard, in love with power, in love with self. He boasted that he had bedded the empress. Transgression was the path to God. He could barely write, but he preached with peasant force. Sincerity, piety – the concepts blur around him, as they did around his putative descendant at my elbow. But his effect on the imperial family was fatal. He exacerbated all that was most insular in them. Their reputations shook and dwindled around him. Rasputin more than anyone, said their family tutor bitterly, was responsible for their end. Even now, nostalgia for a lost imperial utopia can find no focus in the last Czar.

'That's where his house was. There.' Viktor pointed across the barren road. I had seen photographs, taken long ago, of a handsome two-storey mansion, fronted by a picket fence and set in a high-walled courtyard. Only a log cottage stood there now. 'Soon after they destroyed the death-house in Yekaterinburg, the Party demolished this one too. They were afraid of it exciting interest. I remember that time well. They were going to break up the roof – a beautiful roof, it was – but the people here got up and protested, so a brigade came with seven tractors and lifted it off whole. They sold it to Kazakhstan for 40,000 roubles. The ruin stood for a long time, then the authorities told our people to take it away. A gang of volunteers got together – fellows who didn't want to lose their Party membership – and they razed it. Somebody built a pigsty out of the remains.'

His tone had slithered into self-pity – or the pretence of it – as if this was his own mansion they had wrecked, his patrimony. He said: 'But that wasn't quite the end. A few years ago, when we were building a greenhouse in that garden, we opened up an underground passage, lined with beams, down to the river. Rasputin had enemies, and he must have used it to get to his boat unseen. He owned a dacha upriver, with a lake and a bath-house, where he would take *women*.' He rolled the word over his palate. It sounded a sweet corruption. His hand came up and covered his heart in the eerie gesture of Rasputin's hand in photographs. I imagined he did this when he was lying. Perhaps they both did. 'Rasputin had *hundreds* of them.'

I crossed to the vanished mansion and looked back. A post-house had once stood opposite where horses were changed beneath Rasputin's windows, but this too had gone. In April 1918, on their way to Yekaterinburg and their deaths, the Czar and Czarina had stopped here under guard while their cart's horses were changed, and stood looking up at the house of the dead prophet. The empress recorded in her curt diary that they could see the frightened family watching them through the windows. Rasputin's daughter wrote that the empress was weeping.

We turned down mud streets past other houses. Some had pitched into the earth or were drowned in hopeless gardens; others stood weathered and pretty, their eaves and shutters painted blue and green, and they opened out at last on lush pastures under an empty sky. Already the Tura had wandered away from the village, leaving a reed-filled inlet to feint at the old landing-stage. Across the flats the river's banks lay so low that a steamer was floating across the grass. This August the current looked too sluggish for danger; but it had drowned Rasputin's only brother as he tried in vain to reach him, and swept away his epileptic sister as she washed clothes on its banks. Then, with his widowed and drunken father, Rasputin was alone.

Viktor too was a drunk, of course. With the collapse of the collective farm two years ago, the land had been parcelled out – 11 hectares to each worker – and he rented his in exchange for vodka. He lived by selling potatoes. As we trudged back to the village he stopped before another house. 'That's where I used to live. I was married for five years – and then one day I came back from Tyumen earlier than I'd said, and found her with another man. I actually found them. . . .' He smoothed his hands lasciviously over an aerial bed.

'And now I'm already a grandfather! I'm forty-six – and Rasputin died at forty-seven!' Suddenly his gaze was a soft question-mark, inviting pity, perhaps a little afraid. For years he had grown older alongside Rasputin; but what would happen when he reached his death? Would he become meaningless? Would he die?

Then he cried out: 'Have you drunk Rasputin vodka? Rasputin's death is on the labels. It says he was born in 1869, but he wasn't, he wasn't! He was older, he was born four years before, on 12 January 1865. Wasn't he? Wasn't he?' If Viktor was right, then he had four years longer before the death of his shadow. But he was wrong. There were only a few months left. And every Rasputin vodka bottle he emptied carried on it this haunting deadline.

But the next moment he had turned buoyant and sly again. 'Anyway, who needs a wife? Not when the women of Tyumen are the prettiest in Russia!'

'You have a girlfriend there?'

His breath was hot in my ear. 'Many! I go to Tyumen every week. And do you know why they're so pretty?' His hand came up to knead my arm in sensuous conspiracy. 'Because after the Revolution all the prostitutes from St Petersburg and Moscow were pushed out to the Urals, then to Tyumen! And these are their descendants. A paradise of them! You can sin all night. . . .' He gazed at me in self-adoration, self-disgust. 'Many every week . . . Paradise!'

We had arrived at the door of Anfissa, the old woman who had accepted me for the night. Her cottage was newly painted, her garden immaculate, her lace curtains drawn. As I pushed at her courtyard door, Viktor vanished like a ghost at cockcrow. Only beyond her neatly stacked ramparts of firewood did the garden disintegrate, and cow-parsley pushed against the privy walls.

Anfissa: her face is boxed in on three sides by short grey locks, and on the fourth her chins cascade seamlessly into her neck. When she smiles her mouth is a mass of steel, which lends her a glittering intimacy. She is kind, in her cautious way, and rather lonely. She has trouble with her legs. 'It's my heart. They swelled up because of my heart, the doctors said.'

She gives me vegetable soup, flecked with scraps of meat of varying ages, and she has baked the light brown bread herself, from local flour. 'That Viktor,' she says, sitting beside me (but not eating), 'I thought he'd taken you drinking. Because that's all he does. His brother drinks even more, and his sister, she drinks. . . . That's the kind of people they are. His parents gave him a house when they died, and he can't even maintain the fence. Now the place is falling down, and still he does nothing.'

From outside, these log cottages look as comfortless as trappers' shacks; but inside Anfissa's the walls were thickly plastered and papered, and an immured brick stove separated its two rooms, heating both. She drew her water from a pump in the street, and sometimes it was dry. But electric wires multiplied over the walls and ceiling, feeding a television, and an ethereal white cat flitted in and out. Everything was wrapped in paper or secured with string or safe in jars. She seemed to be shoring herself up against the changes rocking everything outside.

'In the towns half the factories have broken down,' she said, 'yet the workers somehow find jobs. But here the collective farm is destroyed, and there's nothing. The people who worked for it have left, and the bosses just dismantled it and took everything for themselves. Almost all the cattle have been sold off, so it's hard even to get butter. There's only chaos.'

I asked: 'Why? Why?' but there was no simple answer.

'I don't know why. Who knows? We need money for machinery – half the tractors are laid off – and the farm leader stole all the petrol.' She turned her childlike stare on me. It was a look I was to see often: the bewilderment of a people betrayed, whose certainties had turned to mist. 'In England, if you're a couple, how much land do they give you? . . . Really? . . . Then if you've so little land, why are your lives better than ours?' After a while, after my inability to explain, her wonder became a helpless threnody: 'We used to have fine corn growing here, but now there's nothing. There used to be flax and hemp, but they're gone. It was full of vegetables and fruit before, but now you don't see a thing.' She hitched her skirts from her smooth, blotched legs. 'If it wasn't for these I could work. Now nobody works. My husband used to get up at four o'clock in summer, and came back after dark.'

'In Brezhnev's time?'

'Long ago. He died at forty-seven, I don't know why. He just fell asleep and didn't wake up.'

The past was closing in on her. She had stuck her family photographs in albums at first, out of sight. Then one day it was not enough simply to leaf through them, as if visiting. She wanted them with her, always. So she tore them out and framed them along the shelf of the living-room, above the chest-of-drawers and the bed. She wobbled to her feet. 'When there's nobody here, and life gets heavy, then I look at them.'

It was a gallery of the young – hopeful parents, blond children – but they looked far away. I asked dutifully: 'How many children do you have?'

'Four. But three of them are dead.' A white cowlick had loosed from under her headscarf and was knocking on her forehead. She looked like an ancient girl. 'I had a daughter who fell ill and died at six months. And my eldest son – that's him, with his car and wife – he died four years ago, only forty-four, from a blood-clot in the head. He came to repair their new apartment in Tobolsk, and had been lying there a week before they found him.'

Only one son had survived. Yet Anfissa's grandchildren proliferated along the wall in a parade of cheekiness and summer dresses. Her eyes flickered over them and came to rest on a yellowing photograph at the end. 'That's my youngest son.' A saturnine youth leaned towards the camera, unsmiling. 'He was sixteen. He killed himself on a motor cycle.' Her tone of routine melancholy sharpened into living pain. 'He had such a future.' His snapshot stood separate from the rest, enshrined. Her fingers trembled when she pointed at it. Above it she had plastered a saccharine print of the Virgin, and beneath it stood an icon, sooted by candle-flame, of the Mother of God cradling her Son.

'There,' she said, 'there.' It was the sound a mother makes as she soothes her child to sleep.

I went out into the night, brushing through the cow-parsley, and by the time I returned she had lit a candle beneath the icon and was contemplating her gallery again. I wondered why it comforted her to watch them: this regiment riddled by death. Perhaps in her mind the living and the dead occupied the same remote hemisphere, because none of them ever came to see her, she said, they were all too far away. Or perhaps she slipped back mechanically into the time before tragedy, when her husband had worked a combine harvester all day, and there was flax in the fields, and children.

Before bed I wondered whether to pull the divan into the kitchen and sleep there. But she only said: 'It's up to you. I'm an old woman. Nobody will talk.' She laughed gruffly. 'That's all finished.'

Her bed stood under a garish wall-carpet, and for a moment, before I switched the light off, her stout body under its striped sheet lay framed in Persian glamour. Soon in the darkness her candle flickered and died under the Virgin and her sullen son, and only the lace curtains hung faint patterns of light in the windows. Anfissa's talk came quiet and disembodied in the dark. 'You have a mother? How old is she? . . . So she's older than me . . . Does she *look* older?' An obscure vanity was surfacing.

I lied. 'Yes, of course.'

Silence. Then: 'Your flat in London, is it made of wood? . . . And do you have cattle or pigs? . . . Ah . . . ah . . .' A clock rustled on the wall above my divan. Time became audible. 'But you have no children. How can that be? Think how quickly they die!' She stirred and groaned. 'In England, do you have a war now or not? . . . No? There's always war in this land. And you, travelling here alone, aren't you afraid? It's become terrible in the towns. People are taking to killing now. In Tobolsk too. Last week a mafia boss was pulled from his car and murdered. I heard it on the radio. It's bad for you to go, very bad. You ought to be afraid . . .'

Her voice sank in sleepy misgiving. In her experience, men died young. Her sentences shrank to disconnected words – 'Alone . . . mafia . . .' – until the patterns in her curtains grew dim above my head, and she fell silent, or I ceased to hear.

At the bus-stop beside the Tobolsk road two drunks, who had dogged me out of the village, closed in to beg with whines and threats, and prodded at my rucksack. Nobody knew when a bus might come. As they became more menacing I grew more angry, and they retired to mutter plans in a nearby field. An hour went by. Then, close beside me, I heard a familiar, caressing voice and turned round to see Viktor, tousled and weak-eyed, clambering towards me up the roadside embankment. 'It's early . . . you're leaving early.'

I sat in the dust while the beggars circled round me, sensing competition, and beside me Viktor's gaze flickered up and down the road, his voice a corrupting whisper: 'Pay me. Just a little . . . pay me . . .'

But roubles, I knew, would liquefy down his throat. I had already left money for Anfissa, and she had held the note in front of her a long time in astonishment – fifteen dollars was a third of her monthly pension – then turned away to wash something already clean in her sink, murmuring: 'It's a great deal. I did not expect it.'

Now Viktor handed me a useless Soviet coin. 'For your journey. Take it . . .' and the bolder of the drunks slunk to my other side and passed me a gold disc. I examined it sceptically. It turned out to be a Soviet maternity medal, awarded to women who had borne five children. But the man was not laughing. He said: 'What will you give me? What?' Viktor was pressing me on the other side. 'I'm ill,' he breathed.

I said: 'Go to a hospital.'

'A hospital can't cure my illness.'

'I know.'

He tried to encircle me, excluding the other men. 'Vodka is our medicine now.'

'I don't have any.'

'Then pay me. . . .'

Each of us could hear the others, yet everything transpired in whispers. 'Just a little . . . What? What? . . . Pay me. . . .'

Then, far away down the cratered road, a ramshackle bus materialised, making for Tobolsk. As I climbed in, Viktor's face slithered into smiles, without resentment. 'Remember me' – his stage whisper stroked my ear – 'your Rasputin.'

'I will.'

The road cut through a slushy, formless land – the raw material of creation – easing into pasture where the hay was rolled up like bedding and tributaries of the Tobol river turned figures-of-eight through the loamy soil. A band of forest crossed every horizon and sometimes shadowed the road with an evergreen dark, in which a few silver birches glimmered. From time to time we stopped for passengers to smoke – they crouched by the roadside, puffing with knit brows; and twice we passed road-blocks where the police were disembowelling lorries. 'Drug searches,' said a man. 'We never had that before.'

Three hours later we were wending through a labyrinth of wooden houses and decayed stone churches. On the heights above, behind the walls of a kremlin, the sleek white bodies of cathedral and bell-tower floated under their domes. Almost from the start of Russia's sixteenth-century invasion, until 1824, Tobolsk was the capital of Siberia. Near this site, in 1582, the Tartar centre of Sibir had been sacked by a band of Cossacks who muscled their boats over the Urals and inaugurated the conquest of the whole subcontinent.

The Cossacks' leader Yermak has endured in legend as a primitive paragon. A former river-pirate, he invaded at the instigation of the powerful Stroganov merchant dynasty, to push their fortunes east. Because he and his Cossacks were free men, he was later hailed by Communist propaganda as a hero of the people, who liberated lesser tribes from the Tartar yoke. In fact, Yermak was a brutal mercenary, and his Cossacks a medley of freebooters, itinerant labourers and criminals, and they went with imperial backing. During three years of warfare, with fewer than a thousand men, he shattered the Tartar khanate whose warriors – a remnant of the Mongol Golden Horde – were the most redoubtable barrier to Russian expansion. At the height of his success, Ivan the Terrible rewarded him with an elaborate suit of armour embossed with the imperial arms. But little by little the dispossessed khan Kuchum wore the Cossacks down. While bivouacked one night on a storm-swept island in the Irtysh river, they were surprised and butchered almost to a man. Yermak, it is said, hacked his way to the river-bank and plunged into the current, but the weight of his imperial armour pulled him under.

Instantly his legend spread. The Tartars said they recovered his body from the water, and that his uncorrupted flesh worked miracles. Above his riverside grave sprang up a column of unearthly fire, and every midwinter an arm in golden mail reared like Excalibur above the water where he had drowned. Around the fugitive campfires of Siberia, ballads and folk-tales nourished and distorted him into a Slavic Parsifal or Robin Hood. The Church beatified him.

The Tartar khan Kuchum, a grander figure, continued to harry the Russians from his exile, although almost all his family had been captured or killed. He rejected the soft amnesties which the czars held out to him. He wanted his kingdom back. Still defiant in his blind old age, he was murdered by hostile tribesmen, but like Yermak he entered his people's heart, so that a century later revolts were still sparked in his name.

The Russians' advance eastward grew remorseless. They set out across the continent as other nations embarked over the ocean, and just as spices or silver tempted European empires into being, so Russian Siberia was the creation of the sable. A few pelts from this glossy tree-marten could make a man's fortune. Their revenue poured into the czar's hands. The invading Cossacks exacted an imperial fur-tribute from natives crushed by their firearms, and spread like a disease along the rivers, spiking their passage with log forts. No sooner was the sable hunted out in one region than the Russians advanced on another. In time-dishonoured imperial fashion, they exploited the tribes' disunity, and within sixty years of Yermak's death they had pushed clear across Asia and reached the Pacific.

Tobolsk was the springboard for this conquest. Its lower town is still restless with Tartars. The shells of great churches haunt the wooden streets. Their naves are littered with cattle-dung and broken farm machinery. From here the walls of the kremlin on its hill rear into view, while above them the cathedral domes bulge like overripe vegetables. From below, the cliff rampart looms over 100 feet and seems impossible to breach. Nothing shows but crenellated walls. Then as you draw closer a deep, man-made cutting opens in the hill, hewn out three hundred years ago by Swedish prisoners of war. You climb through concealing trees. From the battlements jut square and round towers topped off by candle-snuffer turrets and flying iron flags. You pass under a heavy arch, pierced with the bolts of vanished gates, and creep cat-like along a sunken way. Above you there surge blue and spinach-green domes dusted with gold stars, whose lanterns bloom into a swarm of secondary cupolas and filigreed crosses. Nothing sounds but the scrape and clink of desultory repairs in the kremlin court-yard where they rise. A light rain starts to fall. You enter the court over rank grass: the heart of old Siberia, spacious and derelict. The seventeenth-century cathedral inherits the first bishopric in Siberia, founded in 1621. There is an episcopal palace and an old merchants' emporium. An enormous bell-tower hovers nearby. Everything is plastered white.

Stubbornly, insidiously, the past is returning. Tobolsk is the seat of an archbishopric again. Students from the reopened seminary walk in their dark jackets along the overgrown paths. But when asked if they want to revert to a theocracy, or install a constitutional czar, they look indifferent. And their priest points to a small tower where the first exile to Siberia was hung. This was not a man, but a 700-pound bell from Uglich, which rang an insurrectionary alarm on the murder of the imperial heir in 1581. The usurper Boris Godunov had the bell publicly flogged and its tongue ripped out, and ordered the citizens of Uglich to drag it over the Urals to Tobolsk, where it was forbidden to ring. The czars were full of madness, says the priest.

Tobolsk eased out of history. First the great overland Trakt road, then the Trans-Siberian Railway, bypassed it to the south. As you walk along the battlements the town heaves below you in a sea of mansions, soft with birch trees and its own decay. Its colours are gentle and dim: dark with weathered wood and rust, streets silenced by rain, a glint of gold where churches are resurrecting.

But it is not a healthy town to live in, says the priest: the flooded river erodes everything, and half the old houses are abandoned. The past is rotting away. You cannot live in it.

2

Heart Failure

Six hundred miles north of Tobolsk, as the twin-engine Antonov crossed the Arctic Circle, the land transformed. The forest had gone, and in its place glimmered a treeless tundra whose earth was a silvery maze of lichen and fungi. No road or railway crossed it. For thousands of square miles the wilderness shattered into a jigsaw of ponds and streams, as if the whole continent had flattened to sponge, where the rivers wound fantastically upon one another, and splintered ten or twenty ways.

Yet a few feet underground the soil was set iron-hard in ice. For eight months of the year the snow seals it. Then out of the permafrost in spring evaporating water oozes to the surface, and these strange, transitory lakes and streams return. The rhythmic upheaval of the soil – its seasonal swelling and shrinking – deposits boulders and stones in mysterious, concentric rings, as if some pedantic intelligence were at work, and carves out circular pools. Yet the region is almost uninhabitable. It spreads like a protoplasm where nature is still forming, or has already disintegrated. To the west the Urals lift in naked stone.

A low, continuous judder in the aeroplane kept me on edge (this, after all, was Aeroflot, and we had only two propellers). An air hostess handed out bowls of fizzy water and some stale sweets. In the seat beside me a woman was plaiting her daughter's hair. Suddenly below us, out of the tundra, shot up smokestacks and a black detritus of factories and ruins. It came like a physical shock: Vorkuta. For years the name had sounded a death-knell.

Coal was discovered here in the early twenties, and by 1934 the mines were sucking down an army of innocent convicts. Soon the place became an evil jewel in the Gulag crown. The numbers of dead ran into hundreds of thousands. Forty thousand alone died constructing the railway west. The last victims were released, sickly and redundant, only in 1959.

North of Vorkuta a loop-road still links its thirty mines, but only eleven pits are still working. That evening I roamed the town in fascinated unease. Its apartment blocks and offices were decomposing untouched, their walls dripping plaster, half the windows smashed. A river lisped over slag. I passed factories ringed with barbed-wire and searchlights, as if this were the only architecture anyone could remember, and every other street dribbled into a tundra hung with skeletal shutes and pit-wheels.

Here the only superfluity is coal. It lies in heaps along the roads, and litters every compound. The streets are laid on coal-dust. When it rains, the puddles shine black. It hazes the air and it worms under your fingernails. Eventually, it eats your lungs.

The cars make a wandering trickle between the pot-holes on Lenin Street. Cloth cap in fist, his statue still looks across Lenin Square at the Miners' Palace of Culture. The pool in front is awash with vodka bottles. Everywhere on ministerial façades the carved insignia survive: red stars and crossed hammers, torches and banner-dripping spears. Along the rooftops leftover slogans set up an archaic clamour. 'To the masses of Vorkuta!' 'The Miners are the Guardians of Labour!' There is no will either to remove or to replenish them. One by one their letters are dropping off.

I came upon some barracks built for convict miners which no one had bothered to demolish. The weed-sown earth crept half-way up their wooden walls, and the aisles where their bunks had been were filled with rubble. Sometimes the prisoners were packed so closely that they could barely turn in their sleep. At the end of each barracks the life-saving stoves had collapsed in cascades of brick, and garbled English graffiti spattered the walls from a later age. 'Lucky Streik', 'Kiss my Ais. . . .'

A young girl stands in Lenin Square. It is almost deserted. She looks about fifteen, but her black skirt barely descends below her hips, and her stockings stop half-way up her bruised thighs. How many days a year in Vorkuta can she dress like this? She appears pathetically tired and young; perhaps it is her first time. Jobs are hard in Vorkuta. But the palm of one hand is pressed against her cheek, as if to deny her presence here. Then a middle-aged man strolls up and says something. Haltingly, she follows him along the pavement. Her fingers keep slipping behind to pull down her skirt, to no avail. The man hails a car beneath the statue of Lenin, and she climbs tentatively in. By now her hand covers half her face.

My hotel was huge, half ruined and the only one left: a monument to Stalin which rang with my footsteps. Four policemen gazed stonily from an office across the hall, and concierges still slumped at their corridor desks. In the cavernous dining-room canned dance-music played for nobody.

I walked in the streets without knowing where to go. I wondered vaguely if I were being followed. The sallow people wandering the pavements could be thinking whatever you ascribed to them. It was oddly quiet. A populace of old men sat remote in the arid squares, and spoke with me in dislocated phrases and half-smiles. They were Latvians and Ukrainians, exiled long ago, and were taking the air with reticent surprise.

For it was warm, with a dense, midsummer stillness. By eight o'clock in the evening the sun was still high, and at eleven the sky held a limpid, refracted light, as if it were illuminating the town through black gauze. But not one in ten windows was lit. Lost in its suburbs, I had a fantasy that the past, like something viscous and unreconciled, was leaking back in, inhabiting abandoned rooms, reclaiming the factories. Those who had died here far outnumbered the living. They had built the city in chains, and lie beneath it. Yet at midnight people were still walking their mongrels in the roads, and reading newspapers.

Next morning I found a cheery Ukrainian to drive the twenty-mile noose-road through the mines. Vorkuta was a wonderful town, Vasil said, because it was close to the Urals, and you could hunt. He'd lived here thirty years, and life had been splendid. 'You should see the rivers and lakes there. *Hundreds!* And chock-full of fish! You can bribe geologists or soldiers to take you out in a jeep, and they drop you where you want. As for this' – he dismissed Vorkuta with a backhand – 'everything will get better! It's the worst moment now. Soon . . .'

But the town was slipping away, and before us unrolled a ghastly no man's land. For miles its grasslands bunched and undulated with the scars of vanished buildings; and some forgotten war, it seemed, had littered its surface with scrap-iron and ruin. All colour had drained away. Even the sky hung in thundery black and white. Pylons and telegraph poles cross-hatched half the land, while enormous hot-water pipes wormed below, their lagging spilt out over the discoloured grass.

Our car shuddered into pot-holes. We were quite alone. Vasil started telling me fishing and hunting tales, and drove more carelessly as he dreamt of salmon and Arctic fox. Ahead our horizon was bloated with slag-heaps and chimneystacks. Polluted tributaries of the Vorkuta river wandered about. Sometimes I could not tell if a mine were working or wrecked. We would pass a ruin with no man or truck in sight, its shutes snapped off and chimneys extinct; then its pit-wheel would start turning. Surely that was the wind! But no. Deep beneath those installations the earth was teeming with men.

Yet above ground, we were driving among ghosts. Every mine was shadowed by the traces of a prison camp or cemetery. They ruffled the soil with terraces, crashed-in barracks, rotted watch-towers. Sometimes I would leave Vasil and tramp away alone. My imagination was failing me. I wanted to shock myself into pity; but instead I felt a distant recoil and bewilderment. The ground seemed sick underfoot. I was afraid of what I might kick there. I walked lightly over its corrugations. I tried to remember any individual who had died here – a Mandelstam, a Babel. He might have stirred some sharp, particular loss. But I knew of no one. Only a nameless nation of the dead, whom I could not quite separate from its persecutors.

These camps were self-contained states. They evolved in a perverted reflection of the world outside. After Stalin's pact with Hitler in 1939, the mass of Russian and Ukrainian convicts were joined by tens of thousands of Poles, and as early as 1940 Russian soldiers recaptured from the Germans were incarcerated here as traitors. With the annexation of the Baltic states, the Latvians, Lithuanians and Estonians poured in – those who'd fought against Hitler and Stalin indifferently – and by the war's end Vorkuta's patchwork of nations embraced Germans, Japanese, Nationalist Chinese, Jewish survivors of the Holocaust, Persians, several French and Americans, even a Tibetan herdsman who had strayed over the Mongolian border.

Inside the camps the swarm of guiltless politicals was tyrannised by the tight-knit criminal fraternity imprisoned with them. These *blatnye* lived by their own savage laws, conducted their own executions, seized whatever privileges were going. The camp administration ignored or used them. The guards could be as vulnerable as the prisoners. Any carelessness, any untoward mercy, and they might be shot. The pervasive feel was one less of sadism than of brute indifference. By overwork, half-starvation and piercing cold, the convicts were ground down into an animal mass. On a daily ration of porridge, three ounces of fish and a few drops of oil, they laboured under a quota system often impossible to fulfil. They perished of typhus, tuberculosis, pneumonia, or dropped dead of heart failure as they hauled the coal-trucks up the pit. Sometimes their comrades concealed their corpses so they could draw their rations; but within three days the bodies' stench betrayed them.

'... And in winter you just cut a hole in the ice, drop in a line, and up they come – graylings by the dozen!' Vasil was anticipating his next expedition. 'And later you get the big one, the salmon. In July last year I was on the Usa, not thinking of anything, and suddenly the rod's torn out of my hands. The creature weighed fifty kilos, I could swear – that's my wife's weight! – and it flashed round and looked at me. . . .'

On either side of us they continued: mine – graveyard – camp – mine – graveyard – all in ruins. Sometimes a village enfolded the barracks where a few ex-prisoners or their descendants lingered, with nowhere else to go. But most places remained only in memory, like the brickyard where 1,300 politicals were executed in 1937 by the ruthless commandant Kashketin. (He was awarded the Order of Lenin, then shot.) But a grey obelisk commemorates them. The punishment camp of Cementny Zavod had shrivelled to a huddle of gaunt tenements and a vomiting smokestack. Pallid women waited outside shops or sat round a vacant netball-pitch. Even five years before, miners' strikes could rock the Kremlin; but now their pay was six months in arrears, Vasil said, and still the depleted gangs were going to work.

Then we reached the shell of Mine 17. Here, in 1943, was the first of Vorkuta's *katorga* death-camps. Within a year these compounds numbered thirteen out of Vorkuta's thirty: their purpose was to kill their inmates. Through winters in which the temperature plunged to −40°F, and the *purga* blizzards howled, the *katorzhane* lived in lightly boarded tents sprinkled with sawdust, on a floor of mossy permafrost. They worked twelve hours a day, without respite, hauling coal-trucks, and within three weeks they were broken. A rare survivor described them turned to robots, their grey-yellow faces rimmed with ice and bleeding cold tears. They ate in silence, standing packed together, seeing no one. Some work-brigades flailed themselves on in a bid for extra food, but the effort was too much, the extra too little. Within a year the first 28,000 of them were dead. A prisoner in milder times encountered a remnant of the hundreds of thousands who were sentenced between 1943 and 1947. They had survived, he said, because they were the toughest – a biological elite – but were now brutalised and half-insane.

Under the mine's disembowelled head-frame, the heaps of slag and rubbish were inhabited by vagrants scavenging for metal. A horde of vicious dogs was on the loose. I started along the pit railway through shrubs and swamps and an undergrowth of ruin. The rails along the track had been torn up yard by yard. I thrust past waste-tips snowed under flocks of gulls. Then I came to a solitary brick building enclosing a range of cramped rooms. The roof was gone, but the iron-sheathed timbers of their door-frames still stood, and their walls were windowless. They were isolation cells. Solzhenitsyn wrote that after ten days' incarceration, during which a prisoner might be deprived even of clothing, his constitution was wrecked, and after fifteen he was dead. Now their concrete was splitting underfoot. Into each cell the skeleton of a door still swung. Outside, wild camomile lapped against the bricks.

I stumbled into a quagmire curtained by shrubs, and waded out again. In front of me the coal trains were wheezing and clanking over the tundra. I began to imagine myself here fifty years ago. *What would I have done?* But knowing how physical depletion saps the will, the answer returned: *You would have been no different from anyone else.*

I came upon a message scratched on a stone: 'I was exiled in 1949, and my father died here in 1942. Remember us.'

'They come in thousands! Flying south in autumn, that's when you get them. Geese, duck, teal! And there's a red salmon that descends the Pechora river from the Arctic into the Vorkuta. . . .' Vasil swung the car past Mine 29, and we clambered out. The pit-wheels hung stark against the sky. A low hill, slushy with reeds and mosses, had sucked in its decayed camp. 'Now this salmon carries a kind of caviar. One day last June . . .' But he never finished. As we plunged into the dank shrubbery it poured out mosquitoes. They were huge. They were the rearguard of the festering trillions called *gnus* – a miasma of midges, gnats, horse-flies, mosquitoes – which breed in the tundra pools in summer. They came at us like helicopters. In the tundra they can put reindeer and cattle to headlong flight, and have suffocated foals (and even, it is said, reindeer and men) by clogging their throats and nostrils. They live for only a few days, and feed on nothing. Some species have no developed digestive organs at all. Yet they flew in with oblivious fury – almost harmless by mid-August – and bit us out of habit or spite. That night I discovered wide, fiery welts over my wrists and ankles – a thousand Lilliputian mouthfuls – which had vanished by morning.

But Vasil was having none of them. When hunting, he yelled,

he wore protective netting, and he didn't plan to get eaten alive in some dump of a mine. So I scrambled alone among foundations of disintegrating wood, charred posts, and a litter of rusted buckets and chains. A spider's web of fences, trickling into the undergrowth, ended at the vestige of a gateway. An iron-bound window had been tossed into the bushes all of a piece. And in barracks still balanced delicately above the earth, the light was pouring through roofs on to those atrocious aisles where the plank beds of men stacked up like battery hens had dropped to the ground, and powder and coal-dust leaked out of the walls.

Opposite the mine I reached the cemeteries. You stumble over these everywhere round Vorkuta, but they hold only a fraction of those fallen. In winter the corpses were piled in open-sided shacks until there were enough to be worth burying, then an NKVD officer smashed their skulls with a pick and they were tipped into a trench pre-dug in summer. But here, beyond memorials to the German and Latvian dead, hundreds of bleached crosses rose from the undergrowth. All were nameless. Their cross-pieces carried numbers – 'A-41 . . . A-87' – and many had rotted off or vanished. (People stole them as souvenirs, Vasil said.) A sledge-hearse, a pick and a single rubber boot lay under a bush, abandoned by the last burial party forty years before.

Mine 29 bears a peculiar tragedy. A few months after Stalin's death in 1953, strikes broke out in labour camps all across Siberia, and this pit was in the vanguard. Its inmates made demands in the name of the whole Gulag: for the release of the very old and the too-young, and for the repatriation of foreigners. They asked for a ban on random shooting by watch-tower guards. They wanted a reduction of working hours. They wanted humanity. One by one the other Vorkuta camps succumbed to threats or lies from Moscow; but Mine 29 held out. Meanwhile, it was surrounded by two divisions of NKVD troops, with tanks. The main gate had vanished among indecipherable foundations under my feet. But as it was battered down, the troops saw the prisoners standing behind it in a solid phalanx, their arms linked, and singing. There were three or four volleys of small-arms, then the heavy machine-guns opened up. For a minute the miners remained massed and erect, the dead held up by the living, then they started to litter the ground.

The fallen were thrown into a common grave – a 'brothers' grave', as the Russians say. In Khrushchev's day somebody raised a cross like a telegraph pole over the slag-heaps where they lay. It has gone; but in the studio of Vorkuta's chief architect hang designs for other monuments. Nobody knows who will pay for them – the government offers nothing – but the architect's dreams continue. Above the Vorkuta river an immense cross will be carved from the earth, he hopes, its marble sides engraved with the names of the dead. Another hill will open on a crowd of carved faces gazing from the ground, struggling to rise. And above the brothers' grave in Mine 29 will stand a granite figure of Mother Russia, with chunks missing from her face, her shoulders, and her heart.

She is an old woman now. In the street she paddles her bulk along with rhythmic scoops of her arms, and her cheeks flush with the labour. But inside her apartment, her eyes clear. She sits upright, distracted by the Mexican television drama which has been running every day for a year. She says it's rubbish, but she watches. Her face is oddly delicate on its thick neck, and her eyes cornflower blue. Even now, at eighty-seven, she intermittently looks pretty, and in her youth her looks were a dangerous blessing.

She worked in the Russian embassy in Berlin, she says, and joined some fragile movement accused of opposing Stalin. She was arrested early in 1938 and taken from Moscow to Vorkuta: a guileless Communist who seems to have believed in legal process. This belief has never been cancelled. She works now where I met her, at Memorial, an organisation devoted to the memory of the vanished millions, the dead she will not forget.

'We lived half underground at first, then in tent-huts until we built barracks. It wasn't the temperature which hurt, but the winds. The winds tore through you.' Her arms wrap her body. 'At first I worked in the mines, then we were thrown into road-building. Then when the road was finished, I was put back in the mines.' Her talk is sometimes sabotaged by laughter, as if she is still incredulous; then her blue eyes seem detached from it all, born survivors.

'Because I was considered – how to say this? – a dangerous criminal, I didn't sleep in ordinary barracks. I was kept separate, in a hut with four others, and two guards. We slept on two shelves. But the worst thing was to receive no letters. My husband was an army doctor, but he repudiated me to protect our children. In any case, what could I have written to him? "I'm fine"! But he repudiated me, and I didn't write. And of course the censor read everything. . . .'

I ask: 'You were never ill?'

'No, never.' Then, almost in afterthought, she says: 'Ah, yes, just once. In 1941 I caught typhus.' I stare at her. A lice-borne typhus killed thousands in the Vorkuta camps. 'I expected these eruptions all over my body, but they didn't come. Instead my temperature soared. Then my hair fell out and they realised I had enteric fever. I was taken into isolation. I was there a long time, a long time.' She seems to be trying to remember something. It flickers away. 'That was all right. I was alone.'

I feel like a voyeur, ashamed, but I ask: 'What was it like, the work?' I think: perhaps, day to day, it was not quite as people have written it, perhaps only the worst was recalled, the uncommon.

She starts to rock a little on the sofa, backwards and forwards, heavily. Her head turns to the television, where the soap opera is proceeding among yachts and tuxedoes. 'It was hardest when we built the roads. So many died! The trouble was exhaustion, especially for the men. Somehow women seemed immune, stronger. Those who came first – scientists and administrators – they weren't used to physical work, and they died easily. But the worst time came in the war. Up to 1941 there was something to eat, if only dried potatoes. But in 1941 there was famine all over Russia, and the labour and hunger killed very many.' Her voice has levelled into calm. 'There were embankments along the road, and when a person died we used to dig a hole and cover his head with his pea-jacket, and heap the gravel over him.' She leans forward, and smooths her hands above the carpet, tenderly. She is laughing, as if from a great distance. 'And later we laid rails over them, and soon the trains were running over their graves. That's where the trains still run, over their graves.' She touches my hand, as if it is I who need comforting. 'Often the ground was harder than stone, so we had to wait until summer. Then a work-team dug a long trench and threw the bodies in, and that was it. After executions too, they'd dig a brothers' grave.' Her body starts to rock again. 'We knew the war might be coming to an end when we got proper funerals, and coffins. And after 1945 whole echelons of Ukrainians, Belorussians and Germans poured in. Then we knew it must be over.'

She is breathing faster on the sofa beside me, and I wonder if I have asked too much of her. I say: 'I'm sorry for asking.'

'Many suffered more than I did. Of course there were all sorts of people there, *blatnye* too, and different things happened. . . .'

It is impossible to guess what she is remembering. The women suffered peculiarly. The female politicals, the 'roses', were tormented by the criminal 'violets', some of whom were slightly insane; and faced by men they were all powerless. Once two brigades of convalescent women were mass-raped by *blatnye*.

But she says: 'I just worked hard, and I kept quiet and nobody was very cruel to me, not very.' When she grows animated I glimpse the girl in her, and wonder if she received protection at a cost, as other young women did, from an official or a soldier. And were the guards cruel, I ask, or only callous?

'They just did what they were told,' she says. 'After all, if we escaped, they would end up like us.'

I don't like this easy understanding. I want her to be angry. 'Did they think you guilty?'

'Yes, yes, they supposed us all guilty.' She stares down at her hands. Her thinning hair silvers her neck in lank curls. 'Well, maybe in their souls they doubted it. Or perhaps later they began to think that so many couldn't be guilty. But they kept their distance from us.'

How fraught, I wondered, was that distance? Was it imposed by a fear of contamination, of some treason spreading like the camp typhus? Or by the complex danger of feeling sympathy? A guard's fraternisation would condemn him. And the great terror, of course, was suppressed, unthinkable: that these people were all innocent.

'Maybe they pitied us a little,' she says, then adds stubbornly, defending them, somehow defending herself: 'But work is work. You do what you have to.'

I balk and say nothing.

But it is easy to misjudge those times – to forget how isolated people became in a world infested by informers, and how all the organs of state control, all authority, reproduced Stalin's paranoia: the obsession with conspiracy, the mass delusion of sabotage – until ascertainable truth became a dangerous rarity. The questioning or torture of each suspect, of course, produced a scream of new names. Often the charges were ludicrous. People were accused of plotting to blow up non-existent bridges, of spying for countries of which they'd scarcely heard. The very illogic of the accusations said: *You have no rights, no mind. Logic is ours.* And each confession, however absurd, subtly exculpated the inquisitor, secured him in some perverted illusion of rightness. It seemed to sanction the suffering of a whole people.

'And you,' I pursue, 'did you ever imagine yourself guilty?'

'No, absolutely not. Nor did the others with me. But I should have been released in 1948, and it didn't happen. I spent another two years in the camps. After my release, when I wrote to the Public Prosecutor, they answered that I couldn't have been freed earlier because I'd been against Soviet Power. And it's true I was against Soviet Power because it was against the people. Then they told me that *I* was against the people. But I was a Party member, and the Party was for the people, and the Power . . .'

I lose her down a great labyrinth. I can't disentangle her shadows. But at last she says: 'The Party was not guilty, absolutely not. I accuse . . . certain people . . . certain people. . . .' She goes vague. In some misty hierarchy, she has selected a scapegoat. She has displaced blame upward, until it all but fades away. She will not indict the whole system. No. Only somewhere, she knew, something had gone terribly wrong. A tragic fluke, it seemed. She sighs harshly. Were it not for this accident, all would have been well. Instead, paradise slipped away. . . .

She tries to explain, thumps the sofa in frustration. I notice her thick, working wrists. The hands on them are like delicate afterthoughts, just as her facial features look petite on the barrel of her neck. It is as if years of labour had bulked out a woman once frailer, more high-strung, and almost subsumed her.

I say at last: 'You didn't return to the Party?'

She says stoutly: 'I never left the Party.'

No, not in her heart. And on rehabilitation her membership was reaffirmed. In the absence of her anger, I find it rankling inside myself. 'They should be asking *you* to rehabilitate *them*.'

But she stares at me blankly. Perhaps she thinks she has misheard. In the oval of her mouth only three or four teeth remain, one hanging by a wisp of root. Then she looks back at the television, where a Mexican socialite pouts and tinkles a cocktail stick. 'That Dulcinea,' she says, 'she's going to the dogs . . . and her Jose can't act, he just gazes. . . .' She cackles lightly. Then she says: 'Why can't people ever record the good things, the everyday things? If there were ordinary accounts of the camps people would understand how we couldn't always weep, how we came up out of the mines into the wash-house, singing. You're a writer, aren't you, so why don't you write that? How we smiled a little, danced and sang a little. Because people must live in hope. . . .'

Her voice had sweetened into a rhythmic patter, until the rhythm seemed to choose the words. 'Once I got an illegal parcel – three kilos of sugar! – and I was secretly fermenting beer when an officer came into the dormitory and oh! it exploded all over him. I was terrified I'd be taken to the isolator, but instead, whenever we came to identity parade, he would name me as the drink-exploder, and everybody would laugh. So write this too. That it wasn't all tears. Write this too.'

'I will.'

But something is plaguing me. I can't bear her acquiescence. I say cruelly: 'But what was the purpose in the end? To so much suffering . . .'

She looks back at me, and suddenly her eyes begin to water. She glances away again. For the first time she seems unable to answer. She repeats: 'Purpose?'

47

And perhaps this is the hardest to bear, the idea that all that suffering and labour, those deaths, were for nothing. Suffering had once had meaning. 'Purpose?' The word seems to torment her. Her eyes are brimming, so that I feel ashamed of what I have asked. Her hand alights on mine. 'I feel bitter for all my life's waste. We hoped for so much better. Look at what a city was founded here! – and now it's destroyed. Schools have been demolished, libraries closed down, workers have gone months and years without pay. Can you trust a government which allows that? Now people just want to make money. They've lost all belief. . . . To think that it's come to this!'

'But this isn't where it ends.'

I feel she hardly hears me. 'It's never possible to forget those years. Never. It's like an illness. I have not told you everything that happened, but you can imagine. . . .'

'Yes.' (I sometimes think I can.)

'You know how many died!' Her voice makes a terrible music. 'They died from weakness, from privation. If there was a blizzard, if there was cold, we still had to work. It wasn't enough to chop the coal from the rock-face, you had to load it into wagons and haul them. We had no pulleys, and it was only in 1942 that they sent down draught-horses. It was very heavy, very. And to remember how many fell down, how they succumbed just like that, hauling the wagons, and then how we dragged them out by the legs. . . .'

Her voice has gone away from me, as if dreaming. I think: perhaps the dead have taken away the sense of reality with them. Nothing so strong, so sad, had happened since. Meaning has predeceased her.

Yet she gets up and surfs through the television channels with grunts of discontent, then switches it off. She says: 'I am eighty-seven, but I want to live to see the future.'

3

The Flight from Science

On either side of the railway to Omsk the wheatfields shimmered in huge rectangles, and fescue grass spread a pinkish sheen over the pasturelands. In this immense sameness, isolated things – a duckpond, a well, a horse-cart – took on a lonely piquancy. I gazed with relief at terrain empty of coal or ruins, whose mounds were natural. A luxurious sense of freedom welled up. For the first time in Russia's history a foreigner could wander Siberia at will. At any little town where I stopped, I might alight and disappear, nursing my business visa – a scruffy paper inscribed with pro forma destinations – against police intrusion.

The exhilaration of this freedom never quite left me. Whenever I pulled out my map and imagined entering the mountains abutting Mongolia, or taking ship up the Yenisei river to the Arctic, I would be hit by euphoria, then disbelief. Something, or someone, would surely prevent me. That was how Russia had always been. I had slipped through a transient gap in the country's age-old xenophobia.

My train followed a wavering belt of dark-earthed steppeland towards Omsk. The retreat of the last Ice Age was enacted visibly beside it. At the rate of a mile a year the steppes were edging northwards into the taiga, which was encroaching at the same rate on the Arctic.

From its inception in 1891 the Trans-Siberian was built here in a hurry, with poor steel and untreated timbers. In these western stretches it was pushed across swamps and peat-bogs at the rate of a mile a day, behind a vanguard of improvised dykes and artesian wells: within a few years the sagging ballast and buckled steel had turned the track to a roller-coaster where the passenger trains never exceeded 13 m.p.h.

A peculiarly Russian blend of fear and confidence drove it forward. The Trans-Siberian, it was hoped, would build up Russia's defences on the Pacific and bind Siberia for ever to the motherland; and it was powered by an old sense of spiritual privilege and mission: the railway would lay a thread of civilisation through Asia's heart.

The faintly clownish name of Omsk precedes the city with a light-hearted expectation. It lies where the railway crosses the Irtysh on a massive cantilever bridge, and you see the curve of the river under a line of stooping derricks as it heads out among sandy islets and meadows, touching the city with an illusion of peace. But beyond, the suburbs bristle with petrochemical plants, textile combines and oil refineries, and the pollution is so thick that driving at night has sometimes been forbidden. They sprawl for miles above the river. Marx Prospect, Lenin Square, Partisan Street: the veteran names follow one another in relentless procession.

Yet the city keeps a modest distinction. Whereas the Second World War razed western Russian towns to the ground, here in Siberia, untouched, they often attain a formal grandeur or rustic exuberance, and seem older than they are. I wandered the streets in surprise. The municipal flower-beds were all in bloom, and fountains played between provincial ministries. Close above the river, nineteenth-century streets dipped and swung in icing-sugar façades. The air in the parks clattered with pop music. Clusters of miniskirted girls paraded their irregular beauty, and children strolled with their parents in sleepy obedience; but their jeans and T-shirts were stamped with stars-and-stripes or Donald Duck. Every other pair of shoes or trousers sported a pirated Western logo. Fast-food restaurants had arrived, offering instant *pelmeni* – the Siberian ravioli – or anonymous steaks with stale mash, and a rash of small shops and kiosks had appeared, selling the same things.

Yet a feeling of boredom, or of waiting, pervaded the city. All style and music, the new paths to paradise, seemed synthetic, borrowed. Real life remained on hold. The pop songs had the scuttling vitality of streams. The bus-shelters and underpasses, stinking of urine, were rife with graffiti: 'Pomponius Nautilus – I love you! . . . Agatha Christie! Sepulchre! The Prodigy!' It took me time to realise that these were pop groups; other graffiti followed them, sometimes scrawled in English, the *lingua franca* of youth. 'Jim Morrison lives! No! . . . I fucked the bitch! . . . Communists are all buggers. . . .' Then, in Russian, enigmatically: 'Why travel with a corpse? . . . The point of life is to ponder the cross on your grave. . . .'

A pervasive frustration pronounced that freedom, once again, had proved illusory. Scarce jobs and high prices were the new slavemasters. The pavements were dotted with the new poor. Yet in this August sunlight I was touched by the traveller's confusion: the gulf between the inhabitant and the stranger. A little architectural charm, or a trick of the light, could turn other people's poverty to a bearable snapshot. The air was seductively still. Naked children were splashing in the polluted river.

I walked over the headland where the old fort had spread, but trees and terraces had blurred away the lines traced by its stockade, and only a stout, whitewashed gate remained. For four years Dostoevsky had languished here in a wooden prison, condemned to hard labour for activities in a naively revolutionary circle in St Petersburg. Sometimes he would gaze yearningly across the Irtysh at the nomad herdsmen, and would walk round the stockade every evening, counting off its stakes one by one as his sentence expired. He transmuted his life here into *The House of the Dead*, and it was here, among convicts who at first filled him with loathing but later with awe, that he experienced a half-mystical reconciliation with the peasant Russian people.

On the site of the vanished prison, fifty years later, rose a fantastical baroque theatre, painted white and green. Now it was showing *The Merry Wives of Windsor*, Alan Ayckbourn's *Season's*

Greetings and Shelagh Delaney's *A Taste of Honey*. The only prison building to survive was the house of the governor, a purple-faced drunkard and sadist in Dostoevsky's day, who would have his prisoners flogged for any misdemeanour, or none. His home has been turned into a museum to the writer he hated.

A century after Dostoevsky's incarceration, Solzhenitsyn was escorted through Omsk on his way to a labour camp in Kazakhstan. He and his fellow prisoners were interned in a vaulted stone dungeon whose single window opened from a deep shaft above them. He never forgot how they huddled together under a 15-watt bulb, while an elderly sexton sang to them, close to dying: how the old man's Adam's apple quivered as he stood beneath the mouth of the hopeless shaft, and his voice, trembling with death and feeling, floated out an old revolutionary song:

> *Though all's silent within,*
> *It's a jail, not a graveyard –*
> *Sentry, ah, sentry, beware!*

My hotel costs five dollars a night. The plaster falls in chunks from its corridor walls, and from the Stalinist mouldings of the ceiling. The night is close and humid. It is over 85°F. I lie on the bed and watch the full moon shining through a pattern of dainty flowers in the lace curtains. I cannot sleep. The sweat leaks from my chest and forehead. And this is Siberia.

Next morning, outside the big, unlovely cathedral, which in Stalin's day had been a cinema, I found a coach-load of pilgrims setting off for a rural monastery. They welcomed me on board. The monastic foundations were only just being laid, they said, and they were going to attend the blessing of its waters. In 1987 an excavator at the site – near the state farm of Rechnoi – had unearthed a mass grave, and the place was revealed as a complex of labour camps, abandoned at Stalin's death. The inmates, mostly intelligentsia, had died of pneumonia and dysentery from working in the fields, and their graves still scattered its earth.

As our bus bowled through ramshackle villages, the pilgrims

relayed the story with murmurs of motherly pity. They were elderly women, for the most part, indestructible babushkas in flower-printed dresses and canvas shoes, whose gnarled hands were closed over prayer-books and bead-strings, and whose head-scarves enshrined faces of genial toughness. When a fresh-faced cantor began chanting a hymn in the front of the bus, their voices rose in answer one after another, like old memories, reedy and melodious from their heavy bodies, until the whole bus was filled with their singing.

We reached a birch grove on the Rechnoi farm. It was one of those ordinary rural spots whose particular darkness you would never guess. As the women disembarked, still singing, the strains of other chanting echoed from a chapel beyond the trees. It was the first of four shrines which would one day stake out the corners of an immense compound. Inside, a white-veiled choir was lilting the sad divisions of the Liturgy. As the pilgrims visited their favourite icons, a forest-fire of votive candle-flames sprang up beneath the iconostasis, and two or three babushkas shuddered to their knees.

In the south transept, meshed in scaffolding, an unfinished fresco of the Deposition from the Cross loomed above us. It was almost complete; but the flesh tints were still missing, as if the artist were afraid to touch too closely on Divinity, and pots of pigment lined the scaffold. So only the painted garments of the disciples semaphored their grief, while their hands and features were empty silhouettes in the plaster: here a face uplifted in dismay, there a blank caress on the unpainted body of Christ – which remained a ghostly void, like something the onlookers had imagined.

Sometimes, whimsically, I felt as if this scene were echoed in the nave where I stood, where around the great silence left by God the worshippers lifted their heads and hands, crossed themselves, and wept a little.

From outside came the squeal of bulldozers in a distant field. They were smoothing the earth of the labour camps into monastery foundations. I strained to catch the sounds, but our singing drowned them in the mournful decrescendos of the Russian rite.

And out of the mouths of these ancient women – whose sins, I imagined, could barely exceed a little malicious gossip – rose the endless primal guilt '*O Lord forgive us!*', over and over, as if from some deep recess in the national psyche, a need for helplessness.

The sanctuary curtains parted on an incense-clouded region inhabited by a very small priest. His hair shimmered down in a phantasmal jumble, like a Restoration wig, and melted into a droop of violet-clad shoulders. Occasionally, feebly, one of his arms swung a censer; in the stillness between responses its coals made a noise like suppressed laughter. As he intoned the prayers he constantly forgot or lost his place, until his chanting dithered into confusion, and three deacons in raspberry robes prompted his responses with slips of paper. He would peer at these through enormous spectacles stranded in his hair like the eyes of a lemur, and try again. But the cause of his panic was plain to see. Enthroned beside him, giant and motionless, sat Feodosy, Archbishop of Omsk.

Towards noon a procession unwound from the church and started across the pasturelands towards the unblessed waters. It moved with a shuffling, dislocated pomp. Behind its uplifted cross, whose gilded plaques wobbled unhinged, the Archbishop advanced in a blaze of turquoise and crimson, his globular crown webbed in jewels. He marked off each stride with the stab of a dragon-headed stave, and his chest glinted with purple- and gold-embossed frontlets, and a clash of enamelled crosses. He looked huge. Beside him went the quaint, dishevelled celebrant, and behind tripped a huddle of young priests in mauve, and the trio of raspberry-silk deacons.

I fell in line with the pilgrims following. It was oddly comforting. An agnostic among believers, I felt close to them. I too wanted their waters blessed. I wanted that tormented earth quietened, the past acknowledged and shriven. I helped the old woman beside me carry her bottles. My feeling of hypocrisy, of masquerading in others' faith, evaporated. As I took her arm over the puddles and our procession stretched across the wet grass, Russia's atheist past seemed no more than an overcast day in the long Orthodox summer, and the whole country appeared to be reverting instinctively, painlessly, to its old nature. This wandering ceremonial, I felt, sprang not from an evangelical revolution but from a simple cultural relapse into the timeless personality of the motherland – the hierarchical, half-magic trust of its forefathers, the natural way to be.

I had already seen it. Every other market, airport or bus station was staked out by a babushka selling prints of icons and religious pamphlets, and nursing an offertory for the restoration of the local church or cathedral. Holy pictures dangled from the dashboards of taxis, decorated people's rooms. God had re-entered the vocabulary, the home, the gestures of beggars blessing themselves in the streets. Far away in Moscow the Church was growing fat on concessions to import tax-free alcohol and cigarettes; while here in Siberia, traditionally independent but conservative, this corrupting embrace of Church and State was paying (I imagined) for our monastery. But the cross wavered and glistened confidently among the birches. Authority, as always here, was salvation. It gave peace in place of thought.

Yet after the Communist hiatus, what had God become? Was he not now very old? And hadn't He lost too many children? On a road beyond the trees a troop of young men and girls were watching us from their parked cars, without expression, as tourists look at something strange.

How had these devotees survived? For sixty years scarcely a church was open in Siberia; the priests had been dispossessed, exiled, or shot. Even the oldest pilgrims trudging through these meadows could scarcely have remembered the Liturgy from child-hood. How had they kept faith?

'We had icons in my home, hidden in the roof.' The young priest was pasty and shy, with absent eyes. He had joined the procession late. 'My father worked in the stone quarries of Kazakhstan, so we lived miles from anywhere. But parents pass these icons down to their children, you see, and my grandmother's family had kept theirs. That's how I came to God, through the icons, through my grandmother. Not suddenly, but out of the heart' – he touched his chest – 'bit by bit. God calls you out.'

We reached a place where a silver pipe, propped on an old lorry

tyre, was spilling warm water into a pool. A blond deacon like a
Nordic Christ planted the processional cross on the far side, and
the archbishop, the priests, acolytes and pilgrims, the babushkas
with their bags and bottles, a few war veterans and one mesmerised foreigner formed a wavering crescent round the water's rim.

The unkempt celebrant, clutching a jewelled cross, was ordered
to wade in. From time to time he glanced up pathetically at
Feodosy, who gave no signal for him to stop. Deeper and deeper
he went, while his vestments fanned out over the surface, their
mauve silk waterlogged to indigo, until he was spread below us
like an outlandish bird over the pool. At last Feodosy lifted his
finger. The priest floundered, gaped up at us – or at the sky – in
momentary despair, recovered his balance and went motionless.
Then, with a ghostly frown, he traced a trembling cross beneath
the water.

A deep, collective sigh seemed to escape the pilgrims. Again the
cavalcade unfurled around the pool, while the archbishop,
grasping a silver chalice, sprinkled the surface with its own water,
and the wobbly cross led the way back towards the noise of the
bulldozers.

But the babushkas stayed put. As the procession glimmered and
died through the darkness of the trees, and the archbishop went
safely out of sight, a new excitement brewed up. They began to
peel off their thick stockings and fling away their shoes. They
were all ready. They tugged empty bottles labelled Fanta or Coca-
Cola from their bags. Then they clambered and slid down the
muddy banks and waded into the newly blessed water. At first
they only scooped it from the shallows. It was mineral water,
muddied and warm. They drank in deep gulps from their cupped
hands, and winched themselves back to stow the bottles on shore.

Then it all went to their heads. Six or seven old women flung
off first their cardigans, then their kerchiefs and skirts, until at
last, stripped down to flowery underpants and bras, they made
headlong for the waters. All inhibition was lost. Their massive
legs, welted in varicose veins, carried them juddering down the
banks. Their thighs tapered to small, rather delicate feet. Little
gold crosses were lost between their breasts. They plunged moun-

tainously in. I stood above them in astonishment, wondering if I was meant to be here. But they were shouting and jubilant. They cradled the water in their hands and dashed it over their faces. Holiness had turned liquid, palpable. You could drink it, drown in it, bring it home like flowers for the sick.

Two of the boldest women – cheery, barrel-chested ancients – made for the gushing silver pipe and thrust their heads under it. They sloshed its torrent exultantly over one another, then submerged in it and drank it wholesale. They shouted at their friends still on land, until one or two even of the young girls lifted their skirts and edged in. Bottle after bottle was filled and lugged to shore. But it was the young, not the old, who hesitated. The old were in high spirits. One of them shouted at me to join them, but I was caught between laughter and tears. These were women who had survived all the Stalin years, the deprivation, the institutional suffering, into a life of widowhood and breadline pensions, and their exuberance struck me dumb. Perhaps in this sacred and chaotic water-hole the world seemed finally to make sense to them, and all this aching, weary flesh at last found absolution.

The procession, meanwhile, had reached the open fields where the bulldozers worked. All the way to the future cathedral, which would stand in the compound's heart, the tarred pipes lay ready alongside their trenches, and the channel was blessed. I caught up with the remaining pilgrims clustered in the big meadows, beside the ghost-cathedral. Here Feodosy, above the lonely swing of a censer, blessed the site 'where nameless thousands had laboured and died', and we stared across fields lacquered in blue and white flowers while the incense vanished over them. Sometimes I wondered if the past were being laid too easily to sleep, forgotten. But the monastery would countermand this, said the shy priest. In future years people would ask: Why is it here? and recognise its building both as a cleansing and a memorial. This was being done for the dead.

The procession moved on. I fell behind with a war veteran hobbling on a stick, and found myself wondering aloud again: why, why had this faith resurrected out of nothing, as if a guillotined head had been stuck back on its body? Some vital artery had preserved it. And as I watched the pilgrims filtering back towards us from the pool, I thought: it was the women. 'Yes,' the soldierly old man answered. 'For me it was my mother. We lived in a remote region near Voronezh – not in a town at all, you understand, just a country village. No church for hundreds of miles. My mother was illiterate, but she remembered all the prayers from the old days, and taught me them.'

I tried to imagine his old face young, and found a puckish boy there. A dust of hair was still brown over his scalp. He said: 'And in the war, when I was on the front, my mother prayed for me and I for her, secretly. She gave me one of these' – he pulled a miniature icon from his wallet. 'Marshal Zhukov kept one in his pocket all through the war – and so did other generals. And nobody knew it.'

He paused from the pain in his foot. Neither his icon nor his mother's prayers had saved him from a German sniper. The bullet had opened up a 10-inch wound, and now he had this trouble walking. 'We didn't have bullets like that in Russia, it was a type of shrapnel. When it hit me, it exploded and shattered the leg bones. Now I try to walk like this . . . or this . . . but nothing works.' He said: 'God must have been looking away.'

When we arrived back at the chapel we found a long table in the shade, laden with salads and jams. The babushkas had returned. Their hands were ready beside their soup plates in two ranks of sun-cracked knuckles and broken nails. The archbishop, presiding at the head, commanded me to sit beside him – 'We have a guest from England!' he boomed. 'We must make him welcome!' – and I looked down an avenue of nodding heads, which turned to gaze at me as one, and murmured: 'England . . . England. . . .' Their cheeks bunched into smiles, and faltering lines of teeth parted in welcome.

Feodosy pounded the table with a bottle. 'This is for you!' he said. 'It's our monastery water! It cures everything!' He read off the label. 'Chronic colitis and enterocolitis! Liver ailments! All gastric problems! Cystitis! Non-cancerous stomach ulcers! Duodenal ulcers . . .'

The babushkas crossed themselves and commended me to God.

They looked deeply respectable. Nobody would have guessed that half an hour before they had been ducking one another half-naked in a water-hole. Yet under the benches their bags bulged with bottles of holy water and they were sitting becalmed, almost smug, in the warmth of their success.

Around me at the table's head the priests had turned pallid in the desanctifying light. Stripped to simple soutanes, they fingered their cutlery nervously around the archbishop. On his far side the celebrant appeared to be defensively asleep. His beard, I noticed, was fringed with white but auburn at the roots, as if it had turned white after some shock and was getting over it now. Only Feodosy survived proximity, and still looked formidable. His black eyes and aquiline nose broke imperiously through the gush of grey hair and beard which swamped his pectoral crosses and lapped at his nape. He hammered out commands at the nuns who had appeared from nowhere to serve us, or shouted down the table. 'Brothers and sisters! Pass the mineral water round! . . . Sisters, bring on the *kasha*.' The vegetable soup was gone in a trice, and soon he was ramming the rice into his mouth with giant wedges of bread. 'And no water! Sisters . . .' I wondered if he had been promoted for his looks. A burst of jet-black eyebrows lent him the glamour of a converted Mephistopheles. Nobody dared ask him questions. He addressed me in explosions of German which I could rarely understand. 'The man who found the first mass grave here – this was the hand of God – it was the local Party Secretary! And now he's become a priest, yes! He's chaplain to a Cossack regiment in Omsk. Sisters! Where is the bread? . . .'

He ladled a dollop of strawberry jam on to my bowl of rice. It was like being back at school. 'And in the spring we'll start the building of the cathedral, yes, God is in this place of tragedy!' He gestured out to the fields. 'There are dead out there.' He turned sombre. 'And everywhere. The monastery will gather information on them, and the monks will pray for their souls.'

'And what will you do with so much space?'

'Do?' he bellowed. 'We'll plant it with roses! Nothing but roses!' The enamel crosses trembled on his paunch. 'An ocean of roses!'

All down the table the faces broke into smiles again, and stray wisps of hair shivered free of their headscarves. As the meal broke up, one of the women tapped my arm and held out a thin blue sash stamped with prayers. 'This is for you,' she said, 'to wear on your train.' Then she committed me to God, and went back among her friends.

I spread the sash in my hands and read: 'He shall give his angels charge over thee, to keep thee in all thy ways. They shall bear thee up in their hands. . . .'

Yes, I thought, I would wear it as a belt. I must have grown thinner, because my trousers were loose. So I knotted it round my waist.

A light intoxication, something welcome and unexpected (for we had drunk only water) descended on me out of the half-healed land. A priest was tolling a carillon of bells on a makeshift scaffold near the chapel, but softly (perhaps he was practising) as if to lay to rest the spirits, and the pilgrims, by twos and threes, were returning to the coach. I climbed in among them. For a moment I wanted to believe that everything was as they believed. I was thankful for their stubborn needs and passions. I sat squashed between two babushkas (there was a shortage of seats) and they began to sing. 'Sing! Sing!' they cried. I hitched up my sash: 'He shall cover thee with his feathers,' it went on, 'and under his wings shalt thou trust. . . .' Yes, I thought, everything will get better. We will abrogate reason and love one another. Perhaps monastic water will turn us near-immortal. The past will forgive us, and the earth will bear roses. . . .

*   *   *

A land of interlaced earth and water, mutable, near-colourless – the sway of fescue grass above the swamps, the wrung-out platinum of winter wheat – spread out from the train window to a bleached sky. Half-way to Novosibirsk, the Baraba steppe was once a place of exiles and Tartar nomads, crossed by a string of Cossack forts. Now wild geese and coots flew from the marshes over a glint of lakes fringed by salinated soil. Here and there the old collectives spread long white barns, but they looked unin-habited. The villages, too, were empty. Distance resolved them into the hamlets of Russian fairy-tale, where the witch Baba Yaga might appear, or a formation of swan-princesses fly in.

In four hundred miles we stopped only three times. I stared out to a faint, light horizon where the forest made charcoal lines. Occasionally a horseman watched his cattle, or a field of rape-seed broke into buttery flower. More often, for mile after mile, the late summer haze turned this into looking-glass country. Its water-smeared earth wobbled against the sky. All matter looked temporary and dissoluble, all liquid so silted that it was half-way to being earth. Yet a farmer beside me said that the summer rains had been too few, and I noticed how low the rivers dawdled in their banks, and how the shrubs were already taking on the burnish of autumn.

We were following the line eastward of the Trakt post road, the precursor of the Trans-Siberian, which by the 1760s stretched from the Urals to the Pacific. In those days the bone-crunching journey – by horse-cart or sleigh – might take a year. When Chekhov embarked on his long tarantas ride towards Sakhalin, coughing up blood and sinking deep into depression, it was raining day and night, the rivers flooded, the ferries groping back and forth in howling wind, and ice-floes on the move. Now, as we rumbled towards Novosibirsk, the largest city in Siberia, trains passed us every three minutes on the busiest freight line in the world, bringing coal from the Kuzbas basin to the smelting fur-naces of the Urals.

You disembark at Siberia's biggest station, then taxi into the third most spacious city in Russia. Space is the sterile luxury of Novosibirsk. In summer it hangs in vacant stillness over the flat-tened boulevards. In winter it starts to move, and howls between the islanded buildings and across the squares. The city is a claus-trophobe's dream. Its roads sweep empty between miles of apartment-blocks and Stalinist hulks moaning with prefabricated pilasters and cornices. As for the people, there are one and a half million of them, but they seem lost in space. They trickle along the pavements to work. You become one of them, reduced. The traffic, too, seems sparse and far away, meandering over a delta of stone and tarmac.

Longing for intimacy, you avoid the 888-room Hotel Novosibirsk. But instead you find yourself in the void of Lenin Square, where the largest opera house in Russia, bigger even than the Bolshoi, crouches like a square-headed tortoise under a dome of silver scales. To reach it you have to sprint 200 yards across traffic-sprinkled space. Then you are turned away. It is closed in August.

So you stand, a little ashamed of your indifference – for this, after all, is Siberia's industrial giant, its centre of heavy metallurgy and machine-tool manufacture, of international trade conferences and joint ventures – you stand on a traffic island christened by a gold-domed chapel: because here, it has been calculated, lies the geographical centre of Russia. You wait, as visitors wait in Times Square or Piccadilly Circus, expecting something to happen. But nothing does, of course. And you are alone. The streets reel away on either side. From the granite steps of the chapel you gaze miles down the main street at the shadow of a bridge over the Ob river, to where on the far bank glimmers a suburb of smoke-stacks and flat-blocks built in Khrushchev's time, now misted in smog. Here the Ob, the fourth longest river in the world, moves imperceptibly towards the Arctic – dropping only two inches a mile – and downstream will fill with industrial waste and toxic oil, becoming so polluted that in winter it sometimes fails to freeze.

Space, in the end, may be all you remember of Novosibirsk. It is Siberia's gift. The vacancy of the land seems to infiltrate every town, or license it to sprawl. The flat-blocks carry on for mile after monotonous mile. Railway stations, whose tracks and sidings multiply ten or fourteen abreast, lie far from their town centres. And the rivers wind in enigmatically from nowhere like sky-coloured lakes, and curl out again to nowhere. When you hunt for them on your map, you may find only blue threads, tributaries of a tributary to some distant giant. The eye is met by eternal sameness. It begins to glaze.

In the mid-1950s, when the Soviet Union reached middle age, the rise of Khrushchev resurrected the vision of a purpose-built city dedicated to science. This utopian artifice would solve the problems of pure knowledge; but it would also deploy its genius in the service of technology and economics, devoting itself in particular to the vast resources of Siberia, by which Russia would at last outstrip the West.

The embodiment of this awesome concept was planned twenty miles south of Novosibirsk in the Golden Valley by the Ob river. Building began in 1958, and within seven years 40,000 scientists, executives and their families had poured in to fifteen newly opened research academies. A garden city grew up in six micro-regions, with its own schools and supermarkets, an elite university, an artificial beach on the Ob reservoir, even ski-runs illuminated at night.

Here in the taiga, far from the watchful Party apparatus in Moscow, a brief, intoxicating freedom sprang up. Akademgorodok became the brain of Russia. It attracted a host of young, sometimes maverick, scientists, many from Siberia. It opened up fields of study previously forbidden. The Institutes of Nuclear Physics and Economics, of Hydrodynamics and Catalysis, shared the forest with academies devoted to geology, automation, thermophysics (for the tapping of volcanic energy beneath permafrost) and a Physiological Institute working on the adaptation of animals and plants to the Siberian climate. And at the centre of this cerebral spider's-web the Institute of Abstract Mathematics sat like a cool agony aunt, advising on the problems of all the rest. Informal communication between institutes was the touchstone of the place's founder, the mathematician Lavrentiev. There were breakthroughs in physics, biology and computer studies. For a few heady years it seemed as if the science-fiction city could fulfil its promise.

Then, with the fall of Khrushchev, ideological controls began to tighten. Science became yoked to industry and was commandeered to show direct economic returns. The heart went out of things. But in a sense the clampdown came too late. There were people working in Akademgorodok – the economist Aganbegyan, the sociologist Zaslavskaya – whose thought became seminal to *perestroika*. Yet ironically it was the chaotic results of Gorbachev's revolution that laid waste the power-house whose institutes I tramped for two days.

They rose in mixed styles, prefabricated, sometimes handsome, recessed among their trees along irregular avenues. There were now twenty-three of them, but the only map I found catered for visitors shopping in the town's handful of emporia. I scanned it in bewilderment. In Soviet times, I knew, maps were often falsified or full of blanks. This one featured the smallest bakery and cafe. But the institutes had become nameless ghosts. Were they too important to divulge, I wondered, or were they just forgotten?

I wandered them in ignorance, staring at their nameboards. 'Institute of Solid-state Chemistry . . . Cytology and Genetics . . . Institute of Chemical Kinetics . . .' We barely shared a language. In between, woodland paths wended among silver birch and pine trees, their trunks intermingled like confused regiments. The earth sent up a damp fragrance. It was obscurely comforting. A few professors strolled between institutes, carrying shapeless bags and satchels, and fell pleasantly into conversation.

One of these chance meetings landed me unprepared in the Akademgorodok Praesidium. The professor who introduced me soon disappeared, and I was left in a passage outside the General Secretary's office, like a schoolboy waiting to be beaten. I thought I knew these interviews. From the far side of his desk a sterile apparatchik would tell me that all was well. The only signs of truth would be chance ones: damp wallpaper or indiscreet secretaries or the way the man's hands wrenched together. But I waited with suppressed hope. I wanted to know the outcome of several key Siberian projects, and sieved my brain for the Russian equivalent of 'nuclear reaction' or 'electric light stimulant', then gave up in despondency. I wasn't even dressed right. I was still wearing my Orthodox prayer-belt, and one of my climbing boots had developed a foolish squeak.

When the General Secretary's door opened, my heart sank. He

loomed big and surly behind his desk, in shirtsleeves. His features were obscure oases in the blank of his face: pin-prick eyes, a tiny, pouting mouth. I squeaked across the room to shake his hand. It was soft and wary. It motioned me to sit down.

Where could I tactfully begin? He wasn't going to help. He was gazing at me in passive suspicion. So I asked after the institute's recent successes.

He went on staring. All his answers came slowly, pronounced in the gravelly bass of authority. Progress had been made in the climatic adaptation of livestock, especially sheep, he said, and in a biochemical substance to stimulate the growth of wheat and rice. . . . But he did not enlarge on this. I thought he looked faintly angry.

Then I hunted for projects safely past, and alighted on the perilous Soviet scheme for steering Siberian rivers away from the Arctic to irrigate Central Asia and replenish the Aral Sea. He said: 'It was a useless scheme, horrible. It would have been an ecological disaster for both Siberia and Kazakhstan. Our scientists here were categorically against it, and the project was scrapped.'

I shifted nervously in the face of his morose stillness. There had been a project, I continued, in which artificial daylight was used to increase fertility in mink, fox, pigs. . . . It had something to do with the effect of the retina on the pituitary gland, I remembered, and sounded faintly repellent; but the General Secretary might approve.

He said: 'I only know they breed different coloured Arctic fox-furs now.' He tossed a batch of imagined stoles dismissively over his shoulder. 'Blue, navy blue, green. Any colour.'

But the remembered words of Soviet apologists, of Lavrentiev himself, were crowding back into my head. Some thirty years ago they promised that nuclear power would by now be centrally heating enormous tracts of Siberia and flooding Arctic towns with artificial sunlight. '*Dramatic changes in Siberia will astound the world, changes that will make Siberia ideally suitable for human habitation.*'

I said: 'There was an idea for melting permafrost by controlled nuclear power. . . .'

The Secretary was unmoved. 'That was just an idea,' he said.

I felt grateful for this honesty. But the voices of the old enthusiasts went on clamouring in me. 'It was proposed to fire coal underground,' I continued, 'to feed hydro-electric stations from underground funnels.'

A cigarette waggled unlit between the Secretary's fingers. 'It didn't work. It was impossible.'

'Then what about the scheme for fuelling power-stations with steam, using the Kamchatka volcanoes?'

He shrugged. 'I haven't even heard of it. And it doesn't fall within the province of this institution. . . .' He was slumped deeper behind his desk, huge in the slope of his beer-gut. His eyes were ice-pale. I imagined they had no pupils. I felt at sea. My jacket had fallen open on my prayer-belt, which guaranteed me immunity from pestilence and the cockatrice's den. I hid it with my arm. I was unsure what a cockatrice was, but the General Secretary might know.

By now my questions, his answers, and the voices from the still-recent past seemed to be interlocked in a formal dance. I lit despairingly on an old success story. 'The hydrodynamic cannon . . .'

'*It slices off whole layers of hard earth,*' Lavrentiev had said, '*and opens coal deposits in a matter of hours.*'

'They were discontinued years ago,' answered the General Secretary. 'They couldn't really do the job. The principle is now used only to press matter, not cut it open. The cannon could only drill a small hole. . . .'

We had reached a strange impasse. It was I who was believing in a future, it seemed, and he who was denying it. But I floated out a last fantasy, something I had childishly hoped to see. Twenty years ago plans were afoot for a whole Arctic town enjoying its own micro-climate. Named Udachny, 'Fortunate', it would either rise in a transparent pyramid or shelter beneath a glass dome or spread along a sealed web of avenues and gardens. It had been promised within ten years. (Lavrentiev: '*Siberia will become the science centre not only of the Soviet Union, but of the world.*')

I asked: 'Where is this town? Wasn't there a scheme?'

'There was a scheme,' said the General Secretary remorselessly. 'But there is no town.'

I went quiet, foolishly dispirited. The voices of the failed future mewed faintly, faded away. Suddenly the Secretary leant forward. 'Look,' he growled. 'Look. . . .' I had no idea what to expect. His face was heavy with anger. 'We have one overriding problem here. *Money*. We receive no money for new equipment, hardly enough for our salaries. There are people who haven't been paid for six months.' Then his anger overflowed. He was barking like a drill-sergeant. 'This year we requested funds for six or seven different programmes! And not one has been accepted by the government! Not one!'

I stared at him, astonished. I realised that all this time his bitterness had been directed not at me, but at Moscow. Far from being a passive mouthpiece, he was furious with his masters. 'I don't know what policy drives our government, or even if it has one! Science is now as cut off from the State as the Church used to be. As far as I can see everything's run by mafia!'

He delved into a box and found me a book about the past achievements of Akademgorodok. It was illustrated with bursting corn-heads and fattened sheep. 'We used to accomplish things,' he said, as I got up to go. Then, as if a boil had been lanced, his anger evaporated. All his face's features, which had seemed numb or absent before, creased and wrinkled into sad life. How curious, I thought, bewildered. He was almost charming.

'The future?' he said. 'When we have a government that realises no country can do without science, Akademgorodok will flourish again.'

He accompanied me to the Praesidium steps, perhaps reluctant to stay in his gaunt office. I started, too late, to like him. As I shook his hand I could no longer sense the brooding menace of the apparatchik; in its place was an ageing caretaker, dreaming of other times.

I walk along the Ob Sea with a young scientist from the Institute of Physics. This is not truly a sea but a giant reservoir, which sparkles tidelessly. And he is not quite a scientist (although he calls himself one) but a research student from the once-prestigious university. He is wondering what to do with his life. The sand under our feet is not naturally there either, but was imported – two and a half million cubic yards of it – to complete the town's amenities.

And now everything is in ruins, he says. 'The younger scientists are leaving in droves, mostly for business. In business you can earn five times the salary you're offered here. Others have emigrated to the States and Germany. All the bright ones have gone.'

Gone to the countries their parents feared, I thought. 'And you?'

A stammer surfaces in his speech, like some distress-signal. 'I'll go too.'

'To work in science?'

'No. Most of us can't use our scientific expertise. We just want a decently paid job, and a future.'

Our feet drag in the sand. The enormous beach is dotted with sunbathers, and some women are walking their dogs along the shallows. He says: 'A few years ago, you know, when people left university, there was terrible competition to get into the institutes. But now they'll take anyone. They'll give you a flat, of course, but what's the point of that if you can hardly afford to eat?' The question is not quite rhetorical. He wants to be a scientist still. But he doesn't see how. 'Only the dim ones stay. They do laboratory work for a pittance. The equipment's getting old. And nobody's working properly.'

We stop by the water's edge. For miles it is fringed by a flotsam of logs, broken loose from their booms somewhere upriver. For a heady moment their resinous smell returns me to my childhood by a Canadian river, where the stray logs became the playthings of a small, naked boy, years before Akademgorodok was even conceived.

The tree-trunks lie beached at our feet, polished by the water. The student is saying without conviction, without love: 'I'll go into business.'

He was an only child. Reclusive, almost biblically innocent.

During the war his mother had escaped with him from the siege of Leningrad; his father had been killed. I had been given his telephone number by chance, and when he clattered up in his institute's car – a professional perk – I had no idea what to expect.

Where did Sasha belong? Not with Russia's troubled present, I think, but with the dreamers who scatter its nineteenth-century novels. His work consumed him. Many evenings he toiled through the night in a big, bleak building called the Institute of Clinical and Experimental Medicine. Even now, during the August break, the receptionist acknowledged him with pert familiarity. He studied in the basement, in a chain of dim grottoes – their electricity had failed – poring over data on magnetic fields. Beside his desk stood a rusty stove and an exercise bike, and two or three enigmatic machines loomed against the walls in a fretwork of tubes and wires. But there must have been electricity somewhere because a fridge wheezed in one corner, and after a while Sasha disappeared to make tea. I waited, as in the den of some harmless wizard. The walls were hung with prints by the mystic painter Nikolai Roerich – grainy mountains inhabited by hermits or traversed by pilgrims.

We drank tepid tea in the dark. Sasha was fifty-six, but boyish, bursting with enthusiasm and trust. A pelmet of chestnut hair fell over his forehead and his eyes were brown and puppyish. He was sad that he could not measure my magnetic sensitivity on the Heath-Robinson machine beside us ('No electricity!') but he hoped I would enter the hypomagnetic chamber next door. 'You've seen these photographs?' He pointed to a cabinet. 'Those detect energy flowing from a patient's fingertips after just three sessions in the chamber!'

I peered at them: they seemed to show a jelly-fish haloed in hair. I said doubtfully: 'What diseases can it cure?'

'It treats epilepsy, but the subject needs to be very sensitive. It's also helped with nervous paralysis and cancer.'

'*Cancer?*'

'Well, it's helped in diagnosis.'

'But what does the chamber actually do?'

Even to myself I sounded peremptory, but Sasha was breathless with evangelism. 'The chamber almost eliminates the body's natural magnetic waves! They decrease by six hundred times! And this allows *other things* to happen – purer waves. Things we can't be sure about. But before treatment we need to know your pre-natal development in each of the weeks between conception and birth. The interplanetary magnetic field, phases of the moon and so on . . .' He looked at me as if I must have this data on me, perhaps in my passport.

'I'm afraid . . .'

But he rushed on: 'The field-structure of our organism is very dynamic. Sometimes it is closed, sometimes not. Recently, for instance, we had a conference in Martinique, and the people there were very open, very. Their magnetic sensitivity, when we tested them, was first-rate. People need to unlock, you see. To open up!'

I began to feel jittery. I stared down at myself, wondering if I would open up, but saw only a scruffy shirt and a prayer-belt. The magnetic waves to which I would be exposed owed much, it seemed, to the astro-physicist N. A. Kozyrev, who had set up telescopic mirrors to record starlight simultaneously from the past, present and future. Kozyrev was Sasha's god. The astronomer seems to have believed that the Universe was awash with a unified time-energy, in which intellect, matter and cosmic forces were bundled up in some Hegelian process that fascinated Sasha but eluded me.

'It all depends on your responsiveness,' Sasha said, leading me to the next room. 'The machine opens up psycho-physical recesses not normally explored.' We stood before two identical chambers: grey, open-mouthed tunnels for the patient to lie in. They resembled MRI scanners or huge, open-ended washing-machines, but were utterly plain.

I said stupidly: 'There are two.'

'Yes, but one is a dummy,' he said. 'If you lie quietly in each, you will sense which is which.' He straightened the mattresses inside them. 'Of course there are some people who stay closed up. Yes. There are, I should say, cosmophiles and cosmophobes. But 70 per cent are sensitive to it. Some get a feeling of flying, others of being lifted out of themselves. It depends on your sensitivity.'

His trust invited mine. I was determined to be sensitive. I climbed into one of the tunnels, feeling like dirty washing, and lay down. 'Lie quietly,' he said. 'Meditate.' I tried to empty my mind, but instead found my self scanning the arc of ceiling above me for some tell-tale sign. Was this the dummy or the real one, I wondered? I thought I discerned a trickle of wiring under its plaster, but decided this was only a structural joint. I lay still. A mill-race of thoughts started up, subsided. I closed my eyes and concentrated only on the darkness under their lids, where an odd grey plasma was floating. The room was silent. My mind attempted a thought or two, then gave up. But I felt nothing. Nothing. After a while I stared down at the circle of light beyond my feet, hoping for some sensation, anything, but saw only Sasha's face peering in. 'Relax. Meditate for five minutes. I have to check my fax machine.'

I meditated. But no, this was the dummy machine, I realised. I simply wanted to go to sleep. So I climbed out and confronted its twin. They both looked makeshift and somehow unreal, like stage props. But as I crawled into the second chamber, I felt a tremor of unease. Now I would be passing (Sasha had said) from Einstein's space into Kozyrev's space. Living matter would enter an immaterial dimension. Hesitantly I lay down and gazed up. I imagined a blank. A long time seemed to go by. I tried to float. But again, nothing.

I thought: I must be cosmophobic. Perhaps I have no psychophysical recesses. Or the dynamic field-structure of my organism is falling to bits. Maybe I never had one. Compared to the man-in-the-street in Martinique . . .

Then I heard a steady, rhythmic whirring. For a moment I could not locate it, then realised it came not from my head, nor from the tunnel ceiling above me, but from the next-door room. I thought: Sasha is pumping something, a generator perhaps. He is trying to activate my tunnel. So at least I know I'm in the right one. I lay down and tried again. The whirring continued, but instead of flying I seemed to be sinking into a bored catalepsy.

My next thought was: the Russian Academy of Sciences is actually *paying* for this stuff, has been paying for years. . . .

After a few minutes, tiredly, I climbed out. Despite myself, an irritated sense of failure arose. I fought it off. I'm not cosmophobic, I thought grumpily, I'm just English. I scrutinised the chambers for any difference: a giveaway trail of cables or an extra metal coat. But there was none. The rhythmic whirring still sounded next door. I peered in and discovered its source: Sasha was riding his exercise bike.

'How was it? How was it?' He jumped off, sweating and jubilant.

I hazarded a guess at which was the real machine, but got it wrong. 'Maybe I'm tired,' I said. 'I didn't feel anything.' I hated to disappoint him. Momentarily I wanted the world to be riddled with cosmic benevolence. 'At least I don't think I did. . . .'

I had fallen plumb into the insensitive 30 per cent. But Sasha brushed this aside. 'Let me show you something else. . . .' My statistic, I could tell, would be lost in his own certainty. He had a way of discounting failure. His wife and son, he had mentioned, lived far away in Estonia – she had returned to the town of her childhood. Yet he shied away from the word 'separated'. They just were not together. He sealed the subject with a hazy smile. Sadness made him afraid, perhaps.

'You know there are certain trajectories of extraordinary magnetic power. . . .' He was burrowing among his files. 'Just look at these, from Stonehenge. I find these most interesting.'

On to my lap he spilled sheafs of paper covered with random sketches. They were the result of an arcane experiment. Here in Akademgorodok one of his colleagues had sat encased in a curved aluminium chamber called 'Kozyrev's Mirrors', constructed to heighten the transmission of his 'time-energy waves'. While he concentrated his mind on a selection of ancient Sumerian images, other participants – sitting among the monoliths of Stonehenge over three thousand miles away – had attempted to receive and sketch his thought-pictures.

'Look, look,' said Sasha. 'This is remarkable.' He pointed to a Sumerian original, which resembled a pair of dragonflies, then he riffled through the sketches. I saw spirals, boats, dogs, phalli, suns, stick-men, flowers, stars. At last: 'There!' Someone in Stonehenge had come up with a hovering bird. 'You see? You see?' He was glittering with faith. Never mind that all the other sketches – page upon page – bore no relation to anything envisioned, or that only the dragonflies and the bird dimly corresponded. Sasha was smiling at them like a cherub. He scarcely needed proof. He already knew.

*   *   *

An old man sits in his dacha in the Golden Valley. These country homes are given only to the elite – he is an Academician – and all along the avenue their stucco façades rear from tangled gardens, until the road gives out against wooded hills. The Academician's sitting-room is filled with kitsch: glass animals, sentimental pictures, statuettes of the Medici Venus, the Capitoline Venus, the Venus de Milo. But there are icons too, and tense, miniature landscapes painted by a Gulag prisoner. I wonder vaguely what these contradictions mean. Sasha, who has brought me here like a trophy, has gone silent. He listens to the Academician, his mentor, with hushed respect. So do the Academician's wife and middle-aged son. The whole house smells of a damp dog which is hurtling through the undergrowth outside.

For a while we sit nibbling *zakuski* snacks and drinking vodka. The Academician hands me his latest book, *Cosmic Consciousness of Humanity*. Then they toast my future Siberian travels ('It's dangerous now, you know') and I begin to squirm in my traveller's disguise, because they want to convert me to their beliefs. Unnoticed I open the Academician's book and read: 'The total world human Intellect in its cosmoplanetary motion is neither derivative from nor some procreation of, the social movement (social-cultural historic development). It is a peculiar cosmoplanetary phenomenon in the organisation and motion of the Universe Living Matter in its earth-adapted manifestation. . . .'

Fearing an attack of cosmophobia, I close it up, and now,

impatient with the trivia of eating, of small talk, the Academician announces: 'We must go upstairs and discuss.'

Years of deference, I suppose, have wrecked him. An old pedagogy and a new evangelism smooth his thinking to unchallenged monologue. In the study where we sit – his son, Sasha, myself – his books are stacked in avenues from floor to ceiling, all nestled in dust. While his wife stays downstairs, washing up, he explains how man's spiritual and mental life is shot through by galactic waves, and I cannot decide if this idea is a vanity or humility (and the Academician does not take questions). He often lifts his finger as he advances point by point, and his message grows in urgency.

'We are at a crisis in the world's development. The West is powerless, blinded by materialism. It can't *see* anything. *It can't think new.* It is only Russia which can show the way. Point Three: she can do this precisely, and only, because everything has been taken from her, and she is open! Yes, open! This is the moment! We have just a brief chance – now! In a few years it will be too late. Now is the moment for classical thinking and cosmic thinking to converge. We must save the world – not only Russia! – and unleash new ways of thought!'

He speaks as if in an echo-chamber, and the message which he finds so new is resonantly old. It rings through the works of the nineteenth-century Slavophils, who half-mystically enjoined the ancient values of the Russian soul. It is the vision of Dostoevsky, Herzen, Tolstoy. Yes, Russia will save the Earth! Truth will rise through suffering! Europe – rational, individualist Europe – is benighted by affluence. Only impoverished Russia can touch the heart of things, and rescue mankind.

I start to lose the Academician's thread. He seems to be talking about experiments with cosmic waves in a Thracian sanctuary in Bulgaria, and in the Arctic Circle north of Dudinka where I will be going. He drops sweeping abstracts and magisterial generalisations. His audience is solemn, grateful. Stray concepts surface in English, sink again. ' . . . Spatio-temporal waves . . . Point Six . . . distant-image interaction . . .' Then he says to me: 'When you sail down the Yenisei, if you go with an open mind, you'll discover a new Siberia! We conducted experiments in Dikson in the Arctic

Circle, and you'll find the magnetic channels between there and here are very powerful.' He asks: 'You've heard of Yuri Mochanov?'

To my surprise, I have. He is a Russian archaeologist whose excavations on the Lena have uncovered evidence of a prehistoric Siberian people. Controversially he has set the age of their stone tools at over 2,000,000 BC, matching Leakey's Africans in the van of civilisation. He still worked in the town of Yakutsk in East Siberia, where I meant to find him.

The Academician is fired up. 'A civilisation at least as old as Africa's! So what does that do to Darwinism? Now the classic view is that man evolved out of Africa, then spread east and north into Asia. But the excavations of Mochanov and others prove something different. They prove that Intelligence emerged in several regions simultaneously – in Siberia, in Africa, in Central Asia. In fact Siberia was the first!'

It all fits beautifully, of course. Here in Siberia – the symbol and repository of Russia's otherness – civilisation itself began. And here the cosmic flow, the great communion, will be re-affirmed. Not that the Academician repudiates science (although he lives in its ruins). In fact his finger is raised again. 'I hold that cosmic influences accompanied by changes in the earth's magnetic field were responsible for a sudden maturation in men's brains at that time. These early civilisations were in tune with the cosmos, but due to various factors they could not, in the end, survive. . . .' His hands return comfortably to his lap. 'Darwin, you understand, is nonsense.'

I sit opposite him, writhing with rebellion at first, then oddly sad. Sasha is glowing. But I see an old man in track-suit trousers and threadbare socks, who has gone off the rails. Sometimes I feel that he is talking not to us, but to himself, and that he is very lonely. I imagine him the victim of that self-hypnosis which sustained the great illusion of Communism itself – where ideas and dreams hover delusively over the wasteland of fact.

How quiet it is here. Young bracken is starting up in the woods, and the wind in the birch trees unlooses a shimmer of chromium leaves. Somewhere among the forests of Akademgorodok the Museum of Siberian Culture is kept like a private collection. It is small and choice. The iron head-dresses of shamans keep company with the fish-skin coats of Nivkhi tribesmen. The curator shepherds me round.

In the central room the tattooed mummy of a warrior lies beside his wood sarcophagus. He comes from the Altai mountains five hundred miles south on the borders of Mongolia. In this region rainwater, seeping through cairns and into the 2,400-year-old graves below, freezes solid with the first snows, and seals wood, leather, cloth, human skin in a cone of ice. The warrior had been entombed among sacrificed horses, whose bridles and trappings are encased nearby. His woollen coat – lined on the inside with marmot fur – is still serviceable.

Galina, the curator, is quick and proud: a small woman in green glasses. She points to another cabinet, and I peer down at air-thin slivers of gold, fragments from a dress. 'That', she says reverently, 'is *hers*.'

There is only one *She* in Russian archaeology now: the Ice Princess of the Altai, excavated in 1993 – a lone woman entombed in barbarian splendour on a remote plateau above China. Nobody knows who she was – shamaness, noblewoman, or bard – and a tempest of controversy soon brewed up about her race. Her mummy was brought to Akademgorodok and placed in a freezer which had once been used to store cheese. Soon fungi were crawling over the body, fading its delicate tattoos, and it was rushed to Moscow, where embalmers restored it. Slavic experts declared that she was Caucasoid, an early European. But the people of the Altai, who claim descent from her culture, protested that she was theirs, and a Swiss forensic pathologist supported them: she was Mongoloid, he said, close to the modern inhabitants.

Galina, a Russian brunette, is not having this. 'In Moscow at our Gerasimov Institute they said that in early times the Altai region was basically "European", but contaminated by the Chinese. Across the Chinese border they have excavated mummies which have never been shown to the public. They've kept them private. That's another indication that the Altai was racially European.' She is looking at me sharply: small, Slavic eyes. West or East, Europe or Asia – for Russians the debate about their own orientation never quite ends. She says suddenly: 'Would you like to see her?'

I am momentarily astonished. I had thought her still in Moscow, awaiting resolution. But Galina unlocks a small, barred room and beckons me in. A display case stands against one wall, covered in sheets of brown paper. She plucks them off, and inside the glass I see a woman lying. She rests on her side, with her hands crossed over her pelvis. Her torso has caved in on a spine striated like a palm trunk, and her head is tilted back. Her embalmed skin shines like ivory. It is hard to look at her. She is turned to the wall, as if repudiating us.

'Where will she go now?' I am whispering.

Galina gazes at her. 'There was an agreement with the museum at Gorno-Altaisk, the capital of the Altai region, that we should study her here. I believe she's ours.' But her voice is making an angry music. 'Now they want her back. Their curator – that Rima Yakimova! – she doesn't even allow us to excavate in the Altai any more – and her people have no money to excavate, themselves. And now we're making a present of our princess back to her!' However she resents this, the political storm has raged beyond her control. We are looking down at Russia's split identity. 'We've done everything for the princess here. Her felt riding-boots, the raw silk shirt and red-and-white woollen skirt she was buried in – they're being restored at this moment. Her jewellery, head-dress, they've all been photographed. Who else does she belong to?'

The princess had been buried with a sacrifice of six horses. On tables in her tomb-chamber archaeologists found a symbolic meal of mutton and horse-flesh. I stare down at her again. She must have been tall for her day. The indigo tattoos of deer or griffins are still clear on her shoulders and forearms. She has long, delicately boned hands.

'That Rima Yakimova, her museum is too small! It has enough exhibits already, and there's no space. They probably won't be able to preserve the mummy in the right atmospheric conditions. . . . This is the last we may see of her.'

She had died in her mid-twenties, from some natural cause. They found her stretched in her sarcophagus facing the east, crowned by a three-foot head-dress decorated with golden cats, and round her neck a circlet of wooden camels, originally gilded. Most of her innards had been removed, and her body stuffed with peat and bark, whose tannin had preserved her. Her skull was filled with the fur of pine-martens; her eyes had been cut out.

We cover her over again. After two and a half millennia she exerts the potency of the recently dead. The archaeologists had asked her to forgive them.

I think in parting: this rancorous and depleted Akademgorodok is not the place for her mummy. I imagine its future journey back to Gorno-Altaisk, close to the wild valleys where the frontiers of China, Kazakhstan, Russia and Mongolia collide, and I mean to go there.

4

Borderlands

Within two days I was moving south into a land where the Siberia I recognised started to fracture. From trains and buses I watched the steppes wrinkle and undulate, until they lifted into the foothills of the Altai, and the stains of industry vanished. The natives here were Mongol-Turkic tribespeople, semi-nomadic herdsmen by tradition, who found their ancestry among those once-great peoples, now shrivelled and scattered, who formed the armies of Genghis Khan.

But by the mid-nineteenth century Russian farmers had crowded into their pasturelands and were pushing them into the remote valleys. As my bus crossed the region's border to its capital, Gorno-Altaisk, a young tributary of the Ob, the Katun river, ran bright and fast alongside, and I imagined mountains bunching to the south-east: those obscure chains of the Altai and Sayan which separate Siberia from the plateaux of inner Asia.

Gorno-Altaisk was tranquil and run-down, squeezed in the river valley. I had nothing to do here. But in its museum, the future home of the Ice Princess, I went into the office of the notorious Rima Yakimova, and at once the voices of Asia and Europe were arguing again. Far from being small and overstocked, as Galina had said, Yakimova's museum was big and half-empty. And she wanted her Ice Princess back.

'In Moscow they say she's Caucasoid, but she's not. She's Asiatic. Even her hairstyle was Asiatic. And she will be coming *here*.' Yakimova was a native of the Altai: wide, Mongolian features, jet-black eyes. 'All we need now is a glass case for her, but we can't afford one yet: it'll cost twelve million roubles.' Her hands flickered emptily at the ceiling.

I said: 'She'll be kept at a special temperature?' I was remembering what Galina had feared (*'This is the last we may see of her'*).

'No. The mummy has been treated. She can lie at room temperature. All we need is a vitrine.' The glass case would cost seventeen hundred dollars. It did not seem so much. 'There is an idea too that she should be returned to the plateau where they found her. Just laid back in the grave. I'm torn about this. Among our people, the dead should never be disturbed. Never. Yet Russian archaeologists came and dug her up. To free her from the ice they poured hot water over her and she went black.' In the dark moon of her face her lips were full and angry. 'They violated her. But these are our graves, our people. Our own archaeologists can work here. They won't pour hot water over corpses.'

'But you have no money.'

'But the dead will lie in peace.'

These were precarious memories. Perhaps it was the nomad heritage, more than any shared blood, which linked the incensed curator through the Mongol armies to the enigmatic princess. Within living memory the Altai people were still accompanied in death by their sacrificed horses. During the Civil War eighty years ago, before they were brutally settled and collectivised, they had searched their ancestral memory and proclaimed an independent state named Karakorum, after the capital of Genghis Khan. The Bolsheviks swept it away.

Yakimova said: 'Power has always lain with the Russians. Everything discovered or dug up here went to St Petersburg or Akademgorodok. That Galina . . .' she murmured. 'The Hermitage is stuffed with wonderful things from the Pazyryk culture, and all of them are *ours*. Why should our people go to St Petersburg to visit their own heritage? There are things in their reserve collection – hundreds of them – which have never been seen. And a mass were sold off to America by Stalin. He sold our past. And now we want it back. *Here!*'

Pazyryk: the word stands for a culture whose name is lost, the people of frozen tombs. I had seen its artefacts in the Hermitage that June: spell-binding things. And now, when I unfolded my map over Yakimova's desk, her finger shot down a long valley nearly three hundred miles to the closed Mongolian border, then jerked north into a desert of plateaux and streams splintered like nerve-ends. With a short sigh, she inked in 'Pazyryk' there. 'But you won't be able to go. It's too far, too wild.'

The road to Pazyryk trickled at dawn through a surge of hills along the jade path of the Katun river. The world had turned young. The flatness of the steppeland, and the sullen meander of its rivers, had sharpened into mountain freshness – a cold, un-scented air and the chatter of glacial water over rocks. The farming villages were lush with orchards – apple, cherry, pear. Chrysanthemums and hollyhocks sent up a rainbow jumble under their cottage walls, where Russian vines multiplied and Russian children played.

Then the hills steepened. Birch woods spread a pale dust over their slopes. Sometimes the Katun forked and spreadeagled over meadows, or circled white-rocked islands, but as the mountains closed in it ran with a harsh brilliance. Its panicky descent turned it milky-green. Altai herdsmen were riding their stocky horses along its banks, and my bus emptied of Russians.

I was surrounded by a dark, hardy people. The women's heads glinted in gold-threaded scarves. The machine-gun patter of their speech, snagged by sudden gutturals and glottals, grated and chir-ruped through the bus. Some of them were beautiful. The wide plane of their cheeks and foreheads, where shallow noses and bunched lips made no commotion, emphasised instead the feathery isolation of eyebrows so admired of the Chinese. A resurgent confidence had long ago given their children Turkic or Mongolian names, so that from time to time an order would go out for little Genghis to stop fighting or for Oirot to sit still.

Beside me a military policeman on his way to guard the Mongo-lian border slumped inch by inch across my chest, fast asleep and still clutching his truncheon. Frontier life was very boring, he said

on waking. You just waited for nothing. His people were closer
to the Mongolians than to the Russians, he agreed, but his job
was just a job. He wasn't guarding anything, really. And even
here, I knew, in this so-called Altai republic of 200,000, the
Altaisky were outnumbered by the Russians. In all Siberia,
peopled by only thirty million, the indigenous natives numbered
just 5 per cent.

As we crossed the Katun, the clouds came down. The river
carved a cold corridor through mist and hills, then disappeared
as if a water-colourist had washed it into the sky. The villages we
passed became desolate, near-empty. Ground squirrels ran in the
pastures. As we climbed higher, the mountains shut us in eroded
walls where the pines moved in Indian file along the lee of ridges.
Long, vertical arteries of grey and russet shale were inching down
the valleys.

Amid the coming and going of farmers and herdsmen, a Turkic
beauty in a woollen trouser-suit climbed on to the bus and sat
among us for an inscrutable hour, varnishing her fingernails, then
got off at a half-demolished hamlet.

'Who on earth was that?'

Nobody knew.

At the head of the pass, and at springs along the way, the pine
trees were dripping with rags in honour of the spirits. Spirits
infested the waters and peaks of all this country. Neither Christianity nor Communism had dislodged them. They were too
pervasive, and too old. The rags shivered in the pines – requests,
tributes – and the river-beds glistened with coins. Here and there
hundred-rouble notes caught among their stones, pulled free
again, floated away.

Towards evening the bus veered north up a track. Behind us,
above the Mongolian frontier, a skeleton of snow-peaks hung in
the sky. We mounted into uplands burnished with autumn shrubs
and spread with shallow lakes unblurred by any trees. The hillsides were littered with stones. Here and there along the valleys
they traced faint circles and avenues, as if we were following some
ancient migratory road.

Then, at sunset, cresting a pass, we looked down on a wilderness of mountains, where only cloud-shadows moved and a pale half-moon was stencilled on the sky. For a few miles more we travelled into tableland. Then the track and the world stopped, and the village of Ust-Ulagan was strewn around its river in a maze of cottages and horse-corrals. Duckboards made wavering paths over its valley, where buzzards coasted on white-barred wings.

I got out into a deserted street, still called Soviet Road. Cows were slumbering in its pot-holes. Angry dogs ran at my heels. The few shops looked permanently shut, their iron doors padlocked and boarded. Tractors decomposed in the grass. I hunted the streets for shelter, but the village had retracted into itself. Smoke was starting to rise from its chimneys into the dusk, and only a few herdsmen were about – stocky men with wind-darkened faces. When I peered into courtyards I saw that these once-nomadic people had raised yurt tents beside their huts; their circular walls rose nostalgically to windowless domes, where the people in summer deserted their Russian cabins and returned to their past.

I found a concrete municipal office. It was shut; but at its rear a door stood ajar on a room where a hunchback was cooking potatoes. He had come from Gorno-Altaisk to inspect the village budget, he said, but of course there was nothing to inspect. All infrastructure had gone. 'Assess the budget! That's my job! To not assess a non-budget.' He was almost a dwarf, and his face too, knotted around a spread nose, looked out of true. He had rigged up some camp-beds beside the office because there was nowhere else to sleep, and he welcomed me in. 'You'll sleep quietly. Nobody laughs or sings in this place.'

His natural cynicism was being justified by events. The tragedy of Russia might drive others to drink or dream, but for him it only corroborated a conviction of the world's absurdity, and he had come into his own. The whole Altai republic was a shambles, he said. 'The farmers in this place haven't been paid for *five years*. So of course they work as if they were independent. It's back to the family group now, back to the old ways.' He himself was half-Turkic, half-Russian. 'Even us civil servants, our wages are slipping behind. . . . We'll end up like the rest.'

We ate his vegetable stew and my biscuits, then turned in early when the electric light failed. There was no running water, and the privy stank. In the dark he said: 'If you die in this place and can't pay for your grave, they toss you into the street.' The idea gave him obscure pleasure. He let out a long, retrospective chuckle, as if he were remembering the follies of a whole week. As I was falling asleep he asked out of the blue: 'And you? What are you doing here?'

What was I doing? My eyes opened on the night. I was trying to find a core to Siberia, where there seemed none; or at least for a moment to witness its passage through the wreckage of Communism – to glimpse that old, unappeasable desire to believe, as it fractured into confused channels, flowed under other names. Because I could not imagine a Russia without faith.

But I said to him: 'I came to look at the grave-mounds of Pazyryk.' They had yielded the world's most intimate nomad artefacts. 'They're only ten miles from here. You know of them?'

I heard a disembodied snort. 'They don't need me. I don't need them.' He turned over to sleep. 'I need my salary.'

Its true name is unknown. Perhaps it never had one. But the civilisation buried in the Pazyryk valley was the easternmost piece in the vast Scythian world which by the seventh century BC stretched from China to the Danube. The Scythians were Indo-Europeans: a tall, hirsute people who at their zenith tormented the Persian empire and subjugated the Medes. Ever since they touched the sphere of Greece, the fear or romanticism of historians staged them as barbarian nomads, wasters of all that was cultured, literate, settled. Even Herodotus, who knew them, said they had no towns.

But here in the Altai, at least, the Pazyryk people were only intermittently nomadic. Sometimes they built wooden settlements behind earth ramparts, like the Huns who followed them, and planted seasonal fields. They may once have been primitive farmers, for their semi-nomadism was a specialised choice, and their culture stood on the shoulders of others, among whom metallurgy in bronze and gold was already refined.

One day somebody – perhaps here in the Altai – conceived the idea of no longer driving a horse, but of sitting on its back. Then mobility became the Scythians' safety, their grace. They fought on stocky geldings, firing twenty poisoned arrows a minute at full gallop ambidextrously. They migrated in cattle-drawn wagons – sometimes even lived in them – and could transport their yurts wholesale. Their only permanence was in death, in the great stone-heaped tombs called *kurgans*. And at Pazyryk, by the action of water filtering into the underground chambers, they were frozen solid in Time.

Their close-cropped pastures spread unblemished as I climbed to the valley at dawn. All around me the herds and flocks of Ust-Ulagan were drifting over the hills, and their horsemen after them. Behind, in this cleansed light, the village looked frailer, stranger. Its corral fences interlaced it like a breaking spider's web. Already, in September, it was preparing for winter, its yards filling with fodder and firewood. Hopelessly remote, powerless to change or to rebel, it was enclosed on its own survival.

After an hour I reached a graveyard of farm machinery, glittering in the void: cannibalised tractors and bulldozers for fields now vanished. A man was there, tinkering with a harrow. 'Russian things,' he muttered.

For a while he accompanied me. Outsiders no longer interfered much in his village, he said. People just bred their cattle, and got by. His face was pure Mongol, amber-yellow, young; a wiry beard and moustache increased its savagery in my history-tainted eyes. We passed a spring trembling under cloth-hung trees.

'I don't know the name of the spirit here,' he said. 'But when I built my house I chopped down wood in another place. Then I left prayers so the spirit there wouldn't be angry with me.'

His tone was crisply practical. He had apologised to nature, compromised; whereas the Russian way was to master, transform, or obliterate it. But their machinery lay in ruins on the track behind us.

'And the Pazyryk graves?' I asked.

'You'll reach them in two hours.' He left me on the track. 'I don't know their names, the people buried there. We just call them *shifri*. Our ancestors.'

Towards noon I reached the edge of the valley. It descended in a broad passage where chestnut horses grazed, until it struck a transverse ravine and spilled out into space. It hung in a natural theatre. Out of the void beyond swam wooded hills, and beyond these again there lifted a far semicircle of mountains, their summits flashed with snow. They bathed the valley in a numinous cold. I stopped involuntarily on its rim, as if at an invisible frontier. No wonder the dead were buried here. Nothing made a sound. Painted clouds were stuck up in a sky too enormous to register their drift. I was gazing south from the Altai's core to where its mountains trailed for another four hundred miles through Mongolia.

But beneath me, at irregular intervals, the valley floor was blistered by five enormous *kurgans*. They had been raised between the sixth and fourth centuries BC – underground tomb-chambers built of jointed logs and heaped overhead with earth and stones. Now their displaced rocks ringed the excavated chambers in petrified craters, and around them a scattering of lesser graves left tracings in the grass.

Two and a half millennia ago Herodotus described the Scythian royal burials in intimate detail, from the forty-day funerary journey around the dead king's dominion to the narcotic vapour-tents where the mourners howled with joy. The chieftain was laid as if immortal in his tomb, his stomach gutted and filled with aromatic plants, his sinews removed, his skin waxed. Beside him lay strangled members of his household, with a dead concubine and many horses. Around his *kurgan* rode an eerie cavalry, fifty strong: its horses and men had been disembowelled and impaled on stakes and wheels, their feet and hooves never touching the ground.

In the Altai, graves were uncovered in which the Scythian passion for gold outstripped all hearsay. Four hundred years ago rumours were already rife of tomb-robbers finding corpses sand-wiched between gold sheets, and archaeologists later discovered a king scaled in 4,000 pointed gold plaques, his head bound in a golden helmet-crown carved with fabulous beasts and landscapes.

But in all these graves only mineral and bone survived. The intimate and evanescent – the precious commonplace – had gone. Only in this Pazyryk valley, and in the grave of the Ice Princess to the south, was everyday life caught on the wing. The rain which seeped down into the crypts, or coursed along the passage left by contemporary robbers (who took only gold), froze in the cold rooms, and sealed them under a lens of ice. Cloth, wood, leather, fur, birch bark, cheese, meat, horses, humans: even their colours were kept. Experts could tell the season of burial by the contents of the horses' intestines and by the state of their coats and hooves, or by the frozen moss-packing wedged among the beams. They could diagnose osteoporosis and toothache in the humans, and count their battle-wounds. Funerary offerings – frozen where their tables had floated on the insurgent rain – still held horse-flesh in small dishes, and a chunk of goat-meat stuck with a knife.

I descended the valley to the lowest *kurgan*, over pasture too thin, it seemed, for long grazing. Insects whirred in the short meadow-grass, and my feet crushed out a dry fragrance over sage and thyme. A cataract of blood-red stones had flooded into the tomb-chamber. But in its centre two posts remained upright, notched for crossbeams which lay bleaching where they had been tossed fifty years before. The stones grated and clacked underfoot. The archaeologists, themselves now dead, had dug here in the forties. Still under suspicion of intellectual heresy, they had emerged gaunt from Stalin's camps. Even here, at the world's dawn, they had to tread warily: the discovery of refinement in a pastoral people would sound ill on Marxist-Leninist ears. The nomad, by definition, was backward, and the Soviets inherited an ancient fear of him.

In this *kurgan* was discovered the oldest carpet in the world. Now hanging in the Hermitage in St Petersburg, its velvet pile shines in vivid reds and greens, damson and faded turquoise. Stags graze along its inner borders; men and horses parade its outer rim. In the centre a geometric field of lotus-blooms is scarcely

dimmed. A thousand years older than anything similar, its prov-
enance can only be guessed.

Other artefacts linked the Altai to Persia, India, China. Around
the dead chieftain, on a 20-foot-high felt hanging preserved in the
Hermitage, a horseman approaches an unknown goddess in praise
or supplication. Perhaps she came from the Black Sea. Nearby, at
the centre of a saddle-cloth swagged with horse-tails glows a
rectangle of Chinese silk, where sacred phoenixes sing on trees in
a wash of cream and gold.

A pale-wooded carriage once stood in this grave on high, fragile
wheels, near a quadriga of mummified horses. In the Hermitage,
it looked as if it would break at my touch. It was the ceremonial
carriage of a ghost. Canopied in black felt, it had perhaps borne
the chieftain's mummy on its last, forty-day cortege, during which
his subjects feasted his hovering soul.

And he too survives in the Hermitage, with his 16-foot coffin
nearby, scooped from a single tree-trunk, and his concubine stored
in the museum basement. She has soft, chestnut hair, and looks
Caucasian; while he stretches thin-boned, Mongoloid, desiccated
to the texture of wood. His head is wrenched back in a kind of
insensate agony, flecked by wisps of black hair.

The trappings of sacrificed horses hang beside him. Their tails
are tasselled or banded stiff in gold, their necks dressed with false
manes of scarlet hair. The masks in which they were buried
blossom into fantastical antlers and horns. It is as if men were
trying to turn horses into spirits. But the mummified beasts themselves lie curled unimportantly beneath, their heads twisted back
to their shoulders, the pick-blows neat in their skulls.

Climbing the valley to the last *kurgans*, the imagined carriage
teetered before me in a straight line (it couldn't corner) over the
stony hillside to its grave. Under my feet the pasture was sprinkled
with minute plants: scented pink stars and purple spires, worm-
wood, miniature buttercups. In the crater which archaeologists
called Kurgan II, someone had sheltered cattle. Bright orange
lichen was crawling over the stones. More than any other, the ice
of this grave had yielded up everyday things: even a wooden
pillow and a four-stringed harp. And pervading everything, the

Scythian animals – once clan totems – interlocked in wood and gold to form jewellery or horse-trappings, with a supple, stylised accuracy. Here too stood the six-legged frame of a vapour-tent with a bronze cauldron filled by scorched stones and cannabis seeds. The mourners, it seems, had withdrawn from a chieftain's corpse still shrouded in narcotic incense.

A curator had guided me through the dim-lit Hermitage corridors, until we reached the vitrines of Kurgan II. The chieftain's head had been severed from his body by tomb-robbers. It is blunt and expressionless. Then they dismembered his concubine, to tear off her jewellery.

His corpse, it seems, was recovered after battle. Three axe-blows show on the crown of its skull. His tattooed skin has been peeled from the mummified flesh like a discoloured scarf, and hangs softly lit before us. It is extraordinary. Outlandish monsters swarm over his shoulders. They entwine each arm in a spiral of flying talons, beaks, wings, crenellated jaws. They overflow his shoulders on to his chest. A big catfish noses up his right leg. They are pricked in soot. The long incision through which his muscles were removed before burial shows clear across the skin, stitched up with sinews. So does the cut by which the skull was trepaned to remove the brain.

The curator, a warm-hearted woman, points out the beasts on this hanging cloth a little sadly. They teemed there to protect him, she says, and to announce his ancestry. They transmitted magic energy.

In his culture, you might guess, the outer shone transcendent, while the inner was dispensable. In death his head and body became a shell, filled only with aromatic grasses, and that was how he entered eternity. The waxed skin, the embalmed face – these were what mattered. Herodotus wrote how the dried skins of fallen enemies were flaunted as trophies or used as handkerchiefs or quivers, and their skulls as drinking-cups. Perhaps this was a way of tampering with their souls.

We look again at the head from Kurgan II. It appears pure Mongol, but a sprout of facial hair suggests mixed ancestry. In these embalmed faces the anthropological war between Asia and Europe sounds again. In Pazyryk, by the fifth century BC, an invading Mongoloid people was subsuming the Indo-Europeans. Under their *kurgans* the aristocracy, even the Ice Princess, have proved Mongoloid; those in the poorer graves, especially the women, are Caucasoid. This brings no comfort to the Russians.

'I don't know what he is,' says the Hermitage caretaker. The chief's eyes gaze back; his upper lip smiles without meaning. 'He may be anything.' She keeps the rest of him in the reserve collection, with the severed pieces of his concubine. 'But she was beautiful!' she cries. 'She had long Botticelli hands and feet!' The caretaker herself is stoutly voluptuous, a Renoir, and envies her. 'A perfect Botticelli!'

We move on from glass case to case. There is nobody else here. We stare down on horses, quivers, whip handles: all the stuff of speed and flight. We both, I think, feel vaguely unhappy. These supremely mobile and elusive people have been grounded before our eyes by a sad miracle of ice and time. They, who hated cities.

* * *

It never fails. You arrive in a small town towards sunset. You know nobody, nothing. The main street is empty, the shops closed, the few offices almost deserted. But you tell yourself: within an hour I'll be under shelter. So you trudge into some municipal building, where a dazed-looking secretary directs you down the street to a resthouse. It doesn't exist. You try the only shop that is open, but the owner points you back the way you came. A drunk follows you, laughing. In the telegraph office – the only building open now – a sour apparatchik shrugs his shoulders. A chill wind is blowing off the mountains. Then you wander past an open door and fall into conversation with the man who peers after you. He suggests a workers' dormitory he knows, or a room with a friend or space in a defunct collective, where they allot you a camp-bed and a soiled quilt, and you find a kind of peace.

So over five days and a thousand miles I edge back north and east out of the Altai and into their companion Sayan mountains, where the head-waters of the Yenisei gather before turning north to the Arctic. At first I hitch-hike (you pay the driver a little), then find a bus, then alight with premature relief at a railway station in Barnaul.

Railway stations are the haunt of the outcast. Petty criminals, drunks, refugees, beggars – some mad, some hobbling from industrial accidents – throng the Stalinist halls and forecourts. In the ticket-office you become a naked supplicant. The powers shout and growl behind their machines: computer, printer, abacus. The queue scarcely moves. Every ticket is individually printed, proof of identity demanded, a whole campaign. The printer crumples up the paper, the computers go blank, the sales clerk disappears. You may spend two hours waiting.

But once aboard the train, a sense of triumph wells up. Outside, the scenery drags by unchanging, but in a few hours or in a day, you know, somewhere new – a former mystery on the map of Asia – will become flesh and stone. So in my low-class carriage, where Kazakh traders heaved their crates of apples or bananas into my space, the stench of sweat and urine was a bearable price to pay for the future that was unravelling along the rails. Zarinsk, Abakan, Minusinsk . . . The train took thirty-six hours to cover seven hundred miles. Twice it broke down.

The towns were easy to vanish in, oblivious of the stranger. I welcomed the bare cafes with their peremptory staff, simply for being there. Bortsch, *pelmeni*, cabbage soup, *solyanka*, sausages: they catered not to pleasure, but to survival.

Somewhere on the tortuous train-ride east, I shared my compartment with a schoolmistress from Krasnoyarsk, and her twenty-seven-year-old son. As night came down and the lights dimmed in our carriage, we lay on our bunks unable to sleep. They were on their way to fish and trek in the mountains of Tuva where I was going, and pointed out the lonely hunters' fires on the hillsides, and envied them. Svetlana's family had grown up in village isolation, united in their love of wilderness. They had built their own dacha in the wilds, and had the old Siberians' disdain for newcomers.

'But most families are newcomers now,' she said. 'They've been here just a generation or two. Others arrive on high-paid jobs, then go back west.' True Siberians were pioneers at heart, she added. But they were few, too few. 'And the land's become polluted. In Krasnoyarsk everyone gets chest infections because of the dam built there, and the Yenisei is so contaminated it doesn't freeze any more. Even in the Arctic, the nickel from the Norilsk factories poisons everything for hundreds of miles. When I was a child I remember reindeer wandering into the village at night and starting all the dogs barking. They used to graze along the Arctic Sea. But now they're gone.'

The country's pollution had stirred up dreams of Siberian independence, she said, but they were chaotic and fragmented. In the nineteenth century there had been visionaries who imagined a United States of Siberia, even allied to those of America. During the Revolution Siberia had made tentative moves towards secession (adopting a flag of forest-green and snow-white), but Lenin quashed them. Since then a new mobility had interchanged its people with those of European Russia, and bound them closer. Now they could not secede from themselves. Bordered as they were by a risen China, patriotism tied even old Siberians to the Moscow they despised. Their independence, if it ever came, would only be wrenched province by province – more economic than political – and few people were interested.

'You used to hear about it,' Svetlana said, 'but not any more. The Urals wanted it, in a way, but not enough.' She stirred uncomfortably. 'I think nobody believes in these solutions now, or perhaps in anything . . .'

'And you?' I asked. It was easier to ask in the dark.

'Oh, I believed in things once!' Her voice wondered at the memory. 'Yes, I wanted to build Communism!'

'I didn't,' said her son from the bunk above. 'Not for a moment.' His voice whined like a mosquito.

His mother went on: 'I was just a village girl. I didn't know anything. But my father came back from the war minus an arm and half a leg. After two years he tore up his Party card and threw it away. He was very bitter. Nothing was done for him, they just let him rot. And he saw how people were starting to disappear around him, taken away into the camps. Then he died. My mother never told me about his disillusion with the Party. She said nothing, while I grew up idealising it.'

She stopped. She sounded more amazed than angry. Hers had been the last generation to believe like that.

'Then bit by bit I got disillusioned. I came to realise about our local Party, how corrupt they were. . . .' That was how people lost faith in Communism, she said, how it collapsed at grass-roots – not through philosophic doubt or horror at Stalin, but because a local Party minion had purloined funds or wangled a holiday on the Black Sea. 'Now I have nothing absolute to teach my pupils. Most of them believe in nothing. Only a few have ideals. . . .'

Her son whined from above: 'They must be thick.' He sounded proud of his generation's unbelief. He thought it their achievement.

'I don't mean ideals about Communism,' she said. 'None of that means a thing to them.'

'Nobody's got ideals about anything,' he said. 'Not one of my generation. Nobody. They just want jobs.'

I could not see him; but I remembered in daylight a pampered-looking youth with a slick of black hair and a shadowy moustache. His face was already fattening.

Svetlana went quiet a moment, then said: 'It seems centuries ago. Sometimes I feel I've lived for centuries.'

The lights of a village flickered over us, and I saw that she had turned her face to the wall, while her son was leaning on his elbows cracking cedar nuts in his teeth. The gloom I felt was not theirs, I knew, but mine. I wanted them to have faith. Faith would paint a future. But instead I felt this regret, which was only foolish. After all, by not believing in anything defined, they had merely entered the modern age.

Out of the dark the upper bunk mewled: 'Now the old Party bosses have just become mafia. They've grabbed everything. They've built mansions in the unpolluted parts of Krasnoyarsk – you can find whole regions of them. They're all into business.'

'What sort?'

The two bunks chorused: 'Everything!'

On the mafia, at least, they agreed. It was ubiquitous, ungrasp-able, the new repository of evil. 'They own shares in the big companies,' said the lower bunk. 'How do they get so much money?'

'They may own a thousand shares apiece,' whinged the upper bunk, 'and guess how many I own? One!'

'They drive Mercedes. . . .'

'And how much do those cost in your country?' The cedar nuts clicked in her son's teeth. 'They're beyond anything here. . . .'

Silence again – the heavy, rhythmic rocking of the train – while I imagined their disparate pasts: she still coloured by hope, he the child of disillusion.

'But things will get better! I'm sure of it!' Her words sounded a Chekhovian yearning, faintly comic. 'People are better educated than they were in my day. My own pupils . . . I've only taught them literature, but that makes them richer in its way. In the end, everything will be better.'

'Oh, education!' the cynical voice parroted above. 'Oh, literature!'

Between 1897 and 1900 the young Lenin was exiled to the village of Shushenskoe for political agitation. Seventy years later, on the centennial of his birth, its centre was emptied and returned to its past. Lenin wrote that the village was a dung-heap, but now it has the informative sterility of an outdoor museum, spreading behind a high fence in ordered streets and spotless cottages. There is a reconstructed shop, a tavern, a smithy, a jail.

I am assigned a guide at the entrance. She is elderly and with-drawn. She speaks in an explanatory patter without worship or blame or any overt feeling at all. We walk down grassy streets. Every roof is intact, every balcony and fence immaculate. We are quite alone. The houses of poor or rich peasants have been fur-nished in period, fastidiously researched. Their courtyards are stocked with winter sledges and summer carts, and wooden tools for harvesting.

Surly caretakers rouse themselves to unlock the two houses where Lenin was billeted. The rooms are polished, exact, austere.

Here are his high desk and wash-basin. Here are the two iron beds where he and Nadezhda Krupskaya slept, after they married in exile. Under the gaze of their wardens, the objects seem heavy with mana. Was this his teapot, his spoon? His ice-skates (made in Germany) dangle from a nail: his feet were small. Under that wattle arbour outside, drowned by hop foliage, he worked in summer on the articles which would become scripture. The floor-boards creak with the warp of later years. I peer into his cracked mirror.

By contrast to the nightmare system which followed, czarist exile could be ludicrously lax. Lenin spent it in a white-heat of activity. He developed ideas for a radical Marxist party, and structured its newspaper. He corresponded with other revolutionaries, held meetings with them, and smuggled out articles to be published abroad. He grew thin with energy, wrote Krupskaya, who would sit beside him coding his secret letters. They were young and in love.

But when we walk in the streets now, the place is like a village for sale, awaiting its first occupants. Why is no one here, I ask?

'Well, it's not busy in winter.'

'But it's *not* winter,' I say, bewildered.

She looks at me ruefully, as if I were in breach of good manners. 'Today there aren't so many people. But there is a school group coming.'

'And what do they learn about Lenin here?'

She stops in the centre of the street, where no one can overhear. The needless manoeuvre belongs to the fearful past, the past which she upholds. 'That's a delicate question. I don't know what they're taught any longer. There are people who think that Lenin was not a genius at all, that he was not even a very talented man. A while ago our President Yeltsin demanded that this museum be closed down.'

'What happened?'

She lets out a pale smile. 'We wrote in protest to him, and to everybody else we could think of. We said this was an exhibition of turn-of-the-century peasant life – and they let us stay open.'

But the cottage museum dedicated to Lenin's political activity

('Lenin's Ideas are Alive and Victorious') had closed down. In summer it staged folk-singing in traditional dress, prettifying the world he had striven to reform. It was possible to walk through the whole village unaware that Lenin had ever lived.

'Look! Visitors!' The woman lights up. She has spied a cluster of schoolchildren at the bottom of the street. But as they come closer to us, giggling, her pleasure fades. Their teachers are telling them about peasant life under the czars.

'This is very hard for us,' the woman says. Something hot and distressed is beating up under her voice. 'We guides have worked here a long time, and this is our place. But suddenly we are told . . . well, for my part . . .' She turns her back on the children before they reach us. Then a hoarse whisper explodes from her: '*Of course he was a great man!*'

Was he? In my confusion, I agree. But perhaps I mean only that he changed the world, which is not the same.

The children trail past us, carefree. They wear pirated Adidas track-suits, and baseball hats labelled 'Sport' or 'California'.

'I wonder what they think,' I say.

She answers wanly: 'I don't know what they think.' We are emerging out of the despoiled theme park and into the world.

The slats were dropping from the ceiling of Shushenskoe's bus station, built for pilgrims who no longer came, and the floors were awash with rain. It trickled down the carved panels of Bolshevik heroes toppling the imperial eagle, and smeared the cheeks of the embossed Lenin. It dribbled between the window-panes of my bus as it veered south-east, and erased the road a hundred yards ahead. Sometimes it would part like mist around a stack of dark hills, where pine forests stood bearded in parasitic lichen, or drift out of glades sodden with ferns and moss. We might have been underwater.

Over the western Sayan we were pushing into a strange, isolated republic, enclosed by the mountains which give birth to the Yenisei. A century ago, as the grip of the enfeebled Manchu empire slackened, this unseen region of Tuva was sucked from the orbit of China into that of Russia, which annexed it in 1944 while the world was looking the other way. But its Turkic-speaking people – once an ethnic *melange* – had always looked to Mongolia. Mongolia had coloured their ancient shamanism with Buddhism, and had invested them with a shadowy history. Their remoteness, and their late entry into the Soviet empire, had left them a majority in their homeland, half-nomadic in many regions, clannish, poor.

As we breasted the frontier pass the rain turned to sleet. Then, as if winter had come suddenly, in the first days of autumn, the sky was thick with snow. It fell incongruously, like manna. It frosted the half-tropical undergrowth, the ferns, the fat-leaved vines, and gusted across the road in small, angry flakes. On one side of us the cliffs threw down icy waterfalls, on the other the road dropped into space. Then we were over the pass and descending cold-lit foothills. We seemed to be entering a deeper wilderness. Above the gleam of bronze and amber undergrowth, the pine forests were dying. Still wrapped in killer moss, the trees fell all of a piece, their roots wrenched up like old cog-wheels, and spread a ghostly litter over the hills. Whole mountainsides were ashen with them.

But beyond us other ranges were unfolding. Our road descended uncertainly. We were crossing into Tuva between stiffening control-posts. Police rolled out iron-spiked cables across the way, boarded the bus, idly opened our baggage. I was only notionally legal here, depending on official whim, and retreated into a sleepy Estonian version of myself. 'What's this?' The policeman prodded my rucksack with a baton. 'A rucksack,' I revealed, and he moved on.

The land breathed out at last in treeless plateaux edged with clouds. We were crossing grasslands studded by *kurgans*, and the air was cold. Where the road roughened into craters, an articulated truck had jack-knifed and overturned. Beside it stood a police car and a crowd of men. The driver was spreadeagled dead over the tarmac. Our bus let out a wavering, collective sigh. Then our driver turned up his radio and we rolled on.

An hour later the little capital of Tuva – a Russian bridgehead named Kyzyl, founded in 1914 – made a concrete blemish on the plain. But once we were inside the town the land which it defiled shone seductively at the end of every street. I walked it uneasily. The Tuvans were in the ascendant now. Their country might lie in economic thrall to Moscow, but since gaining nominal sovereignty in 1991 they had been gathering strength: a sturdy people with high, burnished cheeks – trim women and crop-haired men. Racial riots seven years before had driven several thousand Russian workers home, and a suppressed violence was in the air. The police patrolled in threes. Twice I saw men searched, then arrested. In the desolate main square, where flower-beds were going to seed, Lenin still flung out a shaky arm at the local parliament. But a monumental fountain was adorned with Tuva's disparate animals – camel, reindeer, yak – and a white theatre hoisted a fly-tower strapped with Mongolian carvings.

If you take a bus down the long road two hundred miles towards Mongolia, you find it filled with men returning from market in thick felt boots, sometimes bruised, drunk, with matted hair; women visiting parental villages, their eyes widened by Russian make-up and their tresses drawn back in mother-of-pearl clasps. In between hamlets the grasslands are broken by knolls, where cairns are stuck with the rag-hung poles of an old worship, and herds of black and chestnut horses graze against infinity. A pair of Bactrian camels crosses the road, and somewhere to the east, out of sight, are the mountains of reindeer herders. Squashed beside a peasant woman who feeds the passengers her last sweet apples, I watch this land unfurl with bemused awe.

Only after a long time, the skyline crinkles and streams come slithering out of forested hills. Here and there the dome of a yurt hunches under a curl of smoke, while to the south the suspended snows of the Tannu Ola shine.

Without expectation, I stroll down a grassy avenue to the monument in Kyzyl which the Tuvans love: a granite obelisk mounted on a globe, to mark the geographical heart of Asia. Here the town stops dead, obscured by trees, and steps mount to a terrace. To the east, the Great and the Little Yenisei converge to form one of the mightiest rivers on earth. To the west, a landing-stage rocks against the bank. The river flows at my feet, fast and strong. Beyond it the grasslands roll to naked hills, and above them, washed by unmoving cloud, the Sayan mountains gleam.

Perhaps it is the flow of the river out of emptiness, like something incarnate, time-bearing, at once peaceful and rather terrible, which tightens my stomach. Or maybe it is the idea of an anthropomorphic Asia: Asia with a heart, a womb, a memory. (An Arab once told me that the English, having no hearts, were always searching for them elsewhere.) I stand surprised in the clear light, the silence. The land looks irreducible, like bone. I stare for long minutes, confused, unable to leave. Asia: it has consumed my adult life.

A native woman wanders by, singing one of those plaintive songs you hear all over the Turkic world, like tuneless ruminations. This, and the river flowing, and the mauve hills under that immense sky, touch me with faint vertigo. I have the fleeting notion that they have pre-existed in my head like an inherited memory, as if this were the first river in the world, flowing to a still uncreated sea.

The woman stares at the foreigner craning into the distance, into nothing. It is absurd, of course. The centre of Asia is a geographic conceit, pin-pointed here by a nineteenth-century English eccentric named Proctor. He identified the heart of two more continents, it seems, confirming the Arab's opinion of the English. Other calculations locate the heart elsewhere.

The death of shamanism, Siberia's ancient and intrinsic faith, was announced decades ago. Collectivisation and the breakup of traditional clans undermined the shamans' influence all over Siberia. They were persecuted, re-educated, exiled, shot. They went underground. In Kyzyl's museum, among the mandatory stuffed elks and showcases of modern achievement, a map shows that in 1931 Tuva had 725 shamans, 314 of them women. From contemporary photographs they stare out remote and half-savage. Documents record their repression and execution all through the 1930s.

Nearby hang their reassembled costumes: the feathered or ant-

lered head-dresses, tambourines and flails, the unreflecting gold
plates which were their mirrors. Their long, black coats drip with
a layered mass of clinking discs and rods, so that the shaman's
every movement was accompanied by a commotion of other
movements, half-independent of him. Everything is festooned with
tassels and ribbons. At worst he must have looked squalid, like a
rubbish-heap moving about. More often his regalia enhanced an
eerie power, its sexless shape and decoration echoing his own
ambivalence. The shaman was often homosexual; but no conventional taboos applied to him.

He was the keeper of his people's memory, of their stories and
traditions, and of his own inherited secrets. He had knowledge of
death. He knew the ancestral spirits, and may even in trance have
recruited or repulsed them. Sometimes he gave them peace. Yet
he was separated from his community, often feared. He was called
upon not for simple healing, but to cure deeper sickness, when
patients were being eaten by the malignant dead, or to reverse
tribal ill-fortune. If he were a 'white shaman', he enlisted the good
spirits; if he were 'black', he deflected or coerced the evil.

Often the shamans' calling was bitter and unwilled. In youth
they became solitary and perhaps mad, suffered delusions, dreamt
strangely, fell inexplicably sick. Then people knew that the ancestors had chosen them, and were whispering songs into their ear
or brain. Often they came of shamanic ancestry, and were taught
by an elder, and their practice seemed to release them from some
psychic burden, even to cure them. Sometimes they learnt a secret
language, or the speech of animals. In their initiation they might
undergo dreams of their own death, a traumatic dismemberment
and decay.

Even sceptical Russians were moved by their trances at the sick-
bed: the reverberation of their drums as they danced in the firelit
tent, the fantastical jangle of their ornaments, the weird ecstasy
of their chanting. When they invoked their animal spirit-helpers,
they trilled or screamed with unearthly similitude. Then they
entered a shadowland. They flew through the 26-odd levels of the
Tuvan nether-life, summoning the help of friendly demons,
fighting off the hostile, and plunging – if they dared – into zones

strewn with the corpses of shamans who had failed, until they reached the sunless basement of Erlik, god of the dead. Sometimes they returned carrying the patient's soul in their hands, and reinserted it through the mouth.

The artefacts of the Tuva museum, the photographs and death-notices, implied that all this was long ago. Rumours of shamans surviving in remote areas had surfaced even in the eighties, but went uncorroborated. Yet hanging in the museum was a photograph of the recent opening of Doongyr, the Association of the Tambour. It was a society of shamans. And someone had given me a letter to a Tuvan shaman, if I could find him, enclosing money for the sale of a yak.

I wondered cynically what an association of shamans was. The shaman had always been a loner, protecting his clan against the outside. They fought one another with psychic powers, poached each other's spirits, attempted one another's lives. But a hundred yards off Lenin Square I found a cottage blazoned with a tambour, and peered in on a nest of near-empty rooms. Three Tuvan women in tight skirts and high heels were standing in the passage, and a frightened-looking Russian youth waited on a bench.

The shamans emerged like casual wizards. A young man in a quilted coat sauntered up to inspect us, his head bound by a soiled cloth with a feather sticking up behind. He had small, heartless eyes. They swept over us, then he vanished into an office. I asked one of the women: 'Where do these shamans come from?' She answered nervously: 'From the country.'

They were as strange to her as to me, I sensed. For her they had kept the redemptive power of the forest, the interior. She wore a chiffon scarf, and had lost the speech of animals. These people were her beginnings. They kept the rude potency of Rasputin in St Petersburg.

A door opened on a shamaness. Her coat was hung with rainbow ribbons over trousers and rubber shoes, and bells tinkled on her back. She looked commonplace. I asked her if she knew the whereabouts of my shaman, Kunga-Boo, who had sold a yak. She stared at me without expression, then muttered a street-name and beckoned the Russian youth into her room. I heard the thump of a drum.

I was overcome by a creeping gloom. I didn't know what I had expected, only that this was different. The old shamanic ceremony, its rapt and collusive audience, seemed to have withered to a ten-minute seance. Through open doors I glimpsed linoleum-topped tables with nothing on them but a tambour or a decorated horse-whip. The Russian youth re-emerged, looking bewildered. We smiled wanly at one another. I told myself I was a heartless purist; yet this guild of shamans, I was sure, had mutated out of recognition. The thread with the past had snapped, and they had lost touch with the ancestors. In becoming institutionalised, they only died a little more. The spirits could not bear much common light.

The street was in a poor suburb, and his home was a shack. I reached it through a cemetery and across a causeway of duck-boards over autumn swamp. I had been told only that he was an old shaman, who was wary of talking, and I realised then how my ideas had been stained by Soviet propaganda: the image of a savage charlatan benighting the proletariat. Two women sat on the steps of his semi-detached hut, but they did not know him. Outside his iron door lay a pair of plastic slippers. Their ordin-ariness surprised me. His feet looked the same size as Lenin's.

'Kunga-Boo?' I tapped on the iron. I heard shuffling inside, some stifled words. Maybe he was senile, I thought, or spoke in riddles.

The door opened on a small man with a face of weathered sweetness. He wore old trousers and a threadbare shirt. His jaw was dimpled by scars, which complicated his smile. He accepted the letter and his yak-money without counting it, and put it away indoors, while I hovered at his threshold. Then he returned with thanks, bowing and touching his hands together in a gesture which I read as dismissal. For a second I stared beyond him into the starkness of his room. This was a shaman's home, I told myself: I must remember it. On the bare floor lies a cloth piled with grasses. An immured stove is dropping tiles. He has an aluminium churn for water (I suppose), and a low table is scattered with powdered herbs. Everything looks small, his own size. But his rooms are separated by a crimson curtain, and I cannot see beyond.

Then he bowed and touched his fingers again, and I realised that this was a greeting, and that he was welcoming me in. We sat on low stools, crouched close together. I felt I was in Lilliput. He gave me tea in a blue-patterned bowl. How far I had come! He knew of London only from Soviet schooling: the London of Dickens and Conan Doyle. 'How do you see in all that fog?'

He had scarcely travelled, he said, he did not know the world. 'When I was very small, we lived in western Mongolia. My father used to say our ancestors arrived with Genghis Khan. Then we came north into Tuva – people did that in those days – and settled in a village here. My father was eighty-five when he died, still strong and a great hunter.'

I could not guess his age. He spoke softly, easily, so that I imagined him a craftsman or a teacher. I found myself asking him very simply: 'Your father was a shaman?'

'No, he lived by hunting. He knew about shaman's work a little, and about medicine. But only I am a shaman.' His voice rose with pride. 'When I told my father I wanted to be a shaman, he just said: Good! Do it! The world needs a shaman!'

So the ancestors, it seemed, had not called him. He had called himself. And no one teacher had guided him. 'There are no teachers now. There are only lamas. But I learnt Buddhism alone, reading the scriptures. So I call myself not a white or black shaman, but a yellow, a Buddhist shaman.'

I started to understand. I had read in accounts of nineteenth-century travellers to Tuva how shamanism and Buddhism had interfused. A Russian visiting the Chief Lama even saw in his home, side by side with Tantric banners, the costume of 'his consort, the Great Shamaness'. Lamas and shamans had adopted each other's rituals, sacred instruments, even each other's godlings. And from this blend of faiths there had emerged the *burkhan-boo*, 'godly shamans', who knew the Buddhist scriptures yet who communed with the dead. Born in Mongolia, Kunga-Boo might be the last of this arcane race.

'It's a very hard calling, very hard. I've studied and practised for thirty-seven years, mostly in secret. It had to be secret.'

'And what is it like, this . . . this . . .' but my delicacy collapsed: 'this travelling among spirits?'

'I can cure the sick sometimes. I can exorcise them.'

'By going into trance?' I longed to hear this. I wondered how simply he slid into this dream-journey. Was it induced by the beat of the tambour in the brain? 'How do you enter trance?'

But he only said again: 'I can cleanse the sick. You see, I make my own medicines.' He got up and squatted in front of a table sprinkled with powders on little squares of paper. He touched the grains to his nostrils. 'Here's black locust grass, and this is old flea-grass. And here's pig-plant' – he handed me a root resembling ginseng – 'it's a styptic and skin-healer.' He placed a pinch on his tongue. 'This one is good for chest pains . . . and here's black *saranka*, a wonderful grass, cures haemorrhoids' – he pointed up his bottom. 'Now I'm making a ten-day course of Mongolian *khash* . . . No, it doesn't have a Russian name . . .'

He had wide, coarse hands, but his fingertips edged the grey-green sprinklings into tiny envelopes, while he declaimed an anti-phony of illnesses and cures. Stomach ulcers, headaches, kidney defects: all could be healed or palliated. 'But you must only take a little, very little. Take too much, and they turn and kill you.'

'How did you learn about them?'

'From ancestors. They did it like this.' He was concentrating now, as if they had imposed a duty. 'There's only one ingredient I haven't got.' He spoke out of long frustration. 'Perhaps you can find me some in London. It's *morzh*.'

'What's that?'

'*Morzh! Morzh!*' He was filling with hope. 'England's in the north, isn't it? So you must have it there! They swim in the sea. *Morzh!*' He conjured a dripping moustache, then dangled his forefingers from his mouth's corners.

'Walrus!' I joined his excitement.

'Wall-russ?' His fingers rose again in two questioning tusks.

'Yes, yes!' I jabbed mine down from my lower lip. We stared idiotically at one another.

'You have them in England, wall-russes?'

The image of a club bore went by. 'Maybe in Scotland.'

'I need one.'

I repeated stupidly: 'One.'

'Yes.' He returned to sorting *khash*. Walrus tusk, essence of walrus, walrus fat. Any of them would do, he said.

Was he perhaps only a medicine-man after all, I wondered? Siberia used to teem with native folk-healers and herbalists. Even the Russians copied them. But a shaman was different, defined above all by the tambour, whose thudding, like mystic hoof-beats, carried him on his flight. There was no sign of any regalia in the room where we sat. Kunga-Boo lived in poverty. But I returned, nagging, to my obsession. 'Can herbs help you go into trance?'

I was still hoping, with waning expectation, for a spirit-traveller's tale: for the gliding over seas and chasms, above the bones of his crash-landed rivals, to the gloomy halls of Erlik.

But he only said: 'Herbs are not for that.' He pushed some grains of *saranka* towards me. They were bitter. Then he was silent. There were things he would not speak about. The light was fading from the windows, and he got up and switched on a naked bulb, then slipped away behind the crimson curtain dividing his home.

My eyes wandered the room, searching for tell-tale signs, but noticed little new: a plastic box filled with tomatoes, a miniature incense-burner, a coil of yellow silk. I wondered what he was doing.

Then *Boom!* My hair prickled. *Boom! Boom!* A ginger cat shot out from under the curtain. *Boom-boom-boom!* It was a deep, haunting reverberation.

I parted the curtain. Kunga-Boo had lifted his tambour like a trophy, and was banging it with a padded stick, and over his bed lay all his shaman's regalia. *Boom-boom-boom!* He was beaming like a child. It was as if he had known my interest all along, and had been testing me.

He said: 'This is my coat.' He laid aside the tambour. 'It is very old.' It was long and black, dripping black tassels. He clashed some ribboned cymbals. Then he took the cloudy gold disc that he passed over patients' bodies, and touched it across his own like an astral stethoscope.

'And this is my head-dress.' He held it delicately. From a circlet of gold plates which jangled and overlapped in his hands, there sprouted glossy black feathers. It looked barbarian. As he donned it, a cascade of attached black hair tumbled to his waist, and the vertical war-bonnet transformed him to a Sioux. He stroked it in delight. Then he thwacked his palm with a short, seven-thonged flail, and beat it at the air. '*Vor! Vor! Vor!*' He was laughing. 'That is how I beat them!'

'The black spirits?'

But even now he would not name them. His face set. 'When I dance, I recognise them . . . and what I need to know, I know.' He whipped the air again. 'They flee away!' Then he plucked up the tambour and struck it in a trilling burst. 'When I dance, I chant to the music *manix-hu-ma, manix-hu-ma*' – he pointed to the ceiling – 'and power comes to me out of the sky!'

Next moment, as suddenly as he had taken them up, he laid the instruments aside and went back to the other room. We sat on the little chairs again. The ginger cat sauntered through. I asked: 'Where can you practise?'

He opened empty hands. The sacred places were few now, he said, very few. But three years ago he had built himself a shrine in a secret place in the wilds, and there he danced.

What about the Association of the Tambour in Lenin Street, I asked?

He grimaced. 'Those are very young people. They understand nothing. I don't know if they are really shamans at all, or what they are. I don't know.'

In parting, he gave me his Lamaist incense cup, and a colour snapshot of himself. I gave him a key-ring dangling a miniature London bus, which he examined with wonder. Then he walked back with me a mile in the still-warm darkness.

Clouds had spread from the west, where the evening star left a lone blur of light.

He said: 'The real shamans, the true shamans, have almost gone now. The traditions have faded away. The customs aren't known. There was one old shamaness in a remote part, eighty-six years old. But she was the last. No more than that. And there used to be so many. And people need us.'

We tramped between the headstones and plastic flowers of the graveyard: tilting crosses and red stars. At the end of the path, he stopped. 'Come back next year.' He bowed and clasped his hands. 'Bring me walrus essence!'

His photograph is still on my desk. He is half-smiling. But I have not been back, and walrus is an endangered species, like him, and unexportable. In his snapshot he is wearing his head-dress, but it looks a little tacky. I see that the raven feathers are tied to its discs with old blue string. And he himself appears different, faintly mysterious, so that I want to ask him again how he travels among the dead.

5

To *the* Arctic

From the hill-chapel of St Paraskeva you may look down on Krasnoyarsk in puritan disgust. A pool of slums separates you from its massed concrete, where the Yenisei glimmers dully, and from the west a vast suburb advances on the centre under a pall of smokestacks. The whole city cringes beneath clouds of carbon, coal tar and dust. Southward a bridge charges over the river to where the chimneys shoot up again, belching soot, or sending up wavering pillars of grey. Invisible beyond them, an immense dam and hydroelectric plant, the most powerful in the world on its completion in 1971, shores up a reservoir two hundred and fifty miles long above the drowned villages of 48,000 displaced people.

Where, you wonder, is the town admired by Chekhov, the spacious city of gold merchants? But Krasnoyarsk had swelled with reassembled factories during the Second World War, to become a metropolis of a million. Before 1991 it was closed to foreigners. The satellites surrounding it to the north – Soviet maps omit them – harbour a nest of underground military electronics plants and nuclear reactors, now converting in part to the manufacture of cassettes and Samsung televisions.

Yet once inside the city, this squalor withdraws. Running in long parallels above the river, the streets are lined with the honey-coloured blocks built by Japanese prisoners-of-war, with Corinthian hulks and turn-of-the-century confections in plaster and stone, with the surprise of a wooden mansion here and there, or a nineteenth-century villa. The Yenisei flows grandly under them.

And you forget for a while the polluted and near-identical citadels of the poor which circle them, imagining that this is the city's heart.

The Yenisei mesmerised me. The slim torrent which I had seen at Kyzyl, flowing from the centre of Asia, had now swollen to a flood over a mile wide. And still it was just beginning. With its Angara tributary, it is the sixth longest river in the world, slicing Siberia into two unequal halves as it moves three thousand four hundred miles from Mongolia to the Arctic. I wandered its banks where the great bridge, built by a French engineer in the 1890s, leapfrogged its current south. A smart-looking steamer, the *Mastrov*, was tied up at the quay. I watched it revictualling. Then, feeling like a runaway boy, I bought a ticket to the Arctic Circle, a voyage to the edge of my map and expectation.

But hours would pass before it sailed. Downriver I came upon the paddle-steamer that carried Lenin into exile at Shushenskoe. It had been hoisted clear of the water, the machinery which drove its rusted paddles still oiled and intact. Inside, the museum once sacred to Lenin had diversified, and there I found a steel document-case once belonging to Nikolai Rezanov.

A young nobleman in the service of Grigory Shelikhov, the founder of Russian Alaska, he set out in 1803 with two ships on an imperial trade mission to America, and plotted to spread Russian dominion into California. While buying provisions in San Francisco, he fell in love with the beautiful daughter of the Spanish commandant, but religious impediments delayed their union, and Rezanov sailed home, promising to return within two years.

The legend survives in Siberia that he and his future father-in-law planned to create an independent California under the protection of the czar. But the following March Rezanov died of pneumonia in Krasnoyarsk, and was buried a few hundred yards from the quay where I walked. His fiancee waited. (Consuella's Rock, facing the sea near San Francisco, commemorates her.) Then, on the news of his death, she founded California's first convent and became its first nun.

For more than a century Rezanov's monument stood by the cathedral near the river. Then in the 1930s a parachute school was built on the site, and the tomb, with its perilously pointed urn and spiked railings, was swept away.

As the three-decked *Mastrov* eases from the quayside, a burning expectation starts up. It is puerile, coloured by Conrad. But now the engines tremble the ship's body, and you weigh anchor from the world. On the jetty a small crowd of relatives is waving itself into obscurity. A few jokes carry across the 50 yards of water. Martial music sounds from the ship's loudspeaker, as if we were departing for the front. A small girl, standing on shore beneath her parents, is crying as her grandmother starts to dwindle over the water. Then, as the boat turns into the mainstream, the hand-waves broaden to semaphore and the crowd breaks up and is lost to sight.

The city drifts away from us. It resolves into important cubes and rectangles: the banks, the concert hall, the river station. Our foghorn booms lonely beneath a bridge. We thread between marshy islets where fishermen stand in black waterproofs and do not look up. A flight of duck is heading west. Our engine putters in near-silence. Moored along the quays, the barges barely rock in our wake. Even as we break clear of the last suburbs, long banners of smoke are streaming from unseen factory chimneys to our north.

Then even these vanish, and on either shore the hills flow down under a soft blaze of trees – birches turning amber, dark layers of cedar and pine gashed by the scarlet of mountain ash. Sometimes, when the river narrows, the cliffs steepen into serrated blades which drop sheer to the water. At others, the way smooths out into an island-studded calm, and the light falls flat and glassy on a meandering half-lake.

I stand on deck for hours. My fellow passengers, burly traders in vinyl caps, have blocked the lower deck with crates of peppers and tomatoes which mount to the portholes. Sometimes they stand staring at the river with hunched shoulders, like me, or play cards in the vestibule. But there is no communal life. The boat seems half-empty. Families returning from holiday keep to their cabins, asleep or munching picnics. The buffet is closed, the saloon is closed, the reading-room is closed. The boat appears to run on magic. But the public rooms are panelled in a lemony splendour of varnished pine, and brass fittings run riot. In the music-room (closed) I glimpse a white-painted piano and walls swagged with sashes and lyres. The dining-room curves with the prow, and flaunts silk curtains and palm-court columns. It serves smoked fish, chunks of fatty ham and black bread; then comes sweet coffee and a puny bill.

Outside on the river, every few hours, the jetty of a village marks its link with the world. Bright-painted rowing-boats leave a broken kaleidoscope on the shore, and wooden stairways wobble up to the cottages cresting its bank. Occasionally a church, old and massive above the rooftops, raises a gutted bell-tower or a cupola shorn of its cross. Then we circle in to the landing-stage, where an avenue of peasant women waits behind their offerings of vegetables and preserves. The moment the gang-plank is lowered the passengers swarm out to buy, while a posse of stevedores shouldering sacks of vegetables charges the other way and heaps up the crates on deck still higher.

Within twenty minutes the furious commerce subsides and we cast off again. We move over water which is like imperfectly set metal. The north wind pushes its surface back, while a deep counter-current foments it from below. The boat rolls faintly, sleepily, over its trouble. I gaze down distracted. The whole surface seems to seethe with a strange, molten cold. Steely circles and ellipses glide over it and appear to shimmer with the commotion of millions of aquatic insects which are not, in fact, there, while an oil-smooth sheen spreads black between the ripples.

From the upper deck I watch the West Siberian Plain stretch to the sky in level forest, while on the other side stir the hills of a still huger East Siberia. The taiga seems to unite them, but in fact they are different countries, and the Yenisei cleaves them like a sword. The loamy plains of the west are still feebly warmed by the Atlantic. Their forests are wet with lakes and marshland, and their indigenous natives may speak languages close to those of Finland and Hungary. But the east is embalmed by a fearsome, static cold, and permafrost underlies it almost to the borders of

China. The taiga thickens among mountains, and the western spruce and pines become infested by armies of tough larches which march to the Pacific. Its native groups are of ancient, more Mongoloid stock.

Slowly, to port and starboard, and for hundreds of miles, an odd difference develops. The western bank runs level with the water, but on the east the shore rears up in a 50-foot earthen wall thronged by trees. The wake of our boat leaves a nervous parting between them. The Norwegian explorer Nansen, who sailed the river in 1913, ascribed the difference to the pull of the earth's rotation as it strengthens towards the North Pole. The phenomenon, once noticed, starts to absorb you: the glitter of young birch trees standing in the western water, the horse herds which amble down unchecked. And the eastern shore, like a closed rampart.

As the ship's prow noses towards the pole, you wait in childlike expectation. You imagine the globe of the earth steepening as all the lines of longitude converge in front of you, and that you can see its curve across the skyline. Soon, you conceive, the earth must level out under the crushing weight of sky, and through that slit in the horizon – where the river parts the forest – you will glide over the top of the world and begin to slide down into the south.

Instead, towards evening, the wind drops and we enter a golden vacuum. I think: this is that primal Siberia – elusive, endless – which lingered like a geographic unconscious behind the eyes of early travellers. Its seeming void was a clean slate to write upon. For centuries it courted hearsay and legend, conjured the ideal, elicited fear. Even its name – a mystical conflation of the Mongolian *siber*, 'beautiful', 'pure', and the Tartar *sibir*, 'sleeping land' – suggested somewhere virgin and waiting. Hegel placed it outside the pale of history altogether, too cold and hostile to nurture meaningful life.

It spreads around us an illusion of vacancy. Yet as early as Herodotus there were tales of habitation. His account of a bald, flat-nosed race, and of a tribe which slept for half the year, seem to be rumours of Mongol and Arctic peoples. And as the Russians probed the Urals, they painted in their demons beyond. God had confined the natives in this wilderness because they ate their dead.

There was a people who died every winter when water spilt from their noses and froze them to the ground. Others who submerged in the summer sea lest their skins split. Their eyes were lodged in their chests, and their lips between their shoulders; or their mouths opened upward in their skulls, so they ate their crumbled food by placing it under their hats and pumping their shoulders up and down. These people, it seems, had been here for ever. For in the unknown, time stops.

But later a pagan beauty crept in. Siberia, exempt from religious surveillance, harboured magic cities. Surrounded by clamour, they could be reached only underground; but once inside their walls an unearthly silence fell. In its snowbound purity, its farness, Siberia became the repository of an imagined innocence.

Yet by the nineteenth century other, countervailing images had long been in place: Siberia as a storehouse to be plundered by officials and hunted bare by Cossacks; and above all, long before the Gulag, as a limbo that could receive all the viral waste of the empire – criminal, vagabond, dissident. Through Siberia, Russia would purge herself. Its vastness could quarantine evil.

The pendulum swung back years ago. As Moscow appears to sink deeper into the embrace of the West, so Siberia becomes enshrined in the Slavic imagination as the Russia that was lost, the citadel of the spirit. The mystique of a chaste, self-reliant Siberia rises again. Siberia is more Russian than Russia is, people say, as if it were a quintessential Russia, or the imagined country which Russia would like to be.

Nobody shared my four-berth cabin. Low-wattage bulbs gave it the feel of a dim nest. So I went up and sat astern while the sun dropped, and listened to the cinnamon-coloured water rustling below. Beside me a thickset man seemed half-asleep. Then a flight of duck introduced us. As they passed, his arm lifted automatically and fired an invisible shotgun. 'It's wonderful sport here. You can see hunters' dugouts all along this stretch. Look there . . . and out there. . . .'

I hadn't noticed them before – the hollowed trunks ribbed with planks, just visible among the reeds. Vadim ached to be in one, or crouched in the marshes waiting for the Canada geese to fly in. He spoke of them with the disturbing affection of the hunter for his prey: how they winged down from the Arctic in autumn on their way to India. There were Brent geese and red-breasted geese too, and widgeon and coots from the tundra. And other, near-holy birds – cranes, swans – which no one shot.

And what about the Great Grey Owl, I asked, with its five-foot wingspan and its head the size of a human's? I longed to glimpse one in the dusk. It sports a white outgrowth of eyebrows and moustache, like a cartoon colonel, with facial discs as big as soup-plates, and it can hear a vole moving a foot beneath the snow. Yes, Vadim said, if you kept very still on a river-bank at evening, you would hear them calling to one another – he gave a clouded hoot – yet you never saw one.

Once, he had walked the thirteen hundred miles from Krasnoyarsk to Dudinka which our boat was travelling. It had taken him fifty days, camping and hunting, following the river by tracks. He spoke of it with earthy nostalgia, his hand sometimes crashing on to my shoulder to confirm his shooting of a marten or fording a river. His eyes were steady in a gross, amiable face. He seemed to typify the old Siberia. 'And I saw bears too! And they saw me. But if you don't bother a bear, he doesn't bother you. Only in winter, he's cross if he's hungry. And there were wolverines about. Now the wolverine, he's big' – he circled his arms around an aerial heavyweight – 'and he has a funny habit of following you. You don't often know it, but there he is, just following behind somewhere, and when you pitch camp he hangs around, the wolverine does. Then when you leave for a moment he empties your tent for you.'

Vadim lived in Arctic Dudinka, but was restless for the forest. Hunting was his passion. He knew a place where wild reindeer crossed the Yenisei, and would shoot two or three a year, carving up their flesh where they fell. A forester lent him an isolated shack from which he would set out at night, and as the morning mist lifted from clearings rich in berries, he would shoot the elk which grazed there, and sell their carcasses on the sly.

And sometimes, he said, he caught reindeer and elk in traps. I winced at him, then asked about this, hoping to elicit an instant's regret; but he merely described it: iron leg-traps. He was a poacher.

This was the old Siberia too. The trappers had been merciless, the taiga strangely fragile. During the seventeenth century its sable had been virtually wiped out.

I asked in puzzlement: 'Why won't you kill a swan?'

'A swan!' He looked shocked, rubbed his heart. 'I love them. They fly all the way to California, then back to us. They're beautiful. Oh, I couldn't touch a swan!'

Now the sun had gone. We made no commotion over the water. After a while a deserted village floated past us, its doors and windows blank over the marshland. 'Those are the ruins Khrushchev left,' Vadim said. 'He forced people into bigger units, he hated the little places. So you see them now, fallen to bits. . . .'

In the last windows dim lights flickered, where people had returned, perhaps, to inhabit a remembered happiness. 'My grandfather was exiled out here in 1921 – yes, that early! – just for owning land. He had to live somehow so he became a merchant of sorts and settled in Yeniseisk, where I was born.' Vadim's hand thumped my shoulder again. 'In Stalin's time, even in Brezhnev's, you and I couldn't have talked like this! You're my first Englishman!'

I smiled, despite myself. He had added me to his game-bag, along with the Canada goose and the reindeer.

'As a young man I'd have thought you my enemy.' A vague wonder surfaced in his voice. 'But one year I went to Germany with a Komsomol group, full of the idea that everything of ours was best. You know how it is. My father was a pilot in the war and died of wounds, escorting British convoys to Murmansk. All his three brothers were killed. I was ready to hate the Germans – but Hamburg! I didn't care about its wealth, but the people welcomed me. We were quartered with ordinary German folk, and they were good people. Good. After that I never felt the same about anything. . . .'

He stood up with his back to the water. The Russian tricolour drooped on its pole behind him. 'And now we have to be like them. In Russia these days a fellow has to work *on his own.*

Alone!' He thumped his chest. 'We live in a new time. I'm a crane-operator in the Dudinka docks at present, but I can work as a mechanic, a book-keeper, a lumberjack. I earn more than any of my bosses. The temperature can dip to −50°F, but I can operate in that. And I'm free. Nobody tells me what to do! When one line of work fails, I switch to another.' He pointed his cigarette at the crates lapping the deck windows. 'But this merchandising, just moving stuff about from place to place – that's no good. Russia has to *make* stuff. That'll be our future.'

'Light industrial stuff,' I agreed. 'Things ordinary people want.'

'In the past we had seven bosses to every worker. One ploughed, as we say, and the others just lifted their spoons. But now we'll pick ourselves up!'

I wanted to hear this, to believe he was the future. I wanted to like him. His feet were planted four-square on the deck, as if he would ride a hurricane. I tried to forget the gin-traps.

'Come to my cabin tomorrow and meet my wife!' He was suddenly striding away. 'When I trap sable she makes them into hats!'

I lingered astern for a while in the cool dusk. A few stars had come out. The ship's bell clanged archaically. The darkening woods no longer seemed so empty. In daytime I had found the taiga silent, filled with a greenish light and cathedral peace. But it was empty only of humans. It rustled unseen with a wary life of its own: lynx, elk, fox. Now the brown and black bears would be gorging themselves on berries and seeking dens for semi-hibernation, and a host of birds was winging south and east. Sables and muskrats, with all the martens and rodents of the trees, would be laying in winter stores, and the black-capped marmot, glutted with fat, would be turning in for its fantastical, eight-month sleep. (Its temperature drops almost to freezing; its heart beats once in three minutes. Every three weeks it wakes, urinates, perhaps copulates, then nods off again.) Yet others – even the tiny nocturnal flying-squirrel – never hibernate at all.

But somewhere ahead, where the taiga thins to conifers and the winter snow becomes a compacted, wind-blown dust, the wolves and reindeer multiply and the red fox gives way to the blue.

Arctic lemmings – nervous, overgrown guinea-pigs, snow-white or coppery – would be breeding even now. Every third or fourth year their numbers explode and they ripple across the tundra in a quivering plague. People imagined they swam the sea in quest of Atlantis, but in fact they were searching for cotton-grass. They never turn back, because they have already laid waste everything behind them. So they seem faintly tragic, impelled by madness. In a bumper lemming year, all the predators congregate. Everything, it seems, eats lemmings. The snowy owls hatch ten or more chicks in celebration, and the wolves become so fat that the reindeer graze in peace (and themselves eat the odd lemming). There is a bright green moss which grows only on lemming bones. Even in their river crossings they are not safe, but turn up in the stomachs of pike and salmon. I kept an eye out for them fording the Yenisei – they could swim several miles – but the river was filling with stars.

That night we were joined by the Angara, which had already flowed three thousand miles from its source beyond Baikal, and turns the Yenisei into one of the most powerful rivers on earth. Ahead of us at dawn, low mountains were shaking loose from the sky, and we could glimpse the waves of eastern hills as they started their long surge to the Pacific. The gold of the forests was laced darker now by conifers. The river had cut up under a cold wind, and a flock of seagulls was trailing us astern. By afternoon the cliffs of islands drifted past, and the Stone Tunguska river, already huge, wound from the east to meet us.

In his cramped cabin, heaped with sacks of potatoes bought cheap in Krasnoyarsk, Vadim plied me with tea and vodka, spurned my Romanian biscuits and produced *piroshki* cabbage pastries made by his mother-in-law. 'Homemade! Better!' They were disgusting.

Then he talked politics. His wife Stalina (her father had fought at Stalingrad) reclined plumply on her bunk beside him, cosseted in a wool cardigan. Bulging cheeks had squeezed her eyes and mouth to pampered dots, and beneath a toppling pyramid of golden curls some cotton threads and wisps of her own black hair floated free. While Vadim complained about the ingratitude of the Baltic states or demanded the crushing of Chechnya, she sent out little snuffles of agreement and censure.

'Those people take everything from us,' he said. 'Even in these parts you'll find native Kets and Dolgans and Entsy and God knows who, and they degenerate because they never do an hour's work. But if you want work in Dudinka, you can find it, and live well.' He appealed to Stalina. 'We live well, don't we?'

'We do, we do.' She was plucking the seeds from a dried sun-flower-head and tucking them into her cheeks with moist fingers. I was starting to dislike them both equally.

'During the seventies I worked eight years for the Komsomol,' Vadim said. 'I went out into the tundra and gave lectures to these people in their huts or tents or just under the sky. It's we Russians who brought them education. They never even had an alphabet before. They couldn't even read.'

'Not even an alphabet!' echoed Stalina.

I asked grumpily: 'What did you teach them?'

'In those days it was the history of the Communist Party.' No trace of irony or regret touched him. 'I told them about our writers and cosmonauts and space engineers. . . .'

'Did they listen?'

He looked blank, as at something irrelevant. 'I went from group to group by helicopter or reindeer-cart with a cine-projector run on batteries – and we'd show them films of the Great Patriotic War. Sometimes we'd take their children to the *Internat* boarding-schools in Dudinka – aged seven, they were – and they'd be given an education, September to May, and then go back to the tundra for three months.'

'We gave them education – free!' His wife snuggled under blankets.

'And if they wanted,' Vadim went on, 'they could go on to some higher institute, and they didn't pay a thing! And there were special places kept for them, even if Russians were more deserving.' His face was clenched with irritation. His wife spat out a sunflower seed.

'What did they do in the tundra with your education?'

'Some got training as vets, but most didn't want to do a thing. Now they just come in to loaf about the town and get drunk.'

'They weren't prepared,' I said. I imagined him flying in to these half-comprehending people, haranguing them on the October Revolution; and their children returning from a jobless Dudinka to a tundra they no longer knew. These *Internats* had spawned a whole generation alienated from its own culture and unfitted for any other.

Through the porthole behind me I glimpsed the forests where the Ket people had once flourished. Every year, two centuries ago, they had sailed to a market fair in two hundred boats, and delivered their tribute of furs to the imperial agents. Within a century the vodka and diseases peddled by Russian merchants had decimated them.

'Don't you go near those people,' Stalina warned. 'They'll do anything to you.'

I wanted to snap back; but I was drinking their vodka, nibbling their *piroshki*. I felt a harsh frustration. 'I'm interested in them,' I said angrily. I would track them down somehow: a village, a nomad camp, anything.

'We Russians cheated them when we arrived,' Vadim said suddenly. 'We took their pelts in exchange for a few brass pots.'

Stalina snuffled ominously.

I asked: 'What's happened now, out in the tundra?'

'I don't know what's happpened out there.' Vadim tossed back his vodka. 'Except that the whole system's fallen to bits. In town these people used just to take money from the government. Now they get nothing, and they're unemployable.'

'Things might be better for them in the tundra,' I wondered.

'Yes!' they chorused. 'Yes! They'd be better out there!'

Night. We are wandering over a polished calm, under a sky cold with stars. I remember the Academician in Akademgorodok talking of magnetic power-lines streaming down from Dikson to our north. We are floating along them now. The Milky Way dissects the sky in a white scar, and Venus is so bright that it sheds a path over the water. I had promised the professor to be cosmically sensitive, but I have no idea how. So I empty my mind, and listen in to nothing. Beyond our prow the shores are pincers closing in on the river's light. The foam of our wake diffuses soundlessly behind. Once an enigmatic lamp blinks from the forest, but otherwise we move across a darkness barely distinguishable from the sky. The pulse of our engine is the only sound.

For two more days and nights we sailed downriver, while around us the deciduous green turned to bronze, and the birch trees massed along the shores were blackened by pines, and the crimson flares of aspen flickered out. The seasons were speeding up. Within four days we traversed autumn, until the leaves were falling, and a coniferous deadness began to spread.

The villages grew even fewer, poorer. Their foundation in the late thirties betrayed them as Stalinist concentrations from lesser settlements, but now they too were half-abandoned, their inhabitants migrated to Krasnoyarsk or beyond. As we churned north towards winter, the produce on their wharves shrank to a few sacks of potatoes and carrots, or some buckets of cranberries.

'Up to here you can grow vegetables,' said the barmaid as we reversed from the jetty of Vorogovo. 'North of here it's just fish.' We were on the 65th parallel. 'And these villagers can't sell things like they did. Folk used to come south to holiday up to two years ago, but now no one has money.'

She looked heavy and tired. She worked behind the bar in the ship's hold, where nobody much came, giving out plates of sausage and dry chicken-legs. Blonde curls bustled round her cheeks and neck. She had gentian eyes. Behind her glinted two shelves of champagne, sweet wine and 'Sport-Cola'. She served here four months of the year, she said. It was the only job she could get. 'I worked ten years as a computer engineer in Tyumen and Krasnoyarsk. Then things got very hard with us, you know, and I had to serve behind counters. The wages of a computer engineer in Krasnoyarsk became three times less than I'd earned in Tyumen. But I had a daughter by then, and I couldn't let up.'

She smiled hardily. On the sunk moon of her face her features seemed to have been touched in later, but formed an expression of half-frustrated tenderness. She'd been born in a village beneath the great dam near Krasnoyarsk, she said. Her parents had even helped to build it. 'But we lived upriver, and our home went under. I was a child when we abandoned it. I used to walk in seven kilometres – aged just five, and alone – to sit and watch the dam being built, and to be near my parents. I didn't know it would drown us.' She had left her childhood under the water.

For a while the father of her daughter hovered unmentioned round her talk. Then she said: 'Things with us aren't like things with you. If I was destitute, *he* might have to pay something. But he just writes sometimes, and I tell him everything's fine. But life is so dear now. When I was my daughter's age, everything got paid for. Now I have to find extra for her singing and dancing lessons – she loves them – and it breaks me. It's odd, you know, but I think she's becoming a Christian. She keeps crossing herself. Perhaps she picked up something at school.' She made it sound like measles. 'But when she gets to fifteen it'll be more expensive still and I don't know what I'll do. . . .'

Meanwhile she hunted for winter jobs, and served cold chicken on the Yenisei, and sometimes, when the ship eased up to a jetty, she would stare through the portholes and feel sorry for the villagers.

A traveller needs to believe in the significance of where he is, and therefore in his own meaning. But now the earth is flattening out over its axis. The shoreline is sinking away. Nothing, it seems, has ever happened here. So time slows into aeons, and history becomes geology. People lose their grip on it.

The villages have no jetties, just a few cottages straggling along a bank. Sometimes weather-hardened men in tin motor-boats push out to sell sturgeon still slippery from their sacks, and hold up jars of yellow caviar. Dogs howl from the shore.

So the world is fading away. Even on the east bank the forest thins behind a littoral of sand and scrub. The river has widened, calmed. You stare at it, because there is nothing else to see. Half-hidden currents shimmer over its surface, trembling with some obscure trouble. At other times the boat pushes through a river like black syrup.

Four days ago you boarded ship knowing nobody. Now there are those you seek out, others you avoid. There is the music teacher from Norilsk with her French bulldog and two musical daughters – eager girls with the conservatoire before them ('Maybe St Petersburg!'); the embittered trader selling lettuces in the dying town of Igarka; a sallow youth who is soon to be conscripted, but who longs instead to go to Italy; a Dolgan vet and her hyperactive son; a Ukrainian metallurgist who can't go home (things are even worse in the Ukraine).

During the fourth night, at some sad village, a Polish priest embarked. He was the first Westerner I had seen for a month: an elderly man, lean and self-sure. He sat in a vestibule on the lower deck, where passengers loitered to watch him, and riffled through a portfolio of papers oblivious to them. I sat tentatively beside him. The white hair flowing back from his forehead to his nape lent him a silken aristocracy. For five years now he'd been travelling up and down the Yenisei, he said. 'This is my parish, the Krasnoyarsk Krai – seven times the size of Poland.' His voice was sharp, cultivated. 'But these villages have grown terrible. They've nothing but fish, potatoes and grass. They're saved by picking berries and mushrooms in the woods. And that's everything. Also they're lazy, and – I'm sorry to say this – stupid. Yes, grossly stupid.'

They were around us now, staring. Their frosty eyes seemed less like organs of sight than of a slow, incontinent wonder. Momentarily, disconcertingly, I saw them as he did. Were they just stupid? A teenage boy stood gazing at him – at his trim white beard, at the dog-collar half-concealed by a high-necked cassock – and touched the silver crucifix against his stomach. 'What's that?'

'That's the Son of God, child. He died for you, and He – '

'Is he real silver?'

The priest turned to me. 'You see, they're stupid. Concepts are beyond them. And unfortunately they drink.' He barely lowered his voice. Contempt, I thought, had made him fearless. I blenched for him. 'But I've converted many in the past few years. Germans mostly, exiled here in 1941. But Russians too, and Poles.'

'How did you find them?'

'I just landed and asked.' He was mysteriously buoyant: eyes shining black in his pallor. 'Now we've six chapels along the Yenisei and a congregation in each village, sometimes only eight people, but sometimes forty. I've even baptised some native Entsy.' He brought them the Mass as others might bring famine relief. He belonged to the venerable Melkite Church, which followed the Orthodox rite yet owed allegiance to Rome. Those whom he baptised would scarcely know the difference. But the authorities, of course, did.

'The Orthodox bishop in Krasnoyarsk should be helping us, but he doesn't. He's hostile. He works for the secret police. Has done for years. Trying to preach in Russia now is like speaking to a country hit by the atom bomb. It's been laid waste for two generations. It's worse than working among heathen. The only source of hope is the children and the old women. The rest are blind.' Through the window a small town loomed unlit above its quay. 'And these villages are dying. They're paying for everything that happened.'

We walked out on deck into the cold night. On a hill above the harbour hung a white monastery. This was old Turukhansk, the priest said, a district centre, and corrupt. A century ago it had been famous for the bones of its saint, carried here from the once-great city of Mangazeya, ruined in marshlands far to the north-west. In 1913 Stalin, exiled in Turukhansk, had fathered a child by a native woman, it is rumoured – a boy who disappeared from history.

The priest crammed a woollen cap over his head. He was shivering. 'These villagers have had seventy years of Satan. Now they're leaving here for anywhere they can find work, for anywhere else at all.'

That night we crossed the Arctic Circle.

The cold has crept up on us. The traders look piratical in high woolly hats and padded coats. I blunder about my cabin in a quilted mountaineer's jacket, knocking things over. Women in crumpled dresses and socks are queuing up at the hot-water boiler. Seagulls scream round the portholes.

The dawn has broken over a river three miles wide. On either shore the trees look dwindled and sickly, or are not there at all. The tundra is starting. The clouds lie in some stilled current of their own, making long, flat-bottomed flotillas across the blue. The eye searches for a focus, fails. Muffled up, I sunbathe on the poop, listening to the faint, slow heartbeats of the engine. The earth has smoothed into peace. Its vast circumference is inscribed meaninglessly around ourselves.

That evening some forty people, mostly women and children, sat on gilded chairs around the music-room in the ship's prow, while the priest celebrated Mass. He prepared the room with the confidence of one who knew that a line of potted ferns will mystically stand in for the iconostasis, and that the curved window (where a horned moon was rising over the Yenisei) is an apse enframing God's creation. He handed out service sheets for the Liturgy of St John Chrysostom, selected a woman to intone the responses, ordered me to wipe down a table, and unwound a scarf to serve as an altar cloth.

Casually he donned armbands and a white robe. His patrician hair and aquiline rigour made me forget that he was barely five feet tall. But beneath his creamy commotion of silks, his mud-stained trainers squelched across the floor whenever he enacted a procession. To the faithful, none of this mattered. Some of them already knew the litanies, and when to cross themselves. The children sat in flocks at their mothers' feet. Three surly youths shambled in and out. Nothing separated his liturgy from the Orthodox, except a single, fleeting mention of the Pope.

'What we believe is not the same as what we see,' wrote St John Chrysostom of the Eucharist, 'but we see one thing and believe another.' So the outward, however negligent, sets in motion the inward, and the Liturgy, to the unbeliever, may proceed like a string of spells. All its moments of solemnity – the entrance of the Book and Holy Gifts, the reading of the Gospel and the Epiclesis – were marked by the priest with cursory matter-of-factness. In the absence of a bell he dinged a fork against a tin. In lieu of the Holy Gospel, he processed with an uplifted service sheet; in place of the chalice (since no one was expected to take communion) he cradled an egg-cup. His trainers squeaked with each duty. A kind of exalted arrogance held him up. Once, when he bowed to earth, his head hit a ventilator. He proceeded unmoved. And whenever the woman incanting the responses faltered – her baby was clambering over her legs – he would break in: 'Come on! Read it! Read it!'

Only in his sermon did he take on a paternal and almost tender authority. His voice mellowed. He spoke of the Apostolic succession, as if confirming his right to be with us, a Pole preaching to Russians on a steamboat at the end of the world. His palms lifted in balance, in forgiveness, weighing grace against sin, while behind him in the window's apse a crimson sun descended and an orange moon rose.

*   *   *

A web of nine-storey blocks in storm-stained concrete, an arid anchorage ringed by naked shores: this is Dudinka. To build here is a technical hell. A few feet beneath the surface the ground is frozen iron-hard, but the slight heat exerted by any foundation will melt this permafrost until the structures above it tilt and come crashing down. So every building is raised four feet clear of the earth on a grid of concrete pillars, often sunk in buckets filled with cement and driven deep into the ground. To stoop through these maze-like basements is like wandering a series of primitive temples. The shafts look too thin and random to uphold the storeys massed above them. They become the haunt of children and lovers, strewn with beer bottles, condoms, broken toys. Above this perilous earth the whole cumbersome-looking town hovers light as a skater, barely touching the surface at all.

Cold stamps it even in autumn. Its shops and offices are immured behind double and triple doors. The fat tubes of water mains, impossible to sink in the permafrost, blunder from block to block, lagged in rotting wood and tin, like arteries from some distant heart. Verandas and outdoor stairs sail free of the ground on iron struts. From anywhere in the streets you can see the stark line of the tundra.

I toiled up from the docks, hunted for the only boarding-house, became lost. Around me the people looked too few, dressed in black or grey as if the town were in mourning, and half the buildings shut. Among the Russians went a sprinkling of indigenous natives, but in this urban anonymity they looked defaced. They were part of the early peoples – Turkic, Samoyed, Tungus – scattered all over Siberia and now half-annihilated or absorbed. In the local museum, run by one of those dedicated women (they were always women) proud of their stuffed polar bears and rock specimens, the native culture was being dutifully laid to rest in simulated yurts and reassembled shaman costumes. Valentina understood my indifference to them, and my ignorant desire to locate a living settlement. She had heard of an Entsy fishing-village eighty miles upriver, she said, and knew the captain of an oil-tanker now in dock, who might drop me there next morning.

Perhaps it was the high latitude, the fading sense of time, which detached me a little from the place and from myself. Valentina said the Entsy village was poor and violent, and my curiosity only increased. I remember roaming Dudinka – its desolate suburbs and port – as if it were another planet.

Then I remember supper in Valentina's flat with her drunken neighbour Misha. His wife was away, and Valentina's husband working in Odessa: everybody separated. From time to time Valentina's daughter – an eleven-year-old solitary with a round, dreaming face – ambled from her bedroom to stare at us. I remember the vodka glasses emptying too quickly, and how I had vowed not to fall victim to these orgies. I remember Valentina's face motherly, sensual and blurring. And Misha's voice wondering about the British. 'The British are too cold and serious – except for you, hah! hah! How do you British get girls? How do you ever . . . Hah! hah! hah! . . .'

Our talk slushed into monotone. Two vodka bottles emptied. Misha mistook me for his son. But I was fifty-eight, I slurred (beyond the life expectation of a Russian male). Misha didn't believe me. Nor, in a way, did I. That was the panacea for growing older, you didn't quite believe it. Your body became a mistake. We clasped each other, toasted Valentina. Her moon-faced daughter had escaped bed again and was pilfering the food. Mortality, Misha said, was a dirty trick. If I close my eyes, I thought, my head will spin away like a top. But if I keep them open, they are near-sightless. Valentina has become a silhouette somewhere to my left. In her daughter, the moon has grown legs and is walking about. I remember hoping that Valentina was less drunk than Misha or me, and that she would wake me in the morning to find the tanker captain. Then I stumbled up to Misha's flat. In a moment of clarity, before lurching to his divan, I set my alarm clock, while he capsized on to a mattress with his German shepherd growling beside him.

Occasionally, in a guise not anticipated, you encounter somebody who resembles a friend in the West. It is both funny and disconcerting. So next morning, an American professor had shed a few years and become ship's mate on an oil tanker running between Dudinka and Krasnoyarsk. Standing alone on the bridge, he steered the cargo out of the silent harbour while the short-wave radio crackled unanswered, and we settled ponderously midstream.

Flying level with the ship, a flock of seagulls watched us through button eyes. My head throbbed. The captain, Valentina's friend, was somewhere below deck. He too was drunk. I groped along the gangway which ran the ship's length past its crude-oil containers, and let the wind scour out my head. Behind me a skeleton crew assembled on the bridge: slothful, friendly men with nothing obvious to do. In winter they tried to find work as mechanics. Then in spring, when the river-ice broke up with a noise like cannon-fire, they would join the tankers nosing through the floes again on the oil-run to Dudinka.

The captain emerged from the hold. He looked bloated and

spent, and the crew ignored him. He asked me down to drink in his cabin. In this cramped chamber he would jump ship into oblivion, sometimes chewing on smoked *omul* salmon before cracking another bottle. He was already so far gone that I dribbled away my vodka unseen on to the floor. He wanted to retire to a dacha, he said – he had a wife and a dog in Krasnoyarsk – but his pension was too small. 'What pension? Bread and water!' So he had installed his son – ginger-haired, like him – among the crew; and his red-headed daughter worked as a cook in the galley. Once, he slurred, he had operated on secret service with the Soviet navy in Algeria and Syria: he couldn't have spoken of it before because of the KGB. He couldn't speak of it now because of vodka.

After four hours the ship churned to a stop in mid-river, and through the porthole I saw the eastern bank rearing 80 feet in an eroded rampart, crested by wooden barracks. It was the Entsy village of Potalovo; it looked like a fort. We stumbled up on deck where the crew was winching a metal motor-boat into the water. Whenever they tried to float it, the current smashed it against the ship's sides. The captain clasped me against him, kissed my cheeks. He didn't like where I was going, he said. No, he'd never been there, nobody had ever been there, but he'd heard of it. He refused to accept any money from me – he whose pension would be bread and water. But would I write to him, he bawled down as I descended the ladder, tell him I'd got safely away? As the motor-boat clanged against the tanker's hull, he spelt out his address in bellowing letters above. A minute later, with two sailors, I was roaring towards the shore.

Only a scatter of beached fishing-boats showed that the place was still inhabited. I climbed the steep track up the grass-covered slope, the sailors behind me. There was no sound. The flagstaff above us looked as if nothing had ever waved there. On the summit we found an administrative building which appeared to have been boarded up for years. Dogs were scavenging in its foundations. But beyond, perched on a roof, a bearded gremlin in a woollen hat was hammering nails into shingles. The sailors turned back to the ship with relief, as he shouted at me: 'You want help?' He clambered down. He was the village doctor.

I would have imagined the doctor here a lonely time-server, sunk in drink and apathy, but Nikolai was a fifty-year-old optimist. The village had declined into barbarism, he said, and if I lodged with a family I could be knifed in a fracas, as half his patients had been. He'd give me a bed in his cottage hospital – there was nowhere else. He gestured behind him. A sea of decrepit shacks had opened up beyond the ridge of the river-bank. This was Potalovo, and it was dying. Duckboards sagged and wandered between its huts, and its tracks were all of compacted coal-dust, laid down against the shifting autumn mud. The air reeked of it. Rubbish lay everywhere, and long-broken tractors rusted in their own debris.

We started to walk. 'It's got desperate here. This used to be a fur-trading village, and was a reindeer collective in Khrushchev's day. But you see it now!' A coal-black pond glistened with discarded vodka bottles. 'The reindeer pastures have been ruined by acid rain. It comes down from the nickel-processing factories at Norilsk. And gas pipelines from the Taimyr peninsula too – the wild reindeer are afraid to cross them. So what can these people do? They just fish a bit, and sell their catch to passing steamers. The passengers buy because it's cheaper than buying in the towns. People here are close to starving.'

A few of them, wrapped in overcoats and waterproofs, sat by their doorways in the last of the year's sun. They had slow, bitter faces. Nothing grew here. Their yards held only coal-heaps and butts of river-water. As we passed, their chained dogs hurled themselves at us from ramshackle kennels – white huskies whose snarls choked in mid-leap. A glimpse through windows showed nothing among the sticks of furniture but items of winter survival – blankets, felt boots, clay stoves. A few sledges rotted in the grass. Of some five hundred villagers, the doctor said, those who remained were mostly Entsy – a Samoyed people – with a few Russians like himself.

'But they've lost their culture. There are no household gods left, and nothing of shamanism. A doctor would know if there were!'

They stared after us through torpid eyes. Only Nikolai seemed to possess the energy to change anything. His wire-wool hair bounced at every step. 'You'd think this place quiet, but it's the most troublesome in the world. When these people drink, they fight. They start with their fists, then stick knives into one another. It's vodka, of course. So there are ulcers and liver diseases. And if it gets too much I send them downriver for operations in Dudinka.'

His hospital was a low, wooden ark. Reindeer moss caulked the gaps between its logs, and it buckled at either end from permafrost. I looked at it with alarm. 'How long do you think it'll last?'

'Twenty years!' He laughed. His face was lined by a life-saving optimism. 'Well, I say that. But you know the Uzbek tale of the teacher who promised the pasha that he could make a donkey speak within twenty years? He reckoned either he or the pasha or the donkey would be dead by then!'

Inside the building was a simple range of three-bed wards, a kitchen and a consulting-room. It had no running water, and its lavatory was a hole in the ground. Between the double windows the sealing moss had fallen in faded tresses. It was almost without equipment. But the rooms were all washed white and eggshell blue, and three part-time nurses tended the five children in its narrow, iron beds, while a woman recovering from premature childbirth lay silent in another.

Nikolai pointed me to my ward, then left. I wondered how long I'd be here. The only way out was the river, where days or weeks might go by before a steamer passed.

I edged open my ward door to see a little bow-legged Entsy perched on the far bed. He looked incalculably old. Around his mouth and nose the flesh had hardened into ridges and knolls, and his chin dribbled a wispy beard. Mongoloid blood had pushed his cheekbones wide, and his hair remained pitch-black. 'Hullo. . . .'

His voice was so small, and his Russian so forgotten, that he was hard to understand. 'My home burnt down, I don't know why. So I'm here. And now my eyes are going.' He rubbed his bloodshot right socket and pulled down its eyelid: he thought I was a doctor. 'I can't look at the sun now.'

'You have glasses?'

'I used to. They were stolen from my pocket when I was asleep, drunk.' His tone was matter-of-fact. 'I've not seen things close since then.' He reached out and tried mine. '*Yay-aach*, yes, better, better.' But he took them off again and pointed inwards at his temples. 'The pain comes here . . . and here . . . like knives. The doctor can't do anything. I went to the hospital in Dudinka, where people die. It's better here in this one.'

'Can you stay here?'

'I've nowhere. My house burnt too easily. Another one burnt down a while ago, and the people died. And another on the other side of the village. A man and wife, they were drunk. And they died. All my clothes were finished, except what I had on. I had time to run in once, before it was too late. Only once.'

What had he carried out, I wondered, in those few seconds? Had he salvaged a few hoarded roubles, a precious garment, a sentimental photograph? 'What did you save?'

I strained to catch his voice. It came tiny, self-satisfied: 'My *passport*.'

He pulled it from his jacket as if to be sure it remained. His name, I saw, was Stepan, and his age, to my astonishment, was only sixty-seven. It was a sensible choice to retrieve, I knew; but I felt his degradation. His hand was trembling, until I held it in mine. And I realised I was angry: angry that even into this remote life Moscow had intruded its ossifying order, grounding and claiming him. Without his passport he could not move, did not live. He had risked fire for it.

I sensed something odd about the hand in mine, and looked down to find its forefinger missing. 'What happened there?'

'Somebody crushed it. A tractor maybe.' He was smiling. 'I was lying in the road, I was drunk.'

I got up and emptied my rucksack over my bed in a jumble of clothes and bottles. Two of the worthless-looking bottles contained dollars, and the hospital, I sensed, was porous: people loitered here. But I could think of no other way to safeguard my things than a show of despising them. And Stepan had less than I did. He kept his money and socks under his mattress like a schoolboy. The handful of chattels donated to him – some underclothes and two tin mugs – hung on the wall in a plastic bag. That night I realised that he used one mug for tea and the other for spitting and snorting. He slept in a pair of faded crimson pants.

But who would rebuild his home, he did not know. Only one of his children had survived, and she was far away in Dudinka. 'My wife is over there.' He waved to the north, at the cemetery. 'So I've nothing now.' He laughed and wheezed.

Occasionally by day he went on walks around the hospital fence, letting out hoarse, unanswered cries as something occurred to him. More often he wandered between our dormitory and the consulting-room, his face creased by a frown of unbearable concentration, as though it took all his attention to stay alive. An elastic band which he bound around his head prevented it, he said, from flying apart.

Sometimes he sat in the vestibule, as if waiting for somebody who did not come.

My days in Potalovo multiplied timelessly. Often it seemed deserted. Roaming its streets, I would hear nothing but the chain-rattling dogs or the cries of seagulls flying in, wheeling away. Its utilities were all in ruins. The rail by which goods had been winched up from the river lay derelict, and two months ago the power plant had gone up in flames. A network of poles, tilted askew by permafrost, still carried intermittent electricity from a pocket generator.

More than half the population was unemployed, and the rest – Entsy and Russians together – looked broken by the rigours of their fishing: sombre, hungry, weather-scarred. On a good day they landed big red sturgeon and *omul*, and there would be salted *muksun* for sale, or gang fish or char or northern pike. On other days, or in times of storm, the fishermen hunched in one another's cottages, brooding and dozing. But word had gone round that a Westerner had come, and many people had never seen one. One man snarled at me to get off the duckboards passing his hovel, another ran out and poured berries into my hands. Knots of children yelled out English phrases.

From a gang of louts and mavericks I was dogged by a poacher. In winter, hunters would cross the frozen river and shoot reindeer from the depleted collective on the far bank, he said. 'We get them when they're asleep. You can live off the frozen meat of one for months.' He tried to sell me their antlers, which he kept in a secret shed.

Others of his band were pathetic or desperate. There was an angry-looking Entsy youth (his Russian cronies called him 'Banana-skin'), who pleaded with me to take him to England; an ex-paratrooper who had fallen from his bed while dreaming that his parachute hadn't opened, and had lacerated his face in deep, parallel wounds; a fanatic who had fled here from the Altai after serving time for killing his wife's lover.

The hospital gave no sanctuary. Once the doctor was gone, these outcasts would sidle through the doors and roam the passage, hunting for food, vodka, anything, ignoring the sharp-voiced nurses. Wheedling, clinging, they promised me furs or reindeer-skins in exchange for an advance of money. The proto-type Ivan of my memory seemed to have multiplied and degenerated in them. He was everywhere now, and in despair. I pushed these men ruthlessly from the wards, crashed my door in their faces, and always afterwards, glimpsing from a window the retreat of their stooped shoulders and resigned backs, I was touched by remorse. It was all right for me, after all. One day a steamer would take me away.

I ate invalid's meals with Stepan in the hospital: thin soup and macaroni or a bowl of rice. On this diet he flourished, while I grew weak. At night the ledge running along the hospital wall became a gangway for huskies, which would cross the dim rect-angle of our window in savage shadows. I lay awake to the whingeing of a child in aching pain, while Stepan retched and spat. Six or eight times a night he would get up to urinate, flicking electric switches uselessly. 'No light . . . *Ye-ach!* . . . no light. . . .' His breathing seemed to drop an octave with every exhalation after he returned to bed, so that once or twice I feared he had died.

At evening the doctor escaped the small, chaotic house where his wife and teenage son wrangled, and lingered in his clinic to talk with me. Above us the walls were banked by pigeon-holes stuffed with patients' records, and a bare bulb flared and winked as the village generator fluctuated. In Nikolai I was reminded of those provincial doctors who inhabit the plays of Chekhov; only here there was no bourgeoisie, no cherry orchard, no voiceable hope. He was alone. These were quiet days, he said, but in a week the monthly pensions would arrive; then people would start to drink, and the clinic would fill up.

'They're even losing their language here. I think this is the last generation that will speak it. They're taught in Russian, their parents know Russian. The children go to the *Internat* schools in Dudinka aged fourteen, or if their parents are out with the reindeer – and there are some still over the river – they leave here aged seven.'

I said: 'I thought the reindeer were almost finished.'

'They are. Even I can remember when there were 11,000 in herds on either side of the river. Now they're reduced to 1,000, and interbreeding has made them smaller. In winter poachers cross the river on sledges to shoot them, and wild reindeer lure others away. That whole way of life is vanishing.'

'And nothing replaces it?'

'Vodka.' He laughed. 'And a few years ago an Arctic fox farm was set up here – 3,000 there must have been – bred for their pelts. But when the river transport dried up it became impossible to feed them, and now they're nearly gone. The river's the only way in and out of here. Without it, there's no food but fish. And no medicine.' This jolted his memory, and he pulled some packets from a drawer. 'Now look. . . . What is your name? Colin! That's Kolya, like mine. Nikolai! Now, Nikolai, sometimes I get English medicines and can't understand the instructions. Can you translate this? Here. . . .'

He handed me a packet of something called Perinorm manufactured in Bombay, and I unfolded a leaflet of smudged directions:

'*Metoclopramide has got central antidopaminergic effect in the hypothalamus and thereby raises threshold for vomiting at chemo-receptor trigger zone. Its effects on the G.I. tract are thought to result from blocking of dopaminergic receptors, potentiation of cholinergic effect. . . .*'

I said bleakly: 'I don't think I can do this. . . .'

'But Nikolai, you're *English*!'

'I know, Nikolai. But this leaflet has a language of its own.'

'It's Hindi?'

'In a way.'

But we struggled through it. He guessed the medical terms by way of Slavic borrowings, and after a while we had discovered our G.I. tracts and resolved the hypothalamus. Noisy triumph greeted each resolution. Our shared name cemented us. I became an expert on vomiting thresholds while he identified the chemo-receptor trigger zone.

Then, suddenly, he was staring at my hands. He removed his glasses, replaced them, looked abruptly serious. 'Is your health quite all right?'

I wondered what he was seeing. 'I don't know.'

'Roll up your sleeve.' He applied a tourniquet and took my blood pressure. I realised with slight alarm that it had not been taken for years. Yet I had passed the terminal age for the average Russian male. Nikolai's frown deepened, either with perplexity or horror, while I kept silent. He peered down my throat through a giant magnifying-glass. The lines of his forehead puckered in a fleur-de-lys above his nose. My imagination broke free. Would he propose chemotherapy, I wondered, or prescribe Perinorm to restore my hypothalamus? Then he picked up my hand, fastidi-ously, by the wrist. 'Your fingers . . . are they always like that? The nails.'

'Just dirty?' I wondered.

'No. They've got vertical lines. And they're very soft. They bend. They're red at the roots.' We stared at them together. I found them vaguely comforting. 'Yet your circulation, your blood pressure, is normal. . . .'

I felt a surge of relief, but I said: 'I thought everybody's nails were like this.'

We took to examining his, which were opaque, clean and hard. He was smiling again. He said: 'You'll survive, Nikolai!' So I wasn't ill, it seemed, I was just peculiar.

'Perhaps it's the difference in our lives,' I said.

He looked at me as if the difference should be flagrant. I was dressed as shabbily as him, after all, and I was travelling in the Arctic on a shoe-string. But my nails were soft. He said: 'So what are you doing here?'

'I'm looking at Siberia.'

'And what do you see?' He gestured out of the window. 'Anything?' Into my silence he pursued: 'What did you expect, Nikolai?'

'Nikolai, it's too long ago to remember!' But I had been looking for patterns, of course. I wanted their security. I wanted some unity or shape to human diversity. But instead this land had become diffused and unexpected as I travelled it. Wherever I stopped appeared untypical, as if the essential Siberia could exist only in my absence, and I could not answer Nikolai at all.

'I didn't expect anywhere as bad as here.'

'This is extreme.'

Perhaps Siberia's essence was wilderness, I thought idly, and human witness destroyed it, like those light particles which the act of observation changes. So I was reduced to knowing it by glancing detail, snatches of talk, the texture of his fingernails.

'And how did *you* land up here?' I asked. I had longed to know this. I was conscious of heroising him, as if he had chosen this post from duty; but I feared some sadder reason, and had recoiled from asking him until now.

But he kept his clarity, even grinned. 'Well, at the time the Soviet Union split up I was an army doctor in Kazakhstan. That's where I was born. In 1992 my unit was disbanded and I decided to become a civilian. I wanted my sons to attend good institutions, so I had to move to Russia, get Russian citizenship. And this was where I got offered.' Then his pride welled up. 'Now my elder son is in the naval college in St Petersburg! He's doing fine. He's even entertained British naval officers. My son with the Royal Navy!'

So the boy was in still-resplendent St Petersburg, while his father eked out his life in a Siberian village, burning with pride. Nikolai had sacrificed himself for his children.

I said: 'How long might you be here?'

'You have to stay a long time to be useful. You have to know your patients' history.' He lifted his chin to the pigeon-holes around us, each stacked with its quota of misery. His beard was salted with grey. 'I only worry that my eyes are failing. I used to read books for pleasure, but now I can't afford to.' He showed me, a little wistfully, a Russian pocket edition of Rudyard Kipling's poems, which he had loved. 'I save my eyes for medical treatises now.'

I felt alarmed for him, and an unfocused sadness. 'What happened?'

'I think it was the long nights. You see, for five months of winter we scarcely see sunlight here. Families just close themselves away, or fish through holes in the ice. I used to read and study for weeks, often by the light of paraffin lamps. But my eyes hated it.' He put on his glasses again without self-pity. 'Now could you just translate?' – pushing a last packet under my eyes: '*Metoclopramide blocks the action of dopramine, thereby inhibiting prolactin releases. . . .*' 'Are you sure you're quite well?'

The only signs of the herdsman's former strength are the gnarled hands clenched over his thighs. The swell of his cheekbones drops fiercely to a faltering jawline. He thinks he is eighty-six, but cannot be sure. He is not happy here.

I stand hesitantly in his room. Its passage is heaped with coal and hung with the antlers of reindeer gathered long ago. He has spent his life with the herds on the far side of the river, but is too weak to sustain that now. The plaster is dribbling from the wattle of his ceiling. His door is locked against drunks.

He says: 'Life was hard over there, but it is better than here. I didn't choose this.'

Over there, in the end, you could live on the miraculous reindeer: eat even its ears and lips and bowel contents, resist the harshest cold in its skins, turn its bones to implements or tinder, ride it to new pastures. This, said the old man, was how things had always been. The reindeer could endure on its reserves like a camel, and possessed a third lung which kept it warm inside. Even after the Soviets collectivised the herders – a tragedy which ignored native knowledge – his people had migrated with their sledge-drawn tents between the Arctic Sea and the Yenisei hinterland. The reindeer could sniff the edible lichen beneath the ice, and paw it up. But unnoticeably, acid rain was depleting the pastures.

The Entsy remembers this. Under his frosted scalp his face has shrunk to a gremlin watchfulness. He remembers the herds withering away.

I have left his door open, and now a drunk Russian barges in and demands a cigarette and a glass of vodka. The old man has neither. The youth curses the prices in Dudinka and the fucking Yenisei and a fucking sturgeon that got away, and he leaves. The Entsy has stayed stoical, as if his eyes were retracted into his skull. Above his bed hangs a pair of thigh-length reindeer boots: sheaths of glistening topaz stripes. They shine like an heirloom. But he wears a vinyl jerkin and rubber shoes now, and picks at a salted *omul*.

'You see how it is. That's what happens here. These people.' His only son died of a heart-attack in the tundra, he says. His wife is dead. (For the first time one of his hands moves: it gestures to the west.) But it is better over there, he remembers, and he wants to cross back over the river.

Beyond the village the tundra spread. Its only trees were stunted larches, which showered down a golden dust of needles at my touch. Its beauty was all underfoot, in a quilt of mosses, heathers, lichens, fungi. In late September – in this moment before snow – they shone in a patina of amber and scarlet. The wind scarcely stirred them. A fruiting of red and indigo currants – bilberries, blueberries, cranberries – hung from stems which were turning ruby, and between them, among lichens unknown to me, the reindeer moss lifted minute, tangled fronds. Half the textures were unexpected. Solid-seeming hummocks gave way to spongy cushions, or sank into bog, while under my feet the moist-looking reindeer moss crackled like wood-shavings.

This wilderness girds the Arctic Sea for more than four thousand miles. After the squalor of the village, it spread a cleansing emptiness. I heard only the squeak of small birds and the sieving of wind through the grass. When I lay down I crushed out a lavender fragrance. Everything, I knew, had evolved in response to cold. The sward grew low against polar blizzards. Thrift and saxifrage clung to their dead but protective foliage through the winter. Other plants formed hair or trapped the sunlight in subcutaneous pockets, or refracted it on to their buds with the parabolic discs of their first leaves.

And because of the permafrost, nothing drained away. I kept slipping into bogs and swamp. Some looked like half-formed pools; mushrooms sprouted in their wells. Others seemed to be old ponds which were transforming to silt-fed clearings. Everywhere lakes broke out in circles and oblongs brimming level with the earth. Their water was auburn, uninhabited, darkly beautiful. Ferns lifted through its surface from a sediment of leaves. They were a little mysterious. Their geometric perfection – formed during the annual contraction and thawing of the ground – still happens unexplained.

At evening the breaking and dimming of sunlight over the lakes followed me dreamily back to the Yenisei. Clouds of mosquitoes rose and settled on my lips, eyelids, nostrils, their biting reduced to a trickle. I emerged a few miles south of Potalovo.

By the time I had climbed the intervening hill, the sun was dropping into the river and I found myself among a maze of free-standing galleries. At first I did not understand. They ran on stilts for 100 yards or more, and had half collapsed. Their flimsy doors slammed in the wind. The place seemed deserted. I heard only an odd clicking, as if a multitude of birds were pecking grain somewhere. Then, as I entered one of the corridors, a terrible screaming broke out. From their cramped cages scores of starved, long-bodied dogs were gazing at me and shrieking. The noise was at once piteous and angry: a little human. I was in the ruins of the Arctic fox farm.

They had lost their wild beauty. Their claws splayed and unhooked painfully over the wire-mesh floor of their cages, and made the unearthly clicking. Their excrement dropped through the mesh on to trays below. They had barely room to turn round. It crossed my mind to release them – all 200 or so – but what would they do? They had known only a few square feet of wire, and impoverished humans needed them. Their heads were unnaturally big on their bodies, and their grey fur was turning white for the winter they would not see.

I turned back along the gallery through the gauntlet of their screaming. It followed me down the hill.

That night I was startled awake. Stepan, drunk, had blundered across the room and grabbed for his bag of belongings on the wall. In the frame of our window, blocking out the stars, the silhouettes of two men were beckoning him away. He lit a nurse's lamp on the floor, then dithered towards my bed. His ancient head seemed to surmount the body of a stunted youth, its muscles barely slackened around his stomach. His hand extended towards me, rubbing its remaining fingers against his thumb. 'Money? . . . money? . . .' I closed my eyes. Then he let out a soft '*Ya-aach!*' and tugged on his pullover, a pair of split trousers, his hat. The faces outside were still pressed against the glass.

The next moment a nurse rushed in and seized him by the arm. 'You've had enough drink!' she screamed. 'You've had enough!' He wrenched himself free, but she seized him again and he collapsed on to his bed and started to sing in a plaintive alto, like a woman. The faces vanished from the window. For a long time I lay trying to sleep, listening to the whimpering of the awakened child, while Stepan's singing faded away.

In the dawn I went out to escape him, past the shuttered houses and growling kennels, to the river. A steamer was expected at noon, and I was hoping to leave. Half the day I waited among the thistles and grass on a high foreland, straining my eyes for the shadow of a ship. But the grey flood of the Yenisei suddenly looked hostile, flowing between dead banks, and nothing came. There had been storms upriver, somebody said.

The richest people in Potalovo are the children. They drive tractors and bulldozers, own houses, sail ships. The fact that all these possessions are wrecked makes no difference. They are a simulacrum of the adult world. So the children keep house in burnt-out cottages, or climb into the cabins of tractors and roam the tundra on vanished wheels. Sometimes they man the bridge of the beached and derelict cargo ship, and steer for the Arctic Sea. Only when they stop being children do they realise that they are inhabiting a world in ruins.

At the age of twelve or thirteen, said Nikolai, they start to drink.

He hated the arrival of the boat-shop which plied the river. That afternoon it had opened its hold on a thin range of expensive goods – vodka, above all – and the villagers had sped out in their motor-boats to meet it. In his dim-lit clinic Nikolai looked through the window at the night and circled his arm. 'Probably this whole settlement is drunk around us at this moment. Almost everyone.'

He dreaded the monthly arrival of pensions. 'Single parents get an allowance for each child, so a man with five children and no wife can feel a millionaire! He'll drink himself sick while the children starve. The women do it too. Everybody. And when the vodka gives out they'll search for anything. There's an American machine oil which is bought galore here. Our machines are all broken, of course, but people drink this fluid by the bottle. Within two to three hours they're asphyxiated. If they get to the hospital I can save them, but they die in their homes or in the streets.' Then, with the hardiness of necessity, he cheered up. 'Listen to this, Nikolai!' He had a Russian book called *A Thousand English Jokes* which he couldn't resist sharing. 'Have you heard the one about the Englishman, the Russian and the parrot? Listen. . . .'

But my mind wandered back to the village, where the life expectation of the Entsy had dropped to forty-five – and half of them died violent deaths. Only Nikolai, with his optimism, his scant equipment and medication, his failing eyesight, saved them from worse.

'And the parrot said . . .'

I asked: 'When will things get better?'

'They're already better! A few years ago these people couldn't even drink river water safely. They used to pump it up into a tank, and for years died of dysentery. Nobody knew why. The doctor at that time didn't realise. Then one summer the tank drained low and they discovered it was revolting. Now they get the water up by tractor, and in winter they gather snow and drink that. Things are better for the first time! Last year was the low point. I think it was the worst we'll have.'

So the people of Potalovo, I thought, were going to survive. They were Siberians, after all. They would adapt, cut down, muck in, suffer, wait.

'Last year,' said Nikolai, 'weeks would go by and we'd scarcely glimpse a boat. But this year, well, you've seen it. Here and there a cargo ship, a tanker. That's how you know the state of things. By the river.'

From outside came the crashing of drunks into his vestibule. Nikolai locked his door. 'I know this lot,' he said. 'If I open to them, there'll be a fight.' He yelled through the door: 'Go away! No, I won't see you! The doctor isn't here! Come back tomorrow! No! He's away!'

The bangs and scrapings faded into the slur of feet over grass. Then silence.

'Listen.' Nikolai reopened his book. 'A duke and a duchess are out with their dog. . . .'

In a window of the children's ward I catch sight of a man staring at me. His hair flies wild round a wind-burnt face. For a second I imagine him another village drunk. Then I realise it is not a window at all. It is a mirror.

For three weeks I have not seen myself. Lines slither down the reflection's cheeks and his eyes are hung with grey crescents. The jaw is ill-shaven and slightly belligerent. Confusedly I try to collate the inner and outer person. I wonder if the mirror is distorting. If it isn't, something else must be. The face looks anxious now. I feel more kindly to anyone who has spoken to it, even the harshest villager. Then I turn away, disowning it.

They have lost their traditions, the doctor said, and even in the home of the octogenarian herdsman I found no pagan totems. People's memory of their nature spirits, and of the old, unapproachable Entsy deity whose son was the god of death, had dimmed away. Nobody any longer knew the oral epics, or the hero Itje, father of the bear and sworn enemy of Christ. The places of sacrifice had been left behind in the reindeer tundra.

Only in the cemetery – the last bastion of conservatism – the importance of death, I thought, may have kept the past alive. On the morning of my departure I discovered it on a hillside beyond the village, hidden among silver birch trees. The painted crosses and sodden wreaths were all I had expected: a people superficially Christianised. And a few headstones carried the Communist star.

But as I climbed higher I found other graves where bleached antlers lay. Their bier-sledges rested beside them, ritually broken; and the skulls of reindeer grimaced from the trees. On almost every grave – I saw this now – the offerings of enamel bowls and kettles had been turned upside down and gouged or split. A doll lay on the grave of a child, dismembered.

When I said farewell to the old herdsman, I asked about this, and it was as I had thought. The offerings, he said, were broken because the afterlife is the opposite of this one. Rivers there flow backwards from the sea. Things turned upside-down here become the right way up over there, and vice versa. Everything whole is broken, and everything broken becomes whole. Otherwise the dead will not find it.

In that inverted world, I thought, Potalovo will be paradise.

A motor-boat was waiting to take me to the steamer, and other craft swarmed about it in mid-river, while the owners tried to sell fish. Only the imbecile Banana-skin was steering his boat in a manic daydream, round and round.

Nikolai stood beside me on the shore with a knot of others. 'These are a good people at heart,' he said. 'I asked around if anybody had anything to give to the Englishman before he left, and look! These are for you!' He handed me a big plastic bag. It was heavy with *omul* salmon. It carried with it a surge of reconciling warmth. Yet I felt somehow shamed, and a little stricken. They were useless to me. I stared out at the river, with a tightening throat. Then the motor-boat took me away.

6

The Great Lake

At Tayshet, once a transit-camp for Gulag prisoners, the Trans-Siberian Railway branches south-east, and the long, lonely and disastrously expensive Baikal–Amur Railway drives on two thousand miles to the Pacific. Conceived grandiosely as an artery for opening up eastern Siberia, and running far north of the exposed route along the Chinese border, the BAM's single track traversed a region increasingly impoverished, and it never lived up to hopes.

But after Potalovo, I travelled it forgivingly. Its bunks over-flowed with passengers' cheap merchandise, and its grimy windows were bolted shut. But I was on the move again. Whenever we crested a rise, the forested hills unravelled beneath us, until the red-gold flare of birch against pine seemed the natural state of half the earth. Once or twice some mammoth industry intruded, and at noon the Bratsk High Dam – once a showpiece of Socialist achievement – rumbled grandly beneath us: on one side a sprawl of lake and factories, on the other the gorge of the Angara river. But always the taiga closed in enormously again, its birch leaves drifting in silence through the massed dark of the conifers.

The only disturbance on the train was caused by me. I felt something move in my hair, and as I ruffled it, three or four squat black spiders dropped out. I had read that the Ixodes tick, which carries encephalitis, fades from the taiga in June, but I was wrong. 'Dangerous! Dangerous!' cried the woman opposite me. She drilled the fingernails of one hand into her forearm. 'They dig themselves in. They murder you!' I gaped at them appalled. These ticks, I knew, could kill or cripple you for life, paralysing your neck and limbs. You are racked by atrocious headaches. But the woman was laughing – everybody in our compartment was laughing – as we trampled on them casually while they dispersed over the floor.

I thought back. I had just flown south from the grim nickel town of Norilsk, and near Krasnoyarsk, early that morning, I had walked innocently into broad-leaved forest. There, I knew, the ticks drop from the trees on to anything warm-blooded (even an Englishman) and might burrow fatally beneath the skin. Up to midsummer Russians only walk the taiga dressed in double layers of clothing.

For the moment, eased by the laughter around me, I gave up thinking about it. But that night I wondered how many more ticks were nestling in the creases of my clothing or body. Lying on my bunk, I began to feel them all over me, needling and burrowing. I imagined them wherever I itched. It was cold, but I started to sweat. The ticks dropped into my dreams. At every station the engine sighed to an unnerving silence, and I woke up. Then night passengers would come barging in under gargantuan packages, gasping and dragging things.

At last I locked myself in the lavatory and dampened my hair from a water-bottle. Then I scrutinised my scalp in a shaving-mirror, hunting for the tail of a buried tick. It would look like a protruding sunflower seed. After half an hour I transferred the inspection to my neck and shoulders. If I glimpsed a quivering tail, I had read, paraffin or salt was the answer. But by now people were battering on the lavatory door; I found nothing; and two hours later dawn was breaking over a new land.

A wash of cloud and stunted pines, their roots twisted about the scree, distilled the view to a Japanese painting, where a faint moon was printed on the sky. Grey rock had broken loose from the forest, and lifted to snow-lit peaks. Soon we were easing downhill. All across the horizon, a curtain of fanged mountains – brilliant and irregular – was glittering above the deepest lake on earth.

*

Severobaikalsk was built in virgin forest for railway workers at the northern tip of Lake Baikal. Its wooden settlement is still there, designed as a temporary town before the BAM builders could move into apartments. But the money dried up. The flat-blocks stopped in mid-construction. Here and there they wait in prefabricated sections, or stand half-finished like forgotten houses of cards. Yet the town remains more handsome than most, austere in its incompletion, a little rural.

A widower and his two sons lived in the wooden suburb. Quiet, preoccupied men, they ran treks into the hinterland and sometimes offered travellers rooms. The father, an engineer, had suffered a stroke; the sons were still at university. We settled down to talk about expeditions along the lake. The younger son, Shamil, was longing to go.

Then their door burst open and in strode two police officials. One was a slovenly officer in uniform, the other a stone-faced woman who called herself the Passport Office. I felt a chill of alarm blowing in from Brezhnev's time. The Passport Office yelled: 'Is there an American living here?' She glared at me. 'Is there an American?' She demanded to see my papers, then cited special laws in this province, Buryatia, requiring me to register at my first hotel. 'Where are you staying?'

'I don't know. I haven't chosen.'

'You don't know! Why don't you know?'

'I've only just arrived. I haven't *chosen*.' This word became tormenting to her, I could tell. I stressed it angrily.

'Are you staying with these people then?'

I sensed this infringed some rule. 'No.'

'Why is your visa incomplete?'

'It isn't incomplete. It's a business visa. I don't have to have Severobaikalsk on it. And I don't have to register anywhere for three days.'

'You're in Buryatia now! Our laws supersede those Moscow ones. They are for your own protection. In order that you don't get lost.'

It was the old, spurious reason for supervision: the self-fulfilling notion that nobody, nothing, could survive without control.

Shamil said: 'Those rules are idiotic. If a traveller comes and camps by the lake, how does he register? What is his address? How can you be responsible for him?'

His brother added: 'And how would you know? And why should you? What's the point?'

The Passport Office balked, then demanded Shamil's passport. He tossed it at her. His father reprimanded her for her inhospitality in a mewing lecture, while the elder son went on eating *shashlik* contemptuously from a bowl, standing in front of the policeman with calculated unconcern. One of the officer's insignia was unstitching from his shoulder.

The woman turned to Shamil. 'You have a Novosibirsk passport! You should register!'

Shamil's face was lumpy with adolescent spots and he wore thick glasses. He took these off as if he was tired of her. He had an awkward charm. 'I'm a student in Novosibirsk,' he said, as if talking to a child. 'But this is my home. I've lived here all my life. I don't have to register to be at home.'

By now I too had lost any fear of them. They appeared only ridiculous: the pantingly didactic woman and the doltish officer with his hat tilted back on his crew-cut head. I was starting to feel a bitter liberation, as if past humiliations were being avenged: the remembered torment of Russian friends. This anger was heady, and might go too far. These, after all, were only pawns. And now the policeman shambled out of the door, demoralised.

The woman tried to save some pride. 'I demand that you register tomorrow,' she said half-heartedly. 'We need three dollars and two passport photographs.' Her pen hung over her note-pad. 'What's your name again?'

She had trouble with the 'Th', as Russians do, and I did not resolve it for her. The youths went on bantering and confusing her. Their father turned his back. When at last she left, she apologised for disturbing us, with no glint of a smile.

'Don't you register!' the brothers chorused. 'It's her problem. It's people like that who make life impossible. Anyway, how did she know you were here?'

'I don't know. I came by taxi.'

'An informer. What was the driver like?'

But I could remember only a shapeless Ukrainian, and a silver skeleton which dangled from his dashboard. 'I thought Stalin was dead.'

'He's drowning in papers and rules,' Shamil said. 'That's typical of this place. Here we were, about to go into the mountains, and these bastards arrive. . . .'

We did drive into the mountains, all the same. Across bridges which we firmed up with logs, across scuttling streams in a temperature below freezing, we reached the snow-line. A military camp stood abandoned except for one bored guard watching a railway tunnel. A gang of other soldiers, toiling to repair an embankment, tried to flag us down for cigarettes. We tramped to the top of a pass against a battering wind, until we saw the snow-peaks.

Shamil's nose and eyes were streaming, but he did not notice. 'Yes, it's beautiful, but it isn't enough. If you want a life, you have to get out of here. Out of Russia altogether. Otherwise you're caught in this bureaucracy. If you can't make use of it, or understand its way of thinking, you sink. So you have to be like a spider. That's how businessmen are here. Like spiders. They diversify, they know how to make contacts, give out gifts. They have to be flexible, because the rules are always changing. They spend half their energy avoiding them. But at heart nothing changes at all.'

He was starting to shiver. The wind burnt our faces. 'Young people don't feel connected with this country, because its system isn't ours. It's an old people's system. It comes from another time. So we'll go to America, or anywhere that will free us. It's not that we don't love Russia, it's just that we have to live properly. We're young men born into an old man's world.'

I took a bus at dawn along the lake's edge, then walked up valleys towards a ruined Stalinist labour-camp. The forest shed a sunless quiet. There was no wind. But the falling of the birch leaves sent up a collective, near-silent murmur. Their trees made golden columns against the mountains. Sometimes I pushed across a pulpy undergrowth of rotted trunks, whortleberries, blackened fungi, but emerged always into this melancholy descent of leaves – millions of them – drifting through the aisles of the forest. Then I entered a defile where pines had lost their grip in an avalanche of lichened scree. A shrike flew silent between the slopes.

The path died through the camp's gates. One of its posts had crashed across the way, the other was reeling in a thicket of willows. A stream lisped in the glade below. A mist of birch leaves covered everything. The log barracks had been dug into the ground against the cold, and their walls shored up with rocks and timbers for roofs now crashed in. Their doors and windows made ghostly frames on the undergrowth. Sixty years of forest had turned this Gulag to an opera-set, cruelly idyllic. Its ruins spread tree-sown above the river. Hell had been landscaped. I climbed about it on soft leaves. A watch-tower had collapsed in the shadows.

This had been a camp for the mining of mica, once used as insulation, and its prisoners had been taken away before the Second World War, when an artificial substitute was found. It had been abandoned as it stood. Wooden ore-buckets, tossed among the rocks, still traced the line of an overhead cableway. Their hasps and bands were intact, and one of the cramp-irons clanked grimly at my touch.

I noticed something silvery under my feet, and dug my hand into the earth. It came up clutching a translucent mass of flakes. For a second I gazed at them uncomprehending. They slithered through my fingers: mica. When I held the slivers to the sky, they separated like tissue-paper. The trees above their waste-tip already stood 40 feet tall.

I followed their trail up a slope and stumbled on the mouth of the mine. It opened in a near-vertical chasm, where gangway timbers had loosened and plunged into the flooded pit. Iron-bound ore-boxes and winches littered the entrance, one still attached to its tackle and holding a glinting sediment. I looked down 30 feet at a coppery pool and the start of passageways. I could hear water dripping. Gingerly I clambered down the pit-side, clinging to the timbers for as far as I could go. The beams, and the whole rock-face, glistened with a dust of mica. Then the galleries vanished underwater.

I returned through the camp feeling a resurrected unease. A cold wind was sifting through its ruin. Its time seemed neither yesterday nor yet in any reconciled past. It had not been destroyed in shame, but left to decay. Why, I wondered, was there so little Russian outrage at the Gulag? Why did its perpetrators live on unpunished? I became dogged by the idea of a helpless national collusion, in which everyone was guilty, everyone innocent. The iron bucket-handles still moved in their sockets.

Months later, after I had returned to London, some silver flakes spilt from my pockets on to the floor, and glittered strangely.

Across the lake at evening – twenty-five miles over placid water – the ranges of Barguzin began. From this northern end the mountains curved south-west under a parapet of frozen clouds, until the haze thickened and they withdrew to a disembodied pallor floating above the lake.

As I stood there a taxi pulled out from a lane, as if it had been waiting for me, and I climbed gratefully in. Then I saw the silver skeleton dancing from its dashboard. I was looking into the heavy features of the Ukrainian informer. Consciously I recomposed my face, smoothing away anger and a tinge of alarm. But beside him sat a Buryat friend – one of the Mongol people from whom the province is named – and on the roof was his newly tarred canoe.

They were on an outing, the driver said, but I noted him now: a burly man whose face, I thought, turned slowly sympathetic around a wedge of grey moustache and pale eyes. Beside him the Buryat glittered with urgency. His black gaze seemed to see only short-distance, but with a passion to pin down, penetrate. Some terrible brightness was in him. His questions stampeded out. Where was I from? How much did I earn? A *month* or a *year*? Had England ever had a Bolshevik revolution? What of Margaret Thatcher? Of Churchill, Princess Diana, Sherlock Holmes?

The newly caulked canoe was off-loaded in front of his house and ramshackle garden, and I was enticed in to drink tea, together with the Ukrainian and a young trapper carrying muskrat skins.

We hung up our coats on elk horns in the hall. The tea became wine, the wine became vodka. The Buryat sprinkled a handful of both over the table. 'That's for God!' He told me of a shamanistic shrine where he went each year to petition fortune for his family and himself. 'My wife is Buddhist – she doesn't go. But I stand and ask for these things to come from the sky. For a blessing.' He couldn't explain it, he said, he hadn't thought about it. But he opened his palms to the ceiling and said almost angrily – because he thought I did not understand: 'From the open sky! From the sky where God is!'

The wine washed down sausage and black bread. 'That's all we have now,' he said. 'I used to be a machine-operator, but now I only trade in muskrat skins.'

The trapper smiled shyly: a glint of teeth between polished cheeks. He came from the most ancient native group, the Tungus-speaking Evenk, scattered between the Yenisei and the Pacific. He seemed to be seated lower than the rest of us, but in fact his thick body was retracted on its stool, and he was tense with bashfulness. He hunted squirrel and the rare sable, he said, but above all muskrat – and a pile of roan skins glistened under his stool. They were gutted whole, like long gloves, with two pinpricks where their eyes had been. 'I lay traps at night,' he said. 'Where their trails are. I see their trails.'

'He hunts elk too,' the Buryat said. 'Do you hunt elk in England? And are there sables? No? No?' His manic sparkle swept over me again. 'How much is an English canoe? How much is a house?'

But slowly the confusions of choice, the perplexities of forestry and mortgages, the absence of *omul*-fishing in the Thames, began to depress him. His brightness leaked away. He said: 'I suppose you find us very poor?'

'There are poor in England.'

'But you say the government gives to the unemployed.'

'Family networks aren't so strong with us,' I said.

'How can that be?'

From time to time the Ukrainian, perched ponderously beside me, offered insights into our differences, denied the existence of

Sherlock Holmes and revised my estimates of Western salaries upward, to everyone's alarm and wonder. His was a disconcerting presence. I imagined his informer's gaze or mind always on me, so that everything I said became suddenly suspect or odd. When I asked the Evenk about the price of muskrat skins, I imagined the Ukrainian thinking: this is industrial espionage on the fur trade. If I commiserated with the Buryat on his lack of work, the secret report might read: 'He is fomenting disaffection among the unemployed.' I knocked back another vodka. This way paranoia lay.

When he drove me back at last into Severobaikalsk he enquired, as I expected, where I was staying. (Shamil's family had lent me an illicit flat.) I mumbled forgetfully. Then I asked him to drop me off in the town centre, and he did so without protest. Perhaps he understood. He wished me well, and refused any taxi money. We were on holiday, he said. I even imagined, in his parting handshake, a tinge of regret.

In late September, in the last mellow days called Lady's Summer, the road through the hills to the village of Baikalskoe blazed with changing forest. This was the fine-poised moment before the first cold wind would tear the colours down. The sunlight shone cleansed and delicate. The undergrowth spread like a forest fire, its berries outrageously crimson or blue, and the willows hung a gold confetti.

I hitch-hiked to a pass above the lake shore. From here, I hoped, I could look down on the City of the Sun in its bay. It should be complete by now. Solar-powered and unpolluting, its forty-five huts had been designed in sympathy with elusive psychic charges. Their layout – following the theories of Elena Roerich, wife of the mystic painter – would lend power and equilibrium to those living there, and the commune's founder, a local industrialist, had hailed their 'sacred geometry' as the cure for Russia's ills. All the country's future cities, he said, would follow in their wake. So the commune would bask in the cosmic waves identified by the Academician. It would be grouped around something called a centre for cultural consciousness, where ecology would be studied like mystic theology. It would save Russia and harmonise the world. In the post-Communist void, it seemed, God was a cosmic flux.

At the head of the pass, where the road turned inland, I found a straggle of pilgrims. Hanging above the bay – sacred to shamanism – a picnic pavilion and even a road sign were dripping with prayer-rags. Vodka bottles, coins, cigarettes, rouble notes and bunches of currants had been laid along the cliff-edge. The tree branches trembled with votive ribbons, and their trunks had turned to maypoles.

I gazed down on a gulf of blue and forest-bronze. Beyond it the headlands pointed to flocks of islands on glassy water, or withdrew to a gleam of lakes. But of Sun City, the blueprint for a redeeming future, there was no sign.

I waited there, dithering between relief and regret, but the pilgrims knew nothing about this lost salvation. They had come for the view's holiness. But that evening Shamil's brother said: 'Oh, that Sun City! Its founder took to the Orthodox Church. It was never built. That's happening all over Russia now. Young people trying to escape the old mess, starting some farming sect or commune in the woods. But they don't come to anything. It seems we Russians have either to leave for the forest or go to America!'

So I tramped along a bay untouched by any later sanctity, and reached Baikalskoe five hours later: a fishing-village where the road ended. Banked steep above the water and ringed by snow-mountains, it had been plucked from a Russian fairy-tale. The tallest building was its rebuilt church, a green-turreted sanctuary on a mound above the harbour, and the filigreed window-frames, shutters and eaves of its cottages were all merry in peasant blues and reds, like cuckoo-clocks. They looked at once quaintly old and spanking new. Cattle drank at the shoreline, and high-prowed black fishing-boats slept in the marshes.

I climbed a bluff high above the lake, to an old place of Evenk sacrifice. Beneath me Lake Baikal became an ocean. Its headlands multiplied to the south, fainter and fainter, while around me the whole northern curve of its water spread kingfisher-blue, edged by a phantasmal range of mountains, sometimes a mile high. All colour, from here, had refined to this drenching blue – even the blue-tinged white of clouds – as if blue must be the colour to which all others purified in time.

It is the peculiar clarity of Baikal which elicits this. As the transparent and slightly alkaline water deepens, other colours are filtered from its light spectrum, until only blue, the least absorbent, remains. Lying over the fault-line between two tectonic plates, whose separation is gradually dropping its floor lower, the waters plunge to a depth of over one mile: by far the deepest lake on earth. Its statistics stupefy. It harbours nearly one fifth of all the fresh water on the planet: equal to the five Great Lakes of America combined, or to the Baltic Sea. If Baikal were emptied and all the world's rivers diverted to its basin, they would not fill it within a year.

It is, too, the oldest of all lakes. The sediment of its decomposed organisms goes down for another mile and a half. Steeped in its own ecosystem, it has endured since the Tertiary Era, for over twenty-five million years. Of the 2,000 species inhabiting its depths, 1,200 are unique to it. Many remain, it seems, from the ancient seas that once covered most of Siberia, and in the pure abyss of the lake retain a kind of evolutionary innocence. Sponges and primitive crustaceans survive almost unchanged. Some 250 aquatic plant types endure only here. But common fish which swim in from its rivers disappear into unexplained extinction. Its waters seem to cherish the strange, but kill the ordinary.

In part their intense oxygenation accounts for this. Even in their greatest depths, mysterious tides circulate the oxygen among organisms that thrive nowhere else. And the lake's purity is intensified by a unique species of *epischura* crab which cleanses the lake of protoplasm, thinning and distilling it to translucent blue. Nothing superfluous survives. Algae and plankton, bones and cloth, are all devoured. Drowned bodies vanish unrecovered.

You try to imagine this frenzy of self-purification while a solitary hydrofoil hurries you across the serene surface for ten hours to the lake's end. There are no connecting roads, so this is the only way. In front of you Baikal curves south-westward for four hundred miles – the distance from Prague to Milan – and only in Siberia could its immensity seem lost. Fifty miles away, on the far shore, the mountains move in a grey-white shadow-play, but the boat hugs the western bank. Often the cliffs rise sheer for miles, scuffed with clinging trees, like a worn-out pelt. Sometimes they unfurl in promontories of schist and basalt. Forest spills from their defiles.

Only a few fishermen's shacks survive in their shadow. Every fifty miles or so a motor-boat filled with red-faced giants in water-proofs and muskrat hats roars up to starboard and hurls on deck some barrels of *omul*, already gutted, for sale in the south; and the crew tosses out thirty or forty empty barrels astern for them to fill next time.

The *omul* is the lake's staple fish: a delicately flavoured relative of the salmon. When it is hauled up, it emits a sharp cry. It spawns upriver, but returns in November, before Baikal freezes; in spring its newly hatched young are swept down into the lake, where their parents are waiting to eat them.

Baikal seems to breed such strangeness. In its shallows a grain-sized crustacean called the 'Baikal horse' inexplicably clutches two stones, as if for ballast. Farther out, 500-pound sturgeons take two decades to reach maturity and carry up to 20 pounds of caviar each. Minute, red-eyed *gammarid* shrimps live a mile down, sometimes packed 25,000 to the square yard, fondling the dark with preposterously long antennae. They share these deeps with the fatty *golianka* – some so translucent that you can read a book through them. The female is viviparous, giving birth to 2,000 ready-swimming young, and after birth may float dead to the surface. But once out of the cold and pressurised deep, her body explodes or simply melts away, leaving a pool of oil and an airy backbone, rich in Vitamin A. The Buryats once used the oil for their lamps.

Only birds commute out of this closed world. In autumn, geese, cranes, swans and a host of waders congregate in its marshes, and migrate south. Tens of thousands of ducks winter in its snow-drifts. And at some prehistoric time the ancestors of the little *nerpa* seal swam up the Yenisei and Angara rivers, it seems, and stranded their descendants here – now 60,000 strong – to become the only freshwater seals.

By noon the far shore has misted away, and as the hydrofoil enters the channel between the western bank and the long, volcanic island of Olkhon, you are sailing over silk. It is the last voyage of the year, and the boat seems almost empty. The island is bitter and rainless: an ancient stronghold of shamanism. The Evenk knew that the sea-god Dianda lived there, and the Buryats peopled it with an evil spirit, the voice of its seismic groaning. The shores are unloosened even here, without rock or weed, and leak out only a salt or mineral trickle. Olkhon is in fact a mile-high underwater mountain, and you are sailing over the lake's abyss.

It is rarely so tranquil. Every few months Baikal shakes. All natives feared and worshipped it. The lake was a divinity, and perhaps an explanation. It was both benign and evil, and they were born from its waters.

In 1861 an earth tremor set church bells ringing along the shores, and flung its waters eastward, creating an instant region of fissures and geysers, and drowning 1,300 people. For much of the year the surface is tormented by violent winds. (Baikalskoe's cemetery is full of young fishermen.) The western *sarma* springs up out of nowhere, pulling the water into misty walls under a pall of dark. With hurricane force it pitches sheep and houses over the cliffs, and ices fishing-boats in freezing rain before sinking them.

Only winter brings a kind of peace. Then the lake freezes so solid that it becomes a lorry road. But without warning, during sharp temperature changes, a six-foot crack may open underfoot and streak for up to eighteen miles across the ice, pulling down trucks and bulldozers to join the tea-caravans of Bactrian camels engulfed a century back.

Beyond Olkhon, the way opens over a plain of ruffled blue, and the snow-mountains have gone. A few settlements appear, and rain. Here at the lake's southern end, where a giant paper mill spreads and the Selenga river carries down effluent even from Mongolia, there lingers the threat of pollution. As long ago as the 1960s, when the factory's cellulose waste began destroying the *epischura*, an infant environmental movement began. The salvation of Baikal became its flagship. The water-level had already risen behind the newly built Irkutsk dam, destroying the shallow feeding-grounds of *omul*, and bird-life was declining. The protesters – the Siberian novelist Valentin Rasputin among them – fought a war against a shifty and irresolute bureaucracy. Baikal became more than itself. As the Soviet empire crumbled, it transformed into the mystic heart of a beleaguered Russia. In one heady triumph, huge filtration systems were fitted to the two pulp and paper plants on the lake and up the Selenga. But the river still carries down urban waste with nitrates from the farmed soil, and the paper plants (according to late reports) still leak into this primordial frailty of sea.

More than 300 rivers and streams fall into Baikal, but only one flows out: the fast-flowing Angara. Past Port Baikal, declined under its cliffs to a station for old ferries, the boat rides the river to the drop of the Irkutsk dam, and makes landfall beside it.

Weeks of visual deprivation turn Irkutsk glamorous. What would I be feeling, I briefly wonder, if I came upon it in Umbria or Castile or New England? Futile questions. It is in Siberia. Its architectural variety and charm, its modest size (little more than half a million inhabitants) and some elusive grace, lend it an old intimacy. Once it was called 'the Paris of Siberia', and I walk it in leisurely euphoria: past the graceful 200-year-old White House of the governor-general of East Siberia (now a library); down the long axis of Marx Street; past the Opera House and the mansions built by exiled aristocrats and jumped-up gold merchants; and on down Lenin Street to the towers and crosses of restored churches, and at last the embracing bend of the Angara river.

Here the 300-year-old Church of Our Saviour sails like a clumsy battleship over parklands. Its six-storeyed bell-tower and eccentric whitewashed sanctuary, clotted with rustic decoration, now enclose an ethnic museum; but outside its apse, the Baptism of Christ and the canonisation of St Innokent, the first Bishop of Siberia, cover the wall in faded murals; while alongside, a crowd of frescoed Buryats are undergoing mass baptism in a pool. Just to the east, above the onion domes and dunce-cap spires of the Epiphany Cathedral, a host of fretted crosses announce reconsecration.

Irkutsk grew up in a mood of rough enterprise. It was founded by Cossacks in 1652 as a garrison-town against the Buryats, but it straddled the burgeoning trade-route between Russia and China. Southward through Mongolia towards Peking went gold, sable pelts and mammoth ivory; northward into Russia came tea, silks and porcelain. The nineteenth century saw the discovery of gold and the intrusion of convicts: Irkutsk became a hub of the czarist prison empire. Small-time traders made suddenly good, peasants and ex-convicts struck lucky in the gold-fields, filled the town with turbulence and possibility. Grand boulevards swept across the boardwalks of mud-clogged lanes, fetid with pigs and open sewers, where palaces might replace hutches overnight. Sturdy, characterful old millionaires walked about in peasant dress. (One found his four-poster bed too beautiful to use. 'I sleep under it,' he said.) People's speech was touched by an antiquated civility long gone from St Petersburg, full of affectionate, slangy diminutives. Parvenus turned themselves into tinsel aristocrats, then lost their fortunes gambling in a week.

A night-life of merriment and debauchery was sharpened by rampant crime. Fur traders and mining concessionaires crammed the vaudevilles and restaurants, or haunted the drinking-dens and gaming tables. Irkutsk became the murder capital of Russia. No day passed without one; sometimes there were over 200 in a month. The nights were bedevilled by professional garrotters; and sledgers would gallop out in blizzards to lasso lone pedestrians and murder them up side-alleys. Nobody interfered. (Poking your nose into others' business was not *sibirski*.) The police were helpless. Householders would routinely fire a warning salvo from their bedroom windows before retiring.

In 1879 a spark in someone's hay-loft started a fire which wiped out three-quarters of the town. Within a few years it was rebuilt, more handsome in brick and stone. It bloomed into a proud paradox. Old-fashioned, pretentious, opulent, squalid, cultivated

– it was starting to confuse its visitors. All but the most jaded or sophisticated were surprised by its magnificence: by the libraries and picture galleries in the handful of finest houses; by the endowment of hospitals and schools; by the balls ablaze with military decorations, Paris fashions and regimental bands playing in the galleries. Upper-class Siberians were starting to commute between their Irkutsk palaces and St Petersburg.

But other travellers reported little but indolence and social pretension. It was *bon ton*, apparently, to have your wardrobe laundered in London, even though you lost sight of it for a year. And the galas, some said, were stereotyped, provincial affairs, attended by the same crowd: the governor and administrative officials, some rich civilians, army officers, and a few classy political exiles.

The merchants, meanwhile, had become a powerful, homemade aristocracy. They financed exploration and sometimes swayed policy under a near-independent governor. And the influx of cultured exiles – especially the 1825 revolutionary Decembrists, and Poles after their failed 1863 uprising – had brought a charge of gentler energies. Gradually the drawing-room pianos were beginning to tinkle, and the library books to be read. After the street-fighting and fires of the Revolution, the remains of these libraries were picked out of the frost and gutters by furtive bibliophiles. Along with charred liturgies donated by old women who had saved them from churches, their skeletal collections now occupy the bookshelves of obscure municipal archives, with the names of half-remembered families on discoloured labels beneath: Yagin, Kazanzevy, Smirdin. . . .

Splendour and rusticity still mingle in the street façades, along with outbursts of pomposity and fuss. I gaze at the rare beauty of stone instead of concrete, comforted by buildings older than myself or than the century, the classical orders trying for grace again. Here and there some playfulness or barbarism erupts in swagged pilasters or columns run amok. But they do not seem to matter. I go down streets where wooden mansions are sunk to their windows in the earth, or mount in tipsy storeys to preposterously scalloped friezes: the homes of peasant princes.

Their gaiety or pride overlaps into the streets. Young women are promenading arm-in-arm again, irregularly beautiful in their shiny tights and lace-up boots. The parks are full of students. Perhaps it is my illusion, but poverty here seems more gently worn, the people more integrated, less transient. They say they inhabit the jewel of Siberia.

Across a tributary of the Angara the white walls of the Znamensky Monastery spread under turquoise domes. Its garden was awash with hollyhocks and sunflowers, and the graves of Decembrists lay lapped in marguerites. Beside them I found a young priest receiving his flock. Standing frail in his black cassock, his black hair tied back from a black beard, he whispered consolation to men twice his age, and from time to time a nun would kneel to kiss his casually proffered hand.

The monastery had just been restored, he said, and out of a sickened world the faithful were returning. He himself was the son of an ardent Communist father, but his mother had been a Christian. He spoke easily of this, while his supplicants drifted away. 'She was half French and half Bessarabian. Even when I was little she took me to church. I remember her singing. . . .' His eyes swam over the graves beside us, as if she were dead (but I did not ask). 'And my father's Communism, I believed in that too. It was only as a conscript in the army that I lost my Communism. In the army men get very close, you know, talk very intimately. . . .'

It had created its own brotherhood, I supposed, its own iconoclasm. 'So you were left with your mother's faith.'

'No, that had already faded. But it was in the army that I began to feel my sin.'

I said hesitantly: 'In what way?'

'In every way. In my work, in my friendships, in my heart.' He looked suddenly bashful: swimming eyes and girlishly parted hair. 'The army can be cruel, you see, very rough. Drinking, swearing . . . and this terrible weight of sin grew in me. That is how I really came to God. Through my guilt.'

In the church, among a glimmering cluster of shrines, he bowed and crossed himself in a sustained fever of submission. An undergrowth of nuns – black cowls, black box-hats – pressed their lips to his hands, sometimes dropped to their knees, while I stood uneasily beside him. The old, nest-like Orthodox comfort intensified around us: a soft blaze of candles dimming the brightness of restoration, kindling the gaze of salvaged icons, gilding the iconostasis where an old woman was kissing her favourite saints (Surely they're listening? Surely they understand?). And beyond this the doors of the sanctuary hung closed on eternal mystery, and from somewhere rose the antiphonal yearning of a choir.

We arrived in front of a casket as big as an altar. Above it hung a full-length icon of St Innokent, the miracle-working Siberian missionary who attempted the conversion of China before returning to die here in 1731. In memory, at least, he looked darkly benevolent, robed and crowned in cream and gold and clutching a pastoral stave. For almost two hundred years he had rested in peace, his body incorruptible, healing pilgrims from his silver sarcophagus in a monastery on the far side of the Angara.

'Then the Communists took him away,' said the priest. 'In 1921 they destroyed that monastery and stole his casket – a beautiful thing – and buried him somewhere in Yaroslavl. But it was documented where he lay, and after *perestroika* he was dug up again and brought here. And his body uncorrupted! Just like yours and mine! The skin! The flesh!' He was gazing at the sarcophagus. In the dimness his lemony skin shone creaseless, like a boy's. 'Still he can heal anything!'

Even as he spoke, a carpet was rolled out and the gilt lid levered back from a glass panel above the saint. In a swirl of black calico, nuns and acolytes were tumbling to their knees before it. 'Come,' said the priest. 'Look.'

I approached with mistrust, my boots squeaking.

But what lay in the silver-lined coffin I could not tell. A pair of gloved hands was knotted over a swell of vestments, and above them a mitre bulged like a jewelled onion from the white cloth covering someone's face.

The priest was whispering close. 'We can't show his face, because the light would hurt it. But in December, on his name day, it is revealed . . . perfect!'

'Will he stay here?' I felt vaguely cheated.

'I don't know. He might be moved to the cathedral when it's restored. But I think things will end before that.'

'What things?'

'All things.' He became urgent. There was something I must understand, he said. 'There's going to be a war, a cataclysmic war. The saint has said so.'

'When?'

'Before his death, he declared it. That on the Last Day the world would be consumed in conflict. I know that it will be between Russia and China. The Chinese are godless, they have a bigger army than we do, they are hungry for land. We will all die by this.'

'And America?'

'America is godless. Nothing good can come from there. Only videos and that music, nakedness, AIDS, everything. America will not help us.' His face had loosened and disintegrated in its fervour, and suddenly to my bewilderment I recognised there the dissolute conscript. The world was crumbling away, he said. He found virtue only in the old, the distant past. The present was licentious, the future unspeakable. He rambled about the ages of Churches – the Armenian, the Ethiopian. The older they were, the better. Beside Russia, he claimed obscurely, the only hope was Spain. Yet Rome was anathema to him; America was anathema; Moscow had become hellfire; Islam was a deformity; and most terrible of all, just to the south, seethed the soulless multitudes of China, who had not listened to St Innokent. From time to time, when the chant of a choir underscored his jeremiads, or he dropped into harrowed silence, I would picture a small boy standing beneath his mother, fluting 'Oh Lord forgive me', while back at home his father growled or drank, or perhaps laughed.

After a while an old man came stooping towards us. He had just lost his wife and daughter in the same week, he whispered, he had nothing left. Then the priest's face cleared, and he strode to the saint's coffin. Gravely he dipped his finger in the oil lamp behind it and anointed the man's forehead and chest. 'You mustn't weep.'

I walked away among the worshippers. A pair of crazed-looking youths was singing in the black knot of a choir. On the fresco behind them St Innokent appeared to be crowning himself saint, while in the sky above him God the Father looked helplessly on. The air was grey with incense. In front of the casket three nuns lay prostrate on their stomachs, one of them sobbing, as if something had to be expurgated for ever.

There are only a few graves around the monastery, but none of them is ordinary. Princess Trubetskaya, who followed her husband into exile in 1826, lies with their three small children under two stones. Nearby is the grave of the Decembrist Peter Mukhanov, whose lover Varvara Shakhovskaya voluntarily shared his banishment. For ten years she lived close to his changing prisons, but they never set eyes on one another again before she died broken-hearted and was buried alone.

But most prominent is a marble obelisk overswept by nautical instruments: copper anchors, capstans, sails, hour-glasses, compasses. The bust above them shows a jowly, high-boned face with far-sighted eyes and a jovial wig. Grigory Shelikhov was dubbed 'the Russian Columbus'. An ambitious fur trader in the north Pacific, he dreamt of a Russian Alaska which would bloom into economic self-sufficiency, complete with cities, shipyards, cathedrals, industries and cattle pastures. In 1783 he sailed with three ships into the Bering Sea, together with his dashing and astute wife Natalya – the first white woman to see Alaska – and within three years had built forts and settlements along the southern coast and islands, and had claimed Alaska for Russia. Soon he was envisioning an empire stretching between the Bering Straits and Spanish California. But in 1795 he suddenly died at the age of forty-eight, and was laid with florid honours under his monument.

The trading company which he established pursued his vision. In 1812 a Russian fort even appeared just north of San Francisco. But in the end these tiny colonies were too precarious and distant for St Petersburg to hold. The Americans and British pressed too hard on them, and they became a drain on the imperial treasury.

In 1867 Alaska, with the last of Shelikhov's dream, was sold to the United States for two cents an acre. But it was a difficult sale. The US Secretary of State, William Seward, who pushed it forward, was vilified for extravagance by the American press and public – 'Seward's folly', it was called – and Congress took over a year to vote him the money. A century later Alaskan real estate was selling for 2,000 dollars an acre, while people still place roses by Shelikhov's grave.

Irkutsk resisted the Revolution. In fact all Siberia – with its wealthy peasant farmers and thin industrial proletariat – inclined haltingly to the Whites, or to Siberian independence. But by 1920 the White Siberian front had broken and the Civil War was all but over. The railway and the Trakt beside it had turned into a slow, chaotic river of the refugee and dying. The White commander, Admiral Kolchak, fled back to Irkutsk with twenty-nine freight-cars carrying the Imperial Gold Reserve, but his authority melted away and he was handed over to the Reds.

He had been a fine naval chief once, but his talents transferred neither to the army nor to politics. His regime was a barbarous and divided one, and Kolchak himself had declined from the clear-sighted strategist of his prime into an irresolute wreck.

Only with difficulty I find the prison where he ended. It had been subsumed by an electric power station. A river flows sunken below, making for the Angara. I walk under its ruined bridge along an embankment whose concrete revetment is sliding into the water. The banks are flecked with rubbish, and overgrown, drooping with willows.

Kolchak was interrogated for over two weeks as the broken White armies fell back on the city, threatening to retake it. His mistress – the grave beauty Anna Timireva – had refused to desert him, and was incarcerated in a cell nearby. The record of Kolchak's ordeal survives. He answered his accusers with dignity and intelligence. He implicated nobody but himself. He sent a secret note to Timireva, warning that if the White forces closed in he would be executed. The note was intercepted. During the second week his interrogators grew more nervous and strident, and he must have known it meant the end. Gunfire could be heard to the west.

Before dawn on 7 February he was taken down to the narrow river. A hole had been cut in its ice. He went calmly, refusing a blindfold. His portly prime minister Pepeliaev was dragged trembling beside him, and a firing-squad placed them together in the headlights of its lorry. Timireva, waiting alone in her cell, heard the distant volley. Then the bodies were pressed under the ice.

The current flows deep here. I clamber back along the ruined bridge. A few years before, some local businessmen had planned to raise a memorial to Kolchak. But still there is only the river.

*   *   *

Three hundred years before Stalin's Gulag, groups of convicts were being ejected over the Urals: the sight of their judicial brandings and amputations, apparently, was offensive to their countrymen. Soon afterwards the need to populate Siberia and to mine its ore drew out a deepening river of deportees, and by 1753, when the death penalty was abolished in favour of lifelong labour, the variety of offences punishable by exile had grown bewildering. Prize-fighting, wife-beating, begging with false distress, illicit tree-felling, vagrancy and fortune-telling might all condemn a man to Siberia, as well as the European innovations of taking snuff (exile was accompanied by ripping out the nostrils' septum) or driving a cart with the use of reins.

By the early nineteenth century the exile system had settled into remorseless stride. Many were simply deported to colonise some remote region and forbidden to return; but a horde of criminals, their heads half-shaven and their cheeks branded with their crime, went shuffling in chains to labour in the Nerchinsk silver-mines or the gold-pits of Kara. They were legally dead. The journey itself – it might take two years – was enough to kill thousands. The transit-prisons were racked by typhus, scurvy, smallpox and syphilis. All along the Trakt the begging-song of convoys tramping into exile – 'Have pity on us, Our fathers' – and the jangle and clank of their chains while they held out their caps for bread, became the very sound of Siberia. The nineteenth century saw a million convicts march into the wild, with their families sometimes trudging pathetically behind them.

In time this dilution of Siberian society lent it a criminal hue which older settlers resented. Discharged prisoners forbidden to return spilled into the community with few skills but robbery, and the roads and woods were rife with vagabond escapees migrating towards the Urals, but rarely arriving. In the end, the vastness of Siberia was their prison and their grave.

Their scourge was eased only by the political exiles, who were far fewer than the criminals but who became, in time, a leavening intelligentsia. Among a medley of cultured dissidents and Polish revolutionaries, those who touched the Russian heart were the Decembrists. Mostly aristocratic liberals disgusted with czarist autocracy, they were guilty of an inept uprising in December 1825, which left their elite Guards regiments leaderless in St Petersburg's Senate Square. After their trial, five of the 121 conspirators were incompetently hanged, the rest imprisoned or banished. In Siberia a belated splendour illumined their cause when some of their wives and fiancees abandoned rank, palaces and even children to follow their men into exile. Thousands of peasant women had done the same and vanished unrecorded, but two Decembrist princesses – the magnificently rich Yekaterina Trubetskaya, and the beautiful young Maria Volkonskaya – came to personify romantic sacrifice.

By the time they settled in Irkutsk in 1844, their hardships were almost over. Their wooden mansions – country cousins to St Petersburg palaces – survive in a still-quiet suburb. They are modestly graceful. Yekaterina Trubetskaya's is the smaller: a gabled house on brick foundations. Her embroidery and escritoire are still here, and a toilette case filled with minuscule instruments. Robust and vivacious, she had been the first to follow her husband, driving four thousand miles by coach and descending into the silver-mines the moment she arrived at Nerchinsk. She was a stocky, plain woman, but when the haggard Decembrists looked up in the lantern-light they imagined an angel.

Two streets from her home, the grey and white Volkonsky

mansion floats out bay windows and pediments with a rural charm. In its reception rooms, still handsome with crimson wallpaper and white ceramic stoves, Princess Maria's musical soirees were attended even by the formidable governor-general, Muraviev-Amursky. (Sometimes she herself played on a clavichord which had been smuggled into her luggage by a loving friend on the night of her departure.) In her early forties she was still commandingly beautiful, as when Pushkin had loved her, and she poured her energies into the renovation of schools and a foundling hospital, the raising of a theatre and concert hall. Gradually this wife of a state criminal became, in popular thought, the Princess of Siberia.

Her home had been alive with guests and servants, and with her two children who softened, perhaps, the memory of the baby she had left behind and never seen again. Her bedroom still overlooks the remains of the garden where her elderly husband, who turned absent-mindedly rustic, worked among the vegetables. She was not faithful to him.

As I wandered alone from floor to floor, with an inventory of artefacts reportedly in place, there were things I could not find. Where were the iron marriage-rings – forged from their husbands' fetters – which these women wore until their deaths? And where the cherished clavichord which had accompanied the princess on her 4,000-mile sledge-ride into exile? When I asked the curator, he said that it had fallen out of tune and had been sent to St Petersburg for restoration three years before. It was still in a warehouse there, he added wearily, and might remain there for years longer. 'We can't afford to pay the bill.'

Few of the Decembrists survived to hear the amnesty granted them after the death in 1855 of the implacable Czar Nicholas I in the thirtieth year of their exile. The survivors returned west as celebrated ghosts. Yekaterina Trubetskaya had died three years too soon; but Maria Volkonskaya went back, and so did their ageing husbands. Some Decembrists tried to eradicate Siberia from their reassembled lives. But others, like Maria, seemed to grow paler in civilisation, and even talked wistfully of the past, as if its suffering was where their meaning lay.

7

Last Days

The world has turned to mist, and my train crawls above invisible valleys. Far in front, its engine groans unseen in the whiteness. As we round the southern tip of Baikal, a stray pylon or smokestack rises memorially out of the fog, as if a town might lie in ruins beneath. The visibility closes down to 200 yards. When we descend along the lake-shore, its waters vanish into the sky. Small waves come lapping out of nowhere. A fishing-boat is anchored in mid-air. Then we are climbing into hills again, winding like a caterpillar through dying forest.

The construction of this loop in 1904 was the railway's final link to the Pacific. Already, in other stretches, permafrost had undermined the tracks and summer marshes engulfed them. Bandits and even tigers harassed the workers, cholera and bubonic plague broke out and convict-labourers ran amok, while floods swept away bridges and poor steel and insufficient ballast buckled beneath the strain.

But this lakeside section, where miles of mountain drop sheer to the water, was the most hazardous. For five years a pair of ice-breaking steamers, manufactured in Newcastle upon Tyne and reassembled on the lake, bypassed the cliffs by carrying the train across the water. The larger ship, belted in inch-thick plates, could bear up to twenty-eight carriages laid keelwise along its deck, while a bronze forescrew roiled the water beneath the prow so that four-foot-thick ice collapsed beneath it. At last, when the lake became a bottleneck in 1904 during the war against Japan, a way was blasted through the cliffs over two hundred bridges, and the great railway was complete.

As the mist starts to lift, we delve in and out of tunnels, then turn inland along the Selenga river. We are close to Ulan Ude now, the capital of Buryatia. The clouds are pouring off the hills on either side, and the river comes gliding out of fog, brimming and calm.

My gaze joins that of the Buryat woman opposite, fixed out of the window. She is visiting her family village, she says, where her mother has fallen ill with cancer. But her hair is dyed ginger, as if she were denying her race. I ask when she was last here, but she only says: 'Too long ago.' It is like travelling back into childhood. This landscape where she was born – the grasslands of Buryatia – seems strange to her now. 'I've been twenty-seven years in Novosibirsk, all my married life. That way you lose touch. My husband's a Buryat too, but we speak Russian even in the home.' She turns away from the window. 'It's not right.'

Her four sisters have arrived already at her mother's sick-bed. She is re-entering her past, before it dies. It is thickening outside our window: Buryatia. Mongols who had settled here a millennium ago, absorbing the local tribes, her people had sometimes allied themselves with czarist Russia against the harsh Mongolian regimes to their south. They were skilled stock-breeders and metallurgists, more numerous and organised than the tribespeople in the far north. Their ancestors had ridden with Genghis Khan. In the ungiving pastures of Transbaikal which we were entering, they had been converted to Buddhism by Mongolian and Tibetan missionaries, and alone among indigenous Siberians they possessed a written language. But even during childhood the woman had sensed in her parents the terror and bewilderment of the thirties: the forced collectivisation, the disappearance of the kulaks and lamas, the destruction of the monasteries.

She sees her Buryat identity fading down the generations. She has not thought of it much before, she says; but now I sense her hunting after half-discarded memories, a definition of her people, her mother, herself.

In a village somewhere east of Ulan Ude, she remembers, her

grandparents kept a scroll painted with the Buddha and fringed in blue silk. It seemed very old. But it was the caressing silk border which the small girl remembered, not the sage it enframed. There were three statuettes of the Buddha too, to which the old people burnt incense and offered meat and fruit. Sometimes the girl would watch secretly to catch the Buddhas eating. She remembers the cupboard where they sat, how its doors opened after Stalin's death, and the sleepy fumes of incense.

'Every morning they offered the Buddhas tea and milk, then sprinkled it to the corners of the porch. That's how Buddhism survived – in secret, the old people remembering. In Stalin's day they rolled up the scroll with their prayer-books in a wooden box, and buried them under the house. But our family's clan still had an altar on a hill, where they offered sacrifices.' She frowns with remembered rebellion. 'I wasn't allowed to go, because I was a girl. But my brother told me about it.'

She goes on looking out at the Selenga valley. Sunlight is breaking over wheat-fields glazed with frost. And now she recalls her grandmother's death, how the village lama came and read prayers secretly over her body. 'Officially the lama did not exist, of course, but everybody knew who he was. Afterwards my grandmother's coffin was carried out of the house for a Communist funeral.' Her eyes flinch from the sunlight behind tinted spectacles. 'My mother will have prayers read too; but my father was buried under the Soviet star.'

She gives a tight laugh. In her Mongol face the lips protrude sensuously almost level with her nose; but her hennaed hair and curly-framed spectacles suggest some violent hybrid, which is perhaps how she feels. I say: 'So you were brought up a Buddhist?'

'No. I became a Communist. That's what we were taught at school.' She looks rueful. 'And now it's gone.' It is growing familiar to me, the native dilemma. She has lost both worlds, and cannot go back. 'But sometimes, at important moments, this Buddhism returns. Before I got married, my mother insisted I see a lama. He compared my husband's horoscope with mine, and looked up the state of the moon in his books. He discovered we were both born in the Year of the Rabbit, which makes for difficulties. But he read some prayers and said we'd be all right. And we've been . . . all right.' Outside the window the suburbs of Ulan Ude are mustering. 'I still feel something for the Buddha.' She touches her heart in the sentimental Russian way. 'But it's hard to believe in anything now. And death frightens me.'

The sixteen parallel tracks at Ulan Ude station were jammed by trucks heaped with gravel, logs, coal-dust, bricks, and by the cylindrical tape-worms of oil tank wagons. They clanked among fumes and dinning loudspeakers as if on rails to Gehenna. From a splitting concrete bridge I glimpsed the Buryat city ringed by smoke and industry. A thicket of cranes marked the Selenga docks. I emerged into a deserted road, tramped down side-streets and arrived suddenly in the square which is Ulan Ude's heart. Then I burst out laughing.

I was looking across a ceremonial space of grotesque pomp, where white and basalt ministries clashed in the perverted pilasters and capitals of Stalinist baroque. Opposite the Buryat parliament, the stucco and black basalt opera house looked built of coal and clotted cream. And in the square's centre, surmounting its crumbling plinth with blank authority, was the biggest head of Lenin in the world. It was the size of an office. If I stood on its beard, I calculated, my forehead might touch its nostrils. It had been sculpted for an exposition in Canada, and since nobody wanted to buy it the municipality of Ulan Ude stepped slavishly in. Iconic, bodiless, it made sense only in the nightmare perspectives of the Soviet past, where a man had displaced divinity. Even now, leaning dangerously on the tower of its neck, the head threatened to roll forward and crash down the square's width, crushing everything in its path.

My laughter spluttered out like a firecracker in the square. I looked round guiltily, but nobody was within a hundred yards of me. A banner slung from the rooftops read: 'May you be young and beautiful – my Ulan Ude!'

But out of the square trickled a provincial, almost domestic main street. Behind a screen of pollarded willows its brick façades mingled with wooden cottages, and alleys trailed off into quiet.

In these old merchants' quarters the Buryats prevailed. Like the Tuvans, they had anticipated the Soviet disintegration by declaring themselves, with delicate contradiction, a 'sovereign state' within Russia, and their old script and language were reviving. But Buryats numbered only a quarter in their so-called republic, and Russians still filled the industrial suburbs, where the collapse of the defence industry had brought a new poverty. Factory walls were slashed with graffiti culled from American movies and videos: 'Sold my soul to Rock . . . Fucked-up Baby . . . Latex Cult . . . Metal up your ass . . . Impaled Nazarene. . . .'

I slunk away as if I had written them.

The main street petered into solitude where an unfinished bridge hung in mid-river and a cathedral loomed above wasteland. Stucco was dropping in chunks from its deconsecrated walls, and when I roamed round searching for an entrance, I found the doors and windows barred. The nearest cottage was a charred shell, in whose fire an old woman, someone said, had died two days before. Her white cat was still wandering the debris. Somebody had tried to salvage or loot the contents, and the ground was littered with enamel basins, hair curlers and broken 78 r.p.m. records: my feet crackled over fragments of 'Pushinka' and 'Quiet Waters'.

For a while I stood among the wreckage, while the cat came purring against my boots. I gathered it up, not knowing what to do. The stench of smoke lingered over the timbers. But suddenly a light appeared under the cathedral's bell-tower; a door opened as if in a ruin and a woman emerged. She managed the collection here, she said, and had adopted the cat, which she took gently from me.

'Collection?' I had heard of a whole museum mured up in the cathedral, but it was closed to public view. Was it possible to . . . ? The cat walked between us like a mascot.

Yes, it was possible. As the woman mounted the tower's stair and unlocked door after armoured door a rich and incoherent maze came to light. Inside had been hoarded not the relics of Christian Orthodoxy but the accumulated treasures of Buddhist monasteries and temples salvaged in the hours before their demolition. Earmarked for display in a museum to promote atheism,

175

then preserved for some future archive of their own, they waited here in glimmering profusion, sometimes stacked pell-mell among Cossack ploughs and harness, more often ranked in half-documented cabinets to themselves.

I examined them in ignorant wonder. In the gloom hundreds of Buddhas lifted their gilded hands in peace or teaching. Gifts from Tibet, Mongolia, China, even Cambodia in the eighteenth and nineteenth centuries, a few were very old. They sat or stood in bronze, gold, gypsum, papier mache. Their smiles filled the dark. Three thousand scroll-paintings crowded the shelves with Tibetan manuscripts and Chinese silks and a medley of temple instruments and regalia – ceremonial horns and the masks of lamaist mystery plays, whose actor-monks glowered out through slavering jaws or demon eyes. Sunlight penetrated only in mote-heavy beams, too weak to fade the sacred banners or illumine the fertility deities coupled in Tantric bliss. I began to lose all sense of age or worth. A horse-headed lute curved beside a ninth-century Indian Buddha, the household altar of a Buryat chief among the bric-a-brac of early tea-merchants.

The collective memory of Buryatia, it seemed, had been incarcerated in these once-Christian walls, and left to die. Of the forty-seven monasteries flourishing in the 1920s, all were gone by 1939. But Buddhism was reviving, said the woman, as she locked the last doors behind me. There were many little monasteries and temples she knew of, newly scattered through the region, and the greatest was only twenty miles away. The outer door clanged shut. The white cat was waiting in the grass. You could take a bus anywhere into the country, she said, and hear the lamas praying again.

Outside, dusk had settled round the cathedral walls. I looked up with a start into the sky, where the first snow of winter was falling, dry and tiny, like grains of salt.

'Free? Freedom to beg, oh yes! That's a kind of freedom!' The grizzled builder elbowed my ribs with each irony. He was angry and a little drunk even at dawn. Outside our bus window the city had splintered into dimming lights around a grey coil of river.

'Things have got terrible now.' He set his jaw at the window. 'You don't see half the cattle you did – and these Buryat farmers are coming into the city. But there are no jobs for anyone, and nobody's getting paid. I've lived in this place for thirty years, and it's never been like this.'

Everything achieved under slavery, it seemed, was being destroyed by freedom. The sparse meadows and dry hills through which we travelled were almost empty. No snow had settled. Only here and there spread tilled fields crammed with cabbages and dotted by canvas shelters where tin chimneys puffed.

'Look at those. Fucking Chinese. They come over the border and rent our fields. Koreans, too. They take our money.'

'Why don't the Russians farm like that?'

'I don't know.' The builder glowered out, thinking. 'I reckon it's all politics. The government here does whatever Moscow tells them. And Moscow . . .'

I turned away to stare at the hills, away from his rancour. Once or twice we passed the haunt of some remembered spirit, where the view of a mountain or the rise of a spring was marked by cairns and rotted prayer-flags. The whole land, it seemed, could be read like a holy book. Such country was its own temple, indestructible. Lamaism had merged with an ancient shamanism to bless it, and its possessive deities had offered a more convincing reality, perhaps, than the Communist shadow-play.

Dawn was now breaking over Ivolginsk, over sparks of colour at the foot of the wooded hills. Beyond marshy pastures and a flimsy stockade, the triple roofs and tilted eaves of a Mongolian temple levitated in bright yellow. I emerged from the bus into biting cold. Around half the monastery stunted birches, hung with prayer-ribbons, spread in a forest of dead white blossoms. I walked delicately through them. The rags dangled stiff with frost. They rasped against my shoulders in a jungle of hope, petition, grief, printed with Mongolian prayers I could not read; dragons, wheels, fire-breathing horses.

I slipped through the frail stockade into the monastery. No one was about. The roofs of its sanctuaries swung skywards in child-like bursts of colour, tossing up gold finials, and the monks lived in prettily painted Russian cottages. I might have strayed into a playground. Guardian lions, sculpted in plaster, patted globes or scowled like soft toys from the grass. A few cows were slumbering in the porches of the shrines.

The monastery had been completed only in 1946, as an isolated concession, and had twice been rebuilt after fire. Perhaps it was this that lent it a funfair transience and gaiety. Its main temple floated up in a wedding-cake of tiered pavilions and canary-coloured roofs. In its topmost walkway a lama was blowing a conch to prayer, as if nothing had changed for two thousand years. His mournful braying seemed to deepen the quiet. One by one the monks struggled from their cottages, sandalled and robed in magenta. A smell of incense and juniper drifted up.

A few pilgrims – booted and wind-burnished cattlemen, prim urban families – were circling the compound around a gallery of prayer-wheels. Small drums and prayer-filled cylinders whirred and squealed under their fingers. The return of their faith seemed less a stormy revival than a simple restatement of identity. In one temple a man was teaching his small daughter to pray. Standing where its Buddha smiled in a thicket of candles, he drew her palms together at her breast, murmuring the timeless '*Om mani padme hum*', while a lone monk clashed his cymbals.

The porch of the chief temple was carved with Buddhist icons: the deer of Benares, the Wheel of the Law. But its sanctum was a tent of violent colour. Gold and crimson pillars swarmed up to a canopy of brilliant draperies and banners. Beneath, in a double aisle of low tables and benches, a few monks were chanting absent-mindedly, and an abbot meditated under his pointed cap. On a throne stood a painting of the Dalai Lama in dark glasses. He had visited Ivolginsk five times, and ordained monks. A pilgrim lay prostrate before it. A cash-register dinged in a corner, where an acolyte was selling candles.

I looked round in bewilderment. Nothing nourished my shadowy Buddhist sympathies. At the sanctuary's end, in lieu of an altar, two ranks of plaster statues gazed from a casement stretched across the whole wall. Avatars and bodhisattvas, disciples and incarnations of the Buddha occupied their lotus seats and thrones like judges in some cosmic court. Reeking of rancid butter-candles, they sat sashed and crowned with paste tiaras. The pilgrims left sweets and biscuits for them. I gave a little money, but scrutinised them numbly. They cradled loaves and orbs, and lifted or lowered their hands in a lexicon of arcane comfort. Years ago I had understood this gestural language a little, but had now forgotten it. They looked like products in a shop window, their bodies wreathed in flowers and jewels. Here was the blue-skinned Buddha of Tibetan medicine, the Goddess of Mercy with her seven eyes, the Laughing Buddha scrambled round by babies. Banked up the wall behind, an audience of minute Buddhas, hundreds of them, spread like sacred wallpaper. And at the centre, seated in a mandala of peacock feathers, a single, vast, sweet-faced Buddha smiled down with cusped lips.

A few pilgrims circled the sanctuary clockwise, at home with the accoutrements crowding the statue's feet: copper horns, salvers, bells. Mysteries. The worshippers' orbit echoed their circling of the enclosure outside, returning them to the older faith, the past reproducing itself within the immense cycle of recurring Buddhas.

But during the twenties, Buddhism here had taken steps to ally itself with Moscow, declaring its philosophy a forerunner of Communism, and for a few years the diametric faiths cohabited. As I stood outside the house of the Chief Lama, I wondered what had happened to his standing. For a century and a half before the Revolution he had been elected in infancy, like the Tibetan Dalai Lama, as the incarnate soul of his predecessor.

But that was all over, said the young monk beside me. He smiled at the idea. 'That's long past.'

I looked into a face of hesitant studiousness, its Mongol bones smoothed under pale skin and a dust of beard. 'Our Lama sits beneath the Dalai Lama now. Tibet is important to us, and Mongolia. Most of us have studied in Mongolia.'

'But your parents were Buddhists?'

'Only in their ancestry, in some part of them. I was brought up without God. It was my decision to become a monk.'

I asked tentatively: 'How was that?'

'I don't know. At school and in the Young Pioneers it was drummed into us over and over that God did not exist. *He does not exist! He does not exist!*' He laughed gently. 'Now it is the Young Pioneers who do not exist.' He spoke as if all this were long ago, but he was less than thirty. 'My parents never tried to prevent me taking vows. But they didn't understand.'

Life was tranquil here, he said. The monks learnt Tibetan language, philosophy and medicine, and sometimes held theological debates. They advised people on their weddings by horoscope, and prayed at *oboos*, the shamanist cairns piled along the mountainsides to ancestral gods. 'We say simple prayers there. It is like remembering the dead.'

'And funerals?'

'We sometimes attend them.' A flicker of unease. 'Although it's difficult.'

I asked in surprise: 'Why?'

'Only for me. It's a personal thing, hard to explain. It's because of . . . pity.'

He could not bear their grief. And no, he did not know why these other monks could stand mourning, while he could not. He took me to the whitewashed stupas which marked the ashes of dead abbots, and to the greenhouse which cosseted a shoot from the bodhi tree in Bihar where the Buddha had gained enlightenment. We went to the library stacked with silk-bound scrolls, and opened the precious 108-roll illumined *Ganjur* scriptures which survived in crimson boxes.

In a circular shrine of his own, the Buddha of the Future waits. A high crown drips pearls over his forehead. His hands hold a ceremonial scarf and his chest is sprayed with jewels. He looks like a woman. 'In July, by our calendar, we hold a three-day ceremony for him,' the monk said. 'Then he is taken out and paraded round the monastery on a cart pulled by a green horse. And thousands of people rejoice.'

We gazed at the figure in silence. It is said he will come again, to usher in his people's golden age. 'Maybe my son will see this,' the monk said. 'But I think not. Some say the Buddha will return in a thousand years. For myself, I think not so soon.'

In the temple a novice was receiving written prayers for submission to the Buddha next morning. Most were softly dictated while he wrote them down. But a pallid Russian youth inscribed his own and folded it with shaking hands.

'Yes, the Russians come too. I think they're frightened. Capitalism is causing more problems than Communism did. Everything's failing. You see our temple too, it's crumbling.' I could not see this; only the dark hills touched it with desolation. 'We are spread very thin – only eighteen monks here – because there are twenty little monasteries scattered about Buryatia.'

'So Buddhism is growing?'

'Yes. Even my parents understand me now. They were proud to see me ordained. That was my day.'

He had felt the Dalai Lama's hands on him.

Dusk drifts down from the hills, and the monastery closes itself away. I find a room in its guest-house, but wander out after sunset. Beneath the temple eaves, tiny bells tinkle in an icy wind, and the roofs are crusted with pigeons.

An old man walks along the avenue of prayer-wheels in near-darkness. Every time he turns one he utters the lotus prayer and flicks forward one of the 108 beads on his string, amassing multiples by a system I cannot understand. He is near the telling of a million prayers now, he says. Under his tangled hair his face has the calm burnish of a statue. 'I do this not just for myself but for everybody. I do this for the world. For all its souls.'

I listen to him tramping down the aisle of wheels, his *Om mani padme hum* droning, repeating, fading. I wonder how he sees the soul. Is he also praying for mine? The soul leaves no tracks across the ashes of the hearth, says local shamanism, and passes noiselessly over dead leaves. Sometimes it takes the form of a bee. Sometimes it can even die.

Long after the old man has moved on, the turned prayer-drums whirr like a flock of birds taking off into the night.

*

I was woken by pigs snuffling under my window, and went out at dawn into the monastery court. The snow was falling in soft, desultory flakes, like apple blossom. The hills had vanished. From the temple summit a lama's conch began to moan like a patient.

I sat shivering in the sanctuary. The monks trickled in, doffing their pointed caps, then flattened themselves full-length before the effete Buddha. They filled fewer than half the cushioned seats, and looked wizened from the cold. At their head, beneath the Dalai Lama's throne, the abbot sat on a wide gold chair and rang a bell at intervals, while a hum of conversational prayer welled up. Along the aisles the tables were set with salvers of ceremonial bread and rice. A domestic well-being was in the air. The brothers chatted together between prayers. A novice went round with a kettle to fill their tea-cups, and the devotions swelled into a pattering hymn.

I waited without expectation. At the end of the central aisle a tiny, Gandhi-like ancient was leafing through folded notes, and I realised that these were the petitions left the day before. As his eyes scrutinised them, the old man's chant scuttled and wavered, blessing them, discarding them, in a thin, formal music. Sickness, mourning, heartbreak, all flickered through his hands and on to some listening Infinity.

By now five or six of the supplicants had crept into the temple and were sitting on benches against the wall. It was impossible to tell for what they were seeking consolation. They gazed blankly at the backs of the monks. A Buryat woman stood haggard near the entrance, kissing one of its columns, while leaf by leaf the petitions passed through the old monk's voice and into silence. Now the shaven heads gleamed closer above their books, and the chanting quickened over a pulse of drums. A few prayers, mounted on little sticks, were hurried up to the abbot, who passed a ritual candle-flame before them. Then the conches brayed through a clash of cymbals; the singing lifted to a gentle climax as the evil spirits were averted; and the supplicants, after cleansing themselves with holy water, went out into the falling snow.

* * *

After the mid-seventeenth century, when schism split the Russian Church, Siberia was settled by waves of religious dissenters. A campaign by the Moscow patriarch to cleanse and reform spiritual practice uncovered in western Russia a conservative mass to whom the old ways were sacrosanct. They had always crossed themselves with two fingers extended instead of the Greek three; they had honoured the Trinity with a double, not a triple, Alleluia; they had used seven loaves on the Eucharistic table instead of one; they had refused to shave their heads; and they had adhered to several other minute liturgical forms strange to the Greek Orthodox, but which had become obscurely precious.

Such things seem trivial to die for. Yet far into the eighteenth century the Old Believers were persecuted as heretics, maimed, burnt at the stake. Some sliced off their index fingers to avoid signing the three-fingered cross; others sent their own infants to paradise by killing them; and hundreds of families immolated themselves in the flames of their homes or churches.

They felt themselves on the brink of Apocalypse. It was a time of Messianic forebodings and prophecies. The divine reckoning was at hand. The double-fingered sign of the cross had entered their psyche as a surety of salvation. It was like a part of their body, a sanctifying magic. But reform augured the advance of Anti-Christ. It was linked in the common mind with contamination from the West: with profane luxuries, an assault on Russian holiness.

So the Old Believers, heavily bearded and multi-loaved, still restricting their Alleluias, either fled or were banished across the length of Siberia. They even reached Turkey and America. Only one bishop remained faithful to them, but he died before ordaining another. They debated laying his stiffened hands on the head of a successor, but his lips could not pronounce the consecrating words, so they gave up. In their forest fastness some of the Old Believers received runaway priests while others declared the whole Church and its priesthood in apostasy. So they administered the Sacraments to one another or were seen kneeling by the roadsides with their mouths gaping at the sky to receive an imagined distillation from heaven.

If the Cossacks were the cowboys of Russia's Wild East, the Old Believers were its Mennonites or Mormons. In time they split into sects or were joined by others yet more extreme. All were marked by ascetic simplicity or violent self-deprivation. They rejected baptism, churches – even prayer. The depraved 'Wanderers' cursed the Czar as Satan, baptised their babies in lakes and buried their dead in forest glades. There were literalists who became herdsmen in obedience to holy writ, and milk-drinking Molokans thirsty for the 'milk of the Word'. There were self-baptisers and non-baptisers, 'Sighers' who prayed breathily in honour of the Holy Spirit, and the 'Prayerless' who abhorred any outward observance at all. There were the pious Stundists and the *Dukhobor* 'Spirit-wrestlers', pacifists, who believed in the primacy of an indwelling spirit, turning even the Bible superfluous. There would even be a sect that deified Napoleon.

Others seemed touched by insanity. The *Khlysti*, with whom Rasputin was linked, whirled into ecstatic dance and self-flagellation crying 'Ho Spirit, Spirit, Holy Spirit, ho, ho, ho', until they fainted to the ground. After initiation a man would bypass his wife and sleep with a spiritual partner, often all three in the same bed, and called the children from his unregenerate past 'young cats' and 'little sins'. As for the *Skoptsi*, they tried to destroy lust by self-mutilation, hacking off their breasts or testicles. In accordance with the Gospels they became blessedly barren, or 'eunuchs for the kingdom of heaven's sake'. Even at the start of the twentieth century travellers might come upon their dreamlike, emasculated villages, whose communities were dying.

Such sects saw themselves in flight from the decadence of European Russia. In Siberia, where worldly authority ebbed away, they could save their souls. For them, with the apostasy of the Czar and of the Church, history itself had died. Its sanctity and meaning gone, they lived outside it, in a tremulous limbo. Frugal and industrious like their Puritan counterparts in the West, the Old Believers, especially, came to form the majority in many Siberian regions. Their lives passed in a dream-filled restlessness, haunted by memories of the past and omens for the future. But in the present they could only wait. They took as their talisman the legendary City of Kitezh, which had sunk beneath the waters of a lake during Mongol invasion centuries before, and would rise from them again when Russia was purified. True believers, it was said, could hear its church bells ringing in the depths.

As I pushed deeper into the valleys of the Transbaikal, I was entering a region where Catherine the Great had resettled 30,000 Old Believers in the late eighteenth century. The snow-clouds bursting over the mountains blurred the Selenga river to a grey welt. I stared ahead in misgiving. The Old Believers, I knew, were wary of all things foreign, including, I imagined, me. Foreign imports such as tea or potatoes (introduced by Peter the Great) had been shunned. Even iron ploughshares caused a rumpus, and communities split over the question of kerosene lamps. In the absence of a Eucharist the family meal, with its dietary taboos, became tinged with the sacramental, and a stranger could not expect to share it. Many products were consensually hated. The mechanical singing of gramophones could debase the Liturgy, and vaccination or property insurance scandalously pre-empted the will of God. Alcohol, of course, was anathema, and tobacco – like a Satanic cousin of incense – sullied the body against which the Cross was signed.

But when my bus clattered over a pass and descended to the town of Tarbagatai, I saw nothing I had expected. No grandly sashed and bearded patriarch stood outside his cottage; no multi-petticoated woman, necklaced in chunky jewellery, dropped her gaze at our approach. This was an ordinary town with its little square and war memorial and handful of bare shops. When I asked after Old Believers, people shook their heads. Those folk had almost gone, they said. Disconsolately I took a room in a run-down boarding-house and continued my enquiries into evening, until someone directed me to a blue-shuttered doll's house.

An old woman was standing in its courtyard clutching an axe. She was less than five feet tall, with a billowing skirt and outsize headscarf. 'What do you want?' she yelled. She looked taut, furious. Snow was fluttering between us. I mumbled about an Old Believer chapel somewhere. 'A chapel? There isn't one! This is my chapel!' She brandished her axe at the door. She made as if to expel me, then changed her mind. 'See my chapel, then!'

I went into two pin-neat rooms, all their furniture snowed under lace. 'There!' She pointed to icons high on a corner-shelf. 'That is the Mother of God and those are the angels. Now cross yourself!' She bunched her fingers in the Old Believer way. Her voice was still stony with unexplained anger. 'Like this! Like this!' She rearranged my fingers. 'Now cross yourself again! . . . Now pray to yourself! . . .'

She had lived here since childhood, she said. Her father had lost both legs in the war, and then died. Her husband had gone under a German tank in the year of their marriage. 'Where have all the Old Believers gone?' she repeated, pushing me outdoors. 'I don't know. To the cemetery, mostly! This was never our part of town anyway. You want Aleksei Akilovich! That's our part! Over the bridge, in Partisan and Lenin Streets. . . . That's where we are. Over the river!'

She slammed the door on me.

Beyond wasteland a wooden bridge arched over a stream, and the town fell quiet. Its houses leaned over alleys deserted in the dusk. The snow was thickening. I felt an intruder. I was probing a community that could not welcome me. Every door was shut, and there were no lights. My leftover gifts – some key-rings and a pocket calculator – might be insulting or even impious. My feet made lonely tracks in the snow.

Behind the tottering courtyard gate of Aleksei Akilovich a horde of mongrels snarled and jangled their chains. I knocked gingerly. After a while I heard someone tramping through mud, and bolts shooting back. Then the gate wobbled and parted. A mastiff on a snapped rope charged the gap and was kicked aside. A voice rasped out: 'Who's that?' and I lurched forward to take someone's hand. But Aleksei stood big and suspicious with his back to the gate. His face was obscured under a battered hat. Above his high boots the trousers were gone at the knee, and stuffing spilt from his jacket. For a moment I could discern nothing of his face behind the coppery beard which deluged his chest. Then I made out his eyes narrowed in scrutiny. 'What do you want?'

'I heard there was an Old Believer chapel here.'

'There isn't.'

'Is there a priest?'

'We have no priests. Nothing.'

We were both shivering with cold. He began to retreat through his gateway. Then, knowing the reverence of Old Believers for books, I said that I was a writer. His hat eased back a fraction. He hovered. The dogs howled and clanked behind him. 'I have books too,' he said. He stepped back from the gates.

I came into the big, littered courtyard where his cottage stood. One of the dogs tore at my trouser-leg, another sank its teeth into my boot. His rooms were stark and filthy, the old pride gone. There was a butt for mixing honey and a table strewn with scraps of half-eaten food and chipped plates. Sections of bee-hive scattered the floor, with a rusty flat-iron. One of the tasselled belts worn at divine service curled discarded in the dust. The only concession to machinery was a tinny clock on a crate. In the second room, where an iron bed was heaped with apples and onions, I stared around at walls of bare log. But a rickety table gleamed with antique books.

Aleksei sat me down beneath a naked bulb. It glowed weakly over the scuffed book-leather and the gush of his beard beside me as he fingered each volume. 'Look . . . look.' When he opened them their spines fell apart on mildewed endpapers and worm-eaten boards. Some were closed by thongs or gilded hasps which seemed all that held them together. Many were prayer-books for the home. They had been left him by old families whose children had lost interest, he said. His calloused fingers trailed along a Church Slavonic script indecipherable to me. 'And this one! Look!' It was a massive liturgy printed in 1547, long before the Great Schism, preserved by the fugitive faithful. Its pages crackled under his hands, with their double Alleluias all in place, together with Old Believer quibbles about the Son of God's eternal reign. On its final page, a hundred years ago, someone had inscribed in faded ink: '*When the last day comes, the people's sins will have grown into mountains, good men will be few and will go unheard.*

A great war will set father against son, and each person will believe only his own heart. Then the sun will darken. . . .'

Aleksei thrust this at me like a writ. 'We ourselves will see this! It will come soon, very soon. This, because our century is a monster, it is perverted.'

I could see him closely now. He must have been about fifty. Under the glimmer of the bulb his head shook with a biblical mass of dishevelled hair, from which two mistrusting eyes gleamed out. Even in his fiercest confidences I glimpsed this lingering suspicion.

'Everything has grown corrupt here, everywhere. Young people have lost all faith, and the old people are dying. Girls go about in those short skirts, even the daughters of our Old Believers, yes. You've seen them? Their legs . . .' His hands clenched and unclenched against his trousers. 'Have you seen them? You see bare legs everywhere now.' But next moment he held up his fingers to form the Old Believer cross and cried: 'At the Last Day those who do this' – his hand shook – 'they will be saved. Only they! The rest will perish.'

I supposed myself included in this holocaust, but he did not seem to notice or hear my 'Why?'

'Everybody drinks, everybody smokes.'

'Even among you?'

'Yes, there's been a great falling away. But if one of us smokes he is corrupting his faith. It's utterly forbidden. As for drinking, well, we can take a little wine . . .'

'*Wine?*' I was astonished. Alcohol had always been anathema.

' . . . and even a *little*' – he pinched his thumb and forefinger together – 'a very *little* vodka.'

I stared at him. He looked back with a kind of caressing duplicity. His eyes shimmered. 'Just a *little*.' He hoped I would smile. He wanted my collusion in the sweet taste of sin. Yet the next moment he had become teacherly and almost angry again. 'But the young people, they smoke drugs. Not from Afghanistan, no. They grow it here, in the fields, a kind of cannabis. They roll the leaves in their hands, and smoke them. And several of them have committed suicide afterwards. They've even drunk petrol and set themselves on fire.' His hands exploded at his chest. 'It's terrible to take your own life.'

Yet he looked covertly excited. Suicide by fire had once been a virtue among his people. Was he trying to tell me something? Was he even a little mad? I couldn't decide. And the suspicion in his eyes continued like a hard flame. 'Nowadays suicides are interred in a cemetery with everybody else, but before, it wasn't so. In the better days, before Communism, they were buried somewhere unconsecrated. Those were called "black graves", and their dead were "slaves of the Devil".'

'So they chose to die that way? By petrol . . .' These suicides seemed to mock the martyrs who had died in flames, and this too perhaps – the debasement and parody of the holy – signalled to him that the Last Day was imminent.

Aleksei closed up his books. 'Our community is vanishing from here,' he said. 'Many have gone into the cities, to other villages or into their graves. When a person dies I'm sometimes asked to read prayers and place candles by him – seven is usual. But now I've lost count of the dead. And their children don't believe. And I don't know how many of us there are left, I can't tell you. But on Sundays some of us gather here – this is our only chapel now. Here we pray.'

I glanced at the dust-filmed floor, the junk-yard furniture. It was hard to believe him. Beside his books the room's only object of sanctity was a single icon whose saint or Virgin had been worn to a cracked shadow. A board nailed to the wall was pocked with sockets where others had been, ranged round an eight-pointed Old Believer cross. All had gone. 'I've been robbed too often. Many of my books were taken too. And my icons. I used to have beautiful icons.'

But I no longer felt sure of him, and my distrust echoed back. He never asked me anything, but his eyes were full of incomprehension and half-found questions. He discovered an illustrated book of icons, and hunted out those that had preceded the Great Schism. 'Look! You see how the hands are?' He touched his third and fourth finger to his thumb and held them up to my eyes. Their black nails and roughened skin seemed to echo the nadir of

189

his people. 'That's how it should be. And the circling of a church or a grave – never walk against the sun.' He thrust his fingers at me. 'The cross! Remember!'

'But why is that so important? Why?'

'Of course it's important!' Yet he looked baffled that the question could exist. From time to time this happened. I would strike something ancient, immovable. Then his eyes would narrow in flagrant distrust, or he would teeter on the brink of anger. Now he almost shouted: 'It's everything, everything! When the way of signing the cross was changed we called it the Victory of the Devil! Satan's triumph! Too many died for that! My ancestors, they died for that! There was a river of blood! Fire and blood!'

I said stubbornly: 'I don't understand it.' But the words only hovered like self-accusation.

He went on to talk about the Stalinist repressions as if they were yesterday. In a village across the river his parents had kept their icons openly, defiantly, on a shelf in the room where he was born. As a boy he had loved the Mother of God. Now he lived alone, almost self-educated, and hunted mushrooms in the woods across the Selenga, and dealt in honey. He had never married.

But the idea of marriage obsessed him. 'I think it's a sin not to marry. Even animals and birds marry.' He held up two fingers. 'Two is godly, one is the Devil! But it's hard to understand them, women. All the same, I need one.' He glared round the dirty and chaotic spaces. 'She would come like a gift!'

I tried to envisage a woman with him: cleaning, mending, making new, yet always confronted in the end by the quicksand of Aleksei.

'I plan to marry an Old Believer,' he said. 'Women of all ages come here to pray. There's one in particular I know, who has a good heart, and she's young . . . very.' His eyes shifted. Neither of us, perhaps, could tell how much he was playing.

I asked: 'Can you fit her in before the Apocalypse?'

He let out only a sombre smile. 'It's true there is little time. You know, when we first came here three centuries ago, the climate was harsh. But God sent his own climate to comfort us. Suddenly the summers were warmer and the winters less severe.

Before, you would never see birds here, but they came with us. Now the weather is growing hard again. It's changing. It is difficult to grow vegetables, or anything. We even have permafrost. This too is a sign.'

'The collective farms have collapsed,' I said. 'That's what's happened.'

But he was not listening. 'The herald of the Last Day will be a Third World War. This is written.'

I remembered the priest in Irkutsk. 'A war between who?'

'Between the Christians and the Moslems. The Iraqi war was a premonition. A far greater war will precede the Last Day.' He stood up. 'That is how we will know.'

By the time we returned through the dark of his courtyard the dogs had gone to sleep. Our feet trailed through fresh snow. At his gate he suddenly demanded: 'Do you always shave your head? You think that's right?'

Before leaving London I'd had my hair crew-cut, but now it lapped my neck. I murmured: 'It's long. . . .'

Aleksei shook his own locks and boomed: 'I prefer to look like God the Father!'

Cynicism, righteousness, blasphemy, all mixed in him. And now, in parting, he lifted his hand above me. 'Remember. Through this you will be saved. Do this.' His fingers cut the air with a schismatic cross. It made a momentary chill wind. I did not know if I had been blessed or cursed. I stepped away, and he became a silhouette in his courtyard, still holding up his fist under a sky ablaze with stars.

The land wrapped itself round us without comfort: waves of forest-blackened hills. Snow stormed in a grey dust across the farther peaks. Along the road the telegraph poles had been eased out of their stone buckets by permafrost, and hung aslant.

In this solitude of arid valleys the village of Kuytun stretched in fresh-painted cottages. They glowed like blue and green toys in the snow. Their streets made corridors of courtyard gates, undermined by the sallyports of dogs, and their windows were sleepy with cats and geraniums. The silver domes of a rebuilding church brandished the Old Believer cross. The only truck I saw belonged to the farmer who dropped me here.

I sheltered under the walls of the half-built sanctuary, and was astonished for an instant to see Aleksei striding towards me. But his sturdy frame and chestnut beard were lit – as he came closer – by a pair of cloudless blue eyes which were not his, and he transformed into the warden of the nearby chapel. Sergei was Aleksei's mirror-image. In him Aleksei had been scrubbed clean and given another chance. A modest self-reliance animated him. In his open face Aleksei's lines had taken more innocent directions. His profile was Hollywood handsome. From time to time he would drop hoary maxims: 'If you work, life will flower', or 'He who attempts will reap . . . '. Within a few minutes he had asked me to his home.

Unconsciously Sergei began restoring to me the cliché Old Believer whom Aleksei had sabotaged. He had built his house of pine logs with his own hands. It was clinically clean. The same linoleum that had dirtied Aleksei's bedroom spread immaculate in Sergei's kitchen. His twelve-year-old son was coming top in school. And here I met the wife I would have guessed: blonde Galina with direct, round eyes and a cherry mouth. They belonged in Russian folk-tale. They owned a pig and four cows. A flock of white chickens scratched in a courtyard. In their storerooms the vegetables they had grown – sacks of carrots and beet – were piled alongside churns of maturing honey and the self-ground wheat from which Galina made a mealy bread.

Beneath their kitchen a trapdoor opened on a cellar just above permafrost level. From floor to ceiling it was stacked with rank on rank of bottled fruits and vegetables: red and purple currants gathered in the taiga, raspberries and strawberries, salads, gherkins, mushrooms (the finest in Russia grew here, they said), boxes of carrots preserved in sand, crates of the once-anathematised potatoes – all their own produce. Winter, they said, could last deep into May.

We roamed about their acre of garden, sniffing tomatoes and picking cucumbers in the greenhouse, and lifted the snow-clogged lids from hives to watch the bees crowding their cells. Once we raised water by one of the spindly hoists which dipped and rose like aquatic birds from wells all over the village. Sergei even had a carpenter's workshop, and a shed full of farm utensils. But the old wood ploughs had all been destroyed in Stalin's day, he said, and the taboo on iron broken. From time to time, as if reassessing things, he would say simply: 'Well, that's how we live, that's how we live.'

All day they lavished meals on me: dumplings, beef stew, currant juice and fresh raspberry jam. Before and after each feast they disappeared into the adjoining room, where I glimpsed them bowing to their icons, crossing themselves over and over with their fingers in order, in an extravagant, secret grace.

These icons had been given by their parents at their wedding: antique, lovely things, each older than the Schism. They glowed on their shelf in vermilions and polished gold. An image of God the Father fulminated just above the electric meter.

'But some have been stolen,' Sergei said. 'We've been burgled four times. Even the church, ransacked. These robbers come from Ulan Ude, not from here. Nobody here would do that.'

I had forgotten that people like Sergei and Galina existed. They seemed to belong in an older, half-mythic Siberia, now drowned under immigration. 'This is the place to be!' he said. 'By December the snow reaches waist-high and the temperature can drop to −50°F. But the air is wonderful – very fresh and still – and the snow stays pure white. You never see that polluted look you get in western Russia. My wife comes from an Old Believer family in the Urals and there, she says, people were dying young because of radiation, and the river water was lethal. But not here! This is a beautiful land!' It was not nature that had made Siberia Hell, he said. It was man.

I thought of his stolen icons, and mentioned those of Aleksei. But he burst out laughing. 'Oh Aleksei Akilovich! I know him! He's a drunk. He can hardly read. I don't know if he was burgled or not, with all those watch-dogs. I think actually he's a little mad.' He twirled his forefinger in his ear. 'He used to live in the woods and sell cedar-cones. And now he does anything.'

For hours Sergei took me round the village visiting friends.

'Nobody knows when the Last Day will come but everyone here is prepared for it. People have made provision – food, clothes – because it will be preceded by a fearful night,' he said. 'That's how we live.'

I remembered his brimming cellar, which I had thought stocked merely against the winter; but he and Galina had a more terrible winter in view. My mind flitted back to my empty London kitchen. I felt vaguely exposed.

In each house we visited the same scene greeted us: the scrupulous cleanliness, a whiff of candle-wax, bed-pillows mounded under a muslin veil, the brick stoves already warming, and always the shelf of icons to which Sergei bowed – because each home, in its way, was a chapel. Bearded patriarchs and stern-faced chatelaines unbent at our arrival, and brought out their cherished liturgies and hymnals. From sheaths of protective cloth the books emerged in chrysalides of split leather and cracked wood, their pages fortified with glued-on parchment. One woman laid on my lap a manuscript prayer-book from a century before the Schism, its ink smudged by rain or snow or tears. Its pages trembled in my hands. I wondered why its corners were charred, and imagined its journey east. Another woman held up the multi-coloured skirts and amber necklaces worn by her grandmother, and sighed a little.

Sometimes, in these pious households, I caught myself thinking of Aleksei Akilovich with heretical warmth, I don't know why. With his ripped-out icon-case and his disintegrating books, he seemed coeval with those wanderers and flagellants whose mingled licentiousness and belief were a quagmire from which the pious had withdrawn. It was easy to romanticise him. All that peasant slyness and naivety, the tarnished shafts of devotion, the never-to-be-fulfilled yearnings, gave an illusion of movement and change beside the stasis of the faithful. He came from the pages of Dostoevsky, they from the sermons of Luther. They were prepared for death or Apocalypse, almost complete. He comprised nothing but loose ends. And I kept thinking about him.

Outside, the snow began to fall, and people were sitting on benches in the street, laughing. 'Winter's here! Autumn's over!'

Later Sergei and I went on to the hills and gazed down. 'It's beautiful, my village!' It was. It shone foreshortened through his field-glasses, like a painted land: a horseman herding his cattle, a cart gliding over snow. Yet the place fell oddly into two halves, with pasture between, and long tracks lay empty which had once been bordered by houses.

'Those farms fell into ruin. Hundreds of them. Their owners were shot or exiled in Stalin's day for being too rich. There were twelve hundred houses in my village then, and now only three hundred!' Their vacant spaces disturbed him. They were the village which should have been: the homes of the diligent and frugal. As we walked they took on a sad presence round us. He remembered their dates and names like a personal hurt.

A modest opulence had followed the Old Belief wherever its people settled. In 1917 they had numbered fifteen million – one tenth of Russia's population – and owned more than half the country's capital. Newly tolerated, they had prospered among the merchant-industrial class, the Cossacks and wealthy peasants. (Sergei himself came from the Don Cossack Pahle family.) They were ripe for Stalin's sickle.

Inside a broken corral two men asked us for cigarettes with the fawning of the chronically drunk. Sergei steered me away. 'Yes, they were Old Believers.' We were wading fast through shin-deep snow. 'Things here aren't like they were. There are five village families who are total drunkards. People are starting to live just for themselves. Our collective for livestock and wheat is falling to bits. We used to have seventy tractors, but now there are only sixteen. Its workers hardly ever get paid, so they pilfer. As for drink, if they can't afford official vodka, they make their own – just sugar, yeast and water mixed. It can kill you.' His eyes lifted to heaven. 'More than half our villagers are pensioners. Young people have gone away to the cities, to Ulan Ude, hoping for work. We're becoming a village of the dead.'

The chapel is a consecrated cottage. It stands in the ashes of its predecessor, ruined in the thirties. Its church bell was retrieved from a Museum of Atheism. Studiously Sergei shows me the old psalteries, translating their dates from the Julian calendar; he lights a beeswax candle to St Sergei and points out the pallets where the faithful strike their foreheads in prayer. The iconostasis is gay with peasant colours. After the Schism, when the established Church adopted the choir-loft, the Old Believers changed nothing. So choir and congregation sing unseparated and the disembodied polyphony of the elevated loft is never heard. Sergei, who serves in the choir of four, points to where they stand, just a step from the congregation.

'We praise with one voice,' he says. 'We become one people.' And suddenly he starts to sing. His baritone rings out in the austere monody of the older worship, preserved here for more than three centuries. His voice is easy and pure. It fills the domestic space with an ancient certainty. He spins out the end of each verse in a long, connective hum, like the chant of the Buddhist monks, a sound of waiting.

'That's how we live,' he says. He still seems to be explaining his people, himself. In surety of justice, he implies, that's how we live.

Our patience is not exhausted. Too much is at stake. So we gather our logs and vegetables. We prune the raspberry bushes and cover them with earth until it's spring. That's how we live. Before winter we kill a calf, and reassemble our sledge to cross the snow-fields.

On Saturdays and Sundays we sing at the Liturgy. The whole church chants as one (remember this) and our ordained priest, who has even painted icons, leads us. And yes, everybody remembers the Old Slavonic, and sings the double Alleluia. That is the way to God's forgiveness. That's how we live.

We do not live like Aleksei Akilovich, so far from grace.

The price of beef is down now, because too many cattle are being slaughtered. But honey fetches a good price. Honey is the future.

We wait for the end of the light. Only others will be taken by surprise. Sometimes we pray for the world, sometimes for ourselves. The dark can only purify us.

*

My bus ran south-west eighty miles to Novoselenginsk. The passengers huddled and chattered as the snow swirled about us. Beyond Goose Lake, an old Buddhist holy place, we laboured through a wilderness of jagged ridges and down again to the Selenga. The falling snow thinned away from a land it had left monochrome. The hills turned to ash, and the sky, above this sudden draining of colour, shone in a startling, artificial blue.

Novoselenginsk looked like the frontier-town it was. Its buildings stretched low along too-wide streets. Snow was gusting through them. There was no one to be seen. Over the asbestos rooftops loomed the wreck of a giant church. Russia petered out here, and nothing identifiable took her place. The land seemed to have pared and simplified itself out of ungiving rock.

Yet in 1818 it was to this antipodes that the London Missionary Society despatched three priests and their families. The Czar granted them a plot of land on the far river-bank from the garrison-town, and here, while learning Russian, Manchu and Mongolian, they laboured for twenty-two years to convert the elusive Buryats. Opposite them the town was being eroded away by the river, dropping piecemeal under its water.

But the mission station saw itself poised near the heart of God's purpose. Just beyond the Mongol-speaking Buryats lay Mongolia itself, and the priests eventually translated the entire Bible out of Hebrew and Greek into Mongolian, and printed it on their own press. And Mongolia was only a stepping-stone. Beyond it spread the greatest prize of all – the ocean of waiting souls that had mesmerised Christian evangelists for generations: China.

The hill between the town and the river was a graveyard of farm machinery – tractors, harvesters, bulldozers – which gleamed indestructibly out of the snowdrifts. As I crested it, leaving Novoselenginsk in a shabby geometry below, there unravelled in front of me the long blade of the Selenga river sliding through its hills. On its far shore the original town had gone, eaten away by the river's current. Only the white shell of its church rose far inland. Below me, a stockaded village lay above the vanished mission, where granite cliffs dropped sheer to the water. It had given up in 1840, and a few years later nothing remained but some outbuildings and a wall enclosing the graves of a woman and three children.

The letters of the senior priest, Edward Stallybrass, survive in the British Museum archives, unflinching in their faith. His handwriting, and that of his wife Sarah, converge indistinguish-ably in a beautiful, forward-flowing script. They seem never to have wavered, only to have underestimated fatally the Buddhism of the inhabitants.

At Mongol New Year, Sarah visited the chief lama temple 'in order', she wrote enigmatically, 'to gratify my eyes and affect my heart'. The feasting and ceremony, the masked plays and deafening music in this 'Great Temple of the Idolators', put her in mind of Hell. But 'I thought the day was perhaps not distant when the gospels in circulation among them would be substituted for their prayers; their instruments attuned to the praises of the Most High; and the great Chair occupied as a pulpit, by one of our devoted missionary brethren'. This vision never materialised. Only a little earlier the Buryats had brought thirty wagonloads of Buddhist texts from Tibet for the price of 12,000 cattle.

I descended into a village which looked half-abandoned. The river had a little withdrawn from it, leaving printless sand-banks. The enclosure and the graves had disappeared. On the site of the mission was only the breached cattle-pen of a ruined state farm, and a litter of rocks. A piercing wind sprang up. Close to the bank, under an icing of snow, I came upon a 20-foot obelisk of rough-hewn stone. Dusting the frost from its iron plaque, I read in Latin an inscription to Martha Cowie, '*Nata in Scotia in urbe Glasguae*', wife of the missionary Robert Yuille. She had died in 1827.

Stallybrass, too, lost his wife, to some unnamed illness. For a moment a heartbreaking loneliness breaks through his piety. 'I can hardly believe that she is to open her eyes upon me no more,' he wrote to his nephew. 'Yet it is true, I wiped the last, cold sweat from her face, and closed her eyes in death. . . .' But instead of final words confirming her love of the Gospels, he wrote, she had only gasped a little, and died.

Beyond the obelisk, and the sheltering cliff, the river loosens into a shining estuary which wanders away in multiple strands towards the south. From where I stood its course was speckled by forest islets, still golden, until the streams drew a watery line beneath wrinkled hills and turned at last towards Mongolia.

In the course of their twenty-two years the missionaries baptised nobody. Even their Buryat servants, wrote an unsympathising visitor, laughed at them behind their backs. The Russian Church hated them, and demanded that any convert join the Orthodox. Eventually, in 1840, it contrived the mission's closure. Within a few years the Buryats believed the place haunted. The bones of Martha Cowie, they said, sat inside her obelisk, awaiting resurrection.

So the missionaries had returned as ghosts, which was natural. They had, after all, left everything meaningful behind them: the pious dead, the impious living, the mirage of China.

8

To the Pacific

A twelve-year-old boy is waiting with his mother in Ulan Ude station. He sits beside me in the lobby and asks: 'Where are you going?' I look into a face of curious, empty sweetness. It is very clear and pale. On his far side the woman touches his hand, as if reminding him of something.

'I'm going to Skovorodino,' I say. 'Then on to the Pacific and Magadan.' It is my last destination.

The woman says: 'I was eleven years in Magadan.'

'Why there?' It is a place horrific in memory: once gateway to the Gulag empire of Kolyma.

'I went there as a girl to work for the Komsomol. I thought it romantic – just reindeer and taiga!' She laughs at her foolishness. 'But people are good there because of the harshness. If you're standing by the roadside in the snow, somebody will stop for you. Here they'll let you die. All Siberia is like that now – people just let you die.' Her words fall into a melancholy music. The boy echoes them with a sad smile. 'I was a Communist believer then. My parents were too. They called my sister Stalina because she was born the day Stalin died. Stalinka, Stalinushka! Then when Khrushchev came to power, they changed her name to Tatiana. Then when Khrushchev was disgraced they changed it back to Stalina; then when . . . Her passport became a mess.'

'But you left Magadan.'

'I lost my belief there. I married and had two children, then we came to Kyzyl as teachers.'

The boy gets up and wanders off to buy ice-cream, and she is staring at his back. 'Then there was him.'

'Your boy?' I ask. But she seems a little too old.

'Yes, by mistake. He's a beautiful boy, very gentle. But he's not normal, you know.' She is looking at the place where he has vanished. 'He has no memory.'

'You mean he's slow?'

'No, he used to be brilliant, two classes ahead of his age. Then when he was seven he had an accident bicycling down a mountain. He hit his head. Since then he can't remember anything for more than a few minutes.' Her voice fills with a stricken tenderness. 'Things just slip away.'

'Don't you get help with him?'

'He's a pensioner. He receives a little over the minimum pension every month.' I wonder about his father, but she says nothing. 'Kolya's coming back.'

He hands me an ice-cream too, a little wistfully, then settles down to play with a clockwork mouse. Sometimes he glances at his mother with the helpless adoration of a small child. While his contemporaries, I imagine, are following sport or wondering about sex, he can imitate all the Walt Disney animals.

They are travelling to St Petersburg, his mother says, in the hope of a new life. 'Some people stay put, others are gypsies like us. That's how we are. Everybody nowadays is just after money, after self, there's nothing else. But God will see to us.' Her elder son lives abroad, she says, and her daughter is estranged from her. She ruffles Kolya's hair. 'My duty is to him. He is my future.'

She gives a little sigh of burden or contentment. She will always have a child now.

For a thousand miles some geologic upheaval had sent the mountain ranges beyond Baikal drifting north-west, mirroring the crevice of the lake. In their peculiar aridity and cold they remained a limbo of tough mining and sheep-grazing. Their winters are thin-snowed, but bitter. For years their most successful beast was a shaggy dromedary which lived on frozen grass. By late October sleet had stripped away the deciduous brilliance of their trees around dun-coloured foothills.

My compartment was monopolised by a Ukrainian porter who sprawled opposite his wife and sometimes stretched out a tattooed arm to pinch her cheek. Around us the bunks were occupied by sleeping Buryat girls, stacked up like dolls, who seemed more delicately in transit than the Russians. I felt I had grown invisible to them all: a down-at-heel Estonian. My boots now squealed as if they enclosed mice, but my snow-proof trousers and quilted jacket, I imagined, edged me into anonymity.

I knew these trains by heart now: their bossy attendant *provodnitsi*, their clamped windows, their stench of urine, raw fish, sweat. I too now softened dried noodles with scalding water from the carriage boiler, brewed up cheap coffee and picked at salted *omul* as the train and the hours crawled on. At dusk I lay curled on an upper bunk reading a biography of Kolchak. A foot above my head a thin, unsteady graffito confided '*Alya + Alyosha = love*'. Then the dark came down.

I tried to sleep. Somewhere beyond Chita the Trans-Manchurian Railway diverged south-east through China. An imperial venture forced on the Chinese in 1896 – war-torn and bandit-ridden – it had completed the Trans-Siberian's link to the Pacific. It was this line, and the track where we travelled, that the White warlord Grigory Semyenov terrorised with gangs of Cossacks, Chinese brigands and Japanese mercenaries, riding the rails in armoured trains named 'The Destroyer' and 'The Terrible'.

Long after midnight we stopped at Nerchinsk, in whose silver-mines Decembrists and Polish patriots had died, and in the darkness I missed the mouth of the Onon valley, birthplace of Genghis Khan. In its upper reaches, after a ravaged childhood, the conqueror gathered beneath him a fateful union of tribes, and in times of crisis would return to pray to the Sky God on the mountain at the river's source. But I looked out on blackness. Genghis Khan's memory haunts all central Asia; for decades it was a Soviet heresy to tell his tale or show his portrait, and his reputation still sheds a dark lustre over all the scattered Mongolian and Turkic peoples.

The motion of the train was so slow, so quiet, as it munched away all night at the twelve hundred miles to Skovorodino, that when an anaemic dawn stole into our carriage I thought we had barely moved. I gazed out of the window to see bare trees flowing over broken waves of hills. It was an unlovely, charred-looking land, drifting into winter. The larches had wasted to leaden fili-gree, and the birches were ghosts. All day the vista scarcely changed, while I became mesmerised by the taiga. Its snow-glazed desolation seemed only to deepen its vastness: one fifth of the forest of the entire earth. Often it runs over a thousand miles deep from north to south, and the suffocating closure of its trees, crowding out all distances, any perspective, has driven people literally mad. Magnetic anomalies can doom even a sane traveller here, while his compass-point swings uselessly. Others start walking in a mania to escape – this is the 'taiga madness' – but return always to their own tracks, until they drop exhausted or lose themselves in quicksand.

As we drew closer to the Chinese border along the northward swing of the Amur river, my Soviet map went empty, and nothing officially existed. But I knew, in fact, that even the static purity of the taiga was an illusion. Logging, especially by North Koreans, and the pollution and fires around gas- and oil-fields, had cut their swathe through it; the state-owned forestry camps along the track, notorious for wastefulness, had followed the economy half into ruin. Now, towards evening, the snow began pouring in grey, driven clouds over the woods, smearing them to shadows or to nothing. Soon its icy tempest was flying past the train, until we were climbing into blinding whiteness, and only hours later in the night did I remember that somewhere we must have tipped over an imperceptible watershed into the railway's thousand-mile descent to the Pacific.

I got off at midnight into piercing cold. In the near-empty station somebody said there was a hotel on the far side of the tracks, and I crossed a crumbling iron bridge and dropped into darkness. Skovorodino was an unknown dot on my map. Nobody went there. For all I knew I was in a military zone. I plunged down a path between locked buildings in pitch darkness, where people were walking. Their talk echoed round me. I asked the voices where a hotel was, but they passed by disembodied, drunk, and I lighted on the guest-house by chance. A sleepy youth blinked wordlessly at my documents, then found me a bed under a wall spattered with mosquitoes. I turned the soiled mattress, and slept.

In the morning I realised by the street names – Soviet Street, Komsomol Street – that I was in the town's heart. Skovorodino was an overgrown railway junction squeezed between hills. The temperature was barely −10°F, but the wind swept my face like cold acid, gusting up snow and dust together. Frozen leaves rasped along the tracks. In an outdoor market red-faced vendors in high woolly hats were selling fish and chickens frozen from their tables. A war memorial was splashed with crimson names: Siege of Leningrad, Stalingrad, the Capture of Berlin. . . . Nothing seemed to have happened since.

But I had come here for the Amur river, which flowed seventy miles to the south, with China beyond. A thin road on my map ended in faded print at Albazin, the site of Chinese–Cossack battles, which must have shrunk to a village on the banks of the great river. The Amur! It was one of those floods, like the Oxus or the Nile, which seem to flow free of geography and into dreamscape.

In Skovorodino there was no petrol, but every other day a diesel engine went down a side-track towards the frontier, and by late afternoon I was crossing valleys of frozen streams in a train full of listless soldiers. We took four hours to cover sixty miles. The driver halted to buy candles at a lonely depot. The soldiers, like the police, seemed to look through me.

It was night by the time we stopped. A few trucks were waiting to take people away, troops to barracks, others to Revnovo village in the forest nearby, and soon I was alone. The sky was starless. I waited where a soldier had said a bus would come for Albazin. The snow began falling in big, intermittent flakes, oddly comforting. Painfully, the train looped and turned back towards Skovorodino. The *provodnitsa* was leaning out of her door as it laboured past me. I shouted: 'Has the bus gone?'

She called back: 'What bus? There's no petrol! No petrol anywhere!'

'Can I walk to Albazin?'

'No! It's eighteen kilometres! And . . .' – her voice faded through the trees – ' . . . there are . . . wolves.'

I watched the train limp back through the pines, until its weak lights disappeared, and the dark and the cold intensified together. I had no idea what to do, only felt the dangerous confidence that something would turn up. For a while I lingered fatalistically, waiting for the bus that would not come. Then I trudged along the railway line towards the station hut. It showed two darkened windows, and I wondered whether to break in. These posts were sometimes obsolete, their lighthouse loneliness overseeing nothing. Tolstoy had died in one, fleeing domestic trouble. The snow was thickening in a luminous curtain before my torch-light. I tramped round the back of the hut, then stopped. Light glimmered under a door.

I hesitated, then pushed through into a bath of hot air. Beaming pleasantly, warming his hands at a stove, Volodya was the kind of Russian heroised or satirised over centuries. He was the copybook peasant prince: an overgrown boy, innocently handsome, unscathed. A station-worker's cap was pushed back on his yellow curls. He did not ask who I was or where I came from, but from his nest of log-books and telephones began to call people to take me to Albazin. 'Misha . . . can you drive tonight? No petrol . . . Yuri, can you take . . .? Petrol finished. . . . Kolya . . . away . . . Petya, Oleg, Vadim – no petrol, no petrol, no petrol. . . .'

'One day petrol will come back,' he said, 'but it'll be more expensive. That's what happend to oil. The mafia manipulate the prices.' He stood up and closed his timetables. 'We'll find some-body tomorrow.'

'But who are these mafia?' I was always trying to locate this ghost. 'Are they the old Communists?'

Volodya weighed me with his candid, rather simple stare. 'They are wherever the power is.'

His cottage was in the forest nearby. His widowed mother, her head bound piratically in a woollen scarf, was watching *Santa Barbara* on television. The soap opera had been going on for five years, three times a week, and it crowded her mind more urgently than Russia's economic recession, the political chaos, or the passing trains. She seemed preternaturally old. All her family had worked on the railways, she remembered – her father a signaller, her husband a station-master, she a ticket-vendor, and now her son kept this lonely post at the end of the line. She did not regret it. For her the railway retained a pioneering afterglow, as the conqueror of the taiga and bearer of civilisation.

After a meal of salad and bread we settled to the television again. It tyrannised all her days. Her cottage had no running water, but her television was huge and new. Volodya went silent before it. They received two channels from Moscow, and an evening one from Blagoveshchensk. In her isolation, it was replacing the world. 'In Brezhnev's years we were told that America was sinking,' she mused. 'Now half *our* people are out of work, and the Americans all seem to live in Santa Barbara. I don't understand.'

Santa Barbara wasn't typical, I said; Europe and America were full of the poor. But she only looked confused, and returned to the screen's comfort. That flickering rectangle – where American soap operas and gangster films mixed with advertisements for cars, jewellery, trips to the Western sun – was starting to encompass all reality. Not that she conceived of bathing off St Lucia or of adorning herself with a necklace of Mirny diamonds. No. She seemed to watch everything with the same undreaming gaze, without envy, disconnected, as you might watch a cartoon.

Only Volodya said: 'You never see a programme about our lives here.'

I slept on their sofa in a room whose carpet-hung walls stopped short of the ceiling, so that Volodya's dreams from a nearby room punctuated mine with obscure cries.

A seventy-year-old farmer with a toppling bobble hat and a cache of petrol arrived early in the morning to drive me to Albazin. The track was clear of snow and his Moskvich saloon skated over it, retching exhaust fumes. He complained about everything, then broke into cynical grins as if none of it mattered very much. In a back seat his portly son, already in middle age and jobless, was hitching a lift back to Skovorodino station. He had put on a heavy overcoat and a muskrat hat to go job-hunting in Blagoveshchensk to the east, but his bootlaces were frayed, and he looked beaten. Compared to his father's tight, nut-brown face, his was flaccid and pale. He might have belonged to another race. From behind his thick-rimmed glasses a pair of heavy-lidded, hopeless eyes seemed to languish with dormant intelligence.

'Everything's terrible!' his father laughed. 'These fields used to be full of wheat and cattle, and now look!' The land around had run to grass and stunted birches. 'There's no funding from the centre. People are just growing things for themselves. In the good days, in Brezhnev's days, you could buy a loaf of bread for a few kopeks. And now? Four thousand roubles! For a single loaf!' But he was grinning.

'Those weren't good days,' said his son.

'Bananas now cost 14,000 roubles a kilo,' his father ran on. 'Meat is 20,000 roubles a kilo!'

His son tapped my shoulder. 'You don't have to listen to him.' He wanted to interest me in himself; he was ashamed of the weathered peasant at the wheel. 'I've always been interested in history and religion, you know, always. When I left middle school I wanted to go to the Philological Institute in Moscow, but for that you need money, and with parents like mine . . .'

His father took no notice, went on driving furiously over the frozen gravel. I closed my eyes.

' . . . so I went to college, and I passed my first exam high, yes. But then I had to go into the army. . . .'

'Should have done you good!' his father said.

' . . . and after that I still couldn't go to Moscow, so I went back to technical college in Ussuriisk. It wasn't very good, but I got my diploma . . . look' – he thrust it into my hands – 'and then I went to Vladivostok and joined the fishing fleet as a kind of . . . restaurant manager.'

'We've got a cow,' his father said. 'That's something.' He milked a phantom udder.

'Why do you have to say that?' his son bleated. He started up again: 'My first fishing trip took two months, and I was sick every day, but after that I got used to it. I saw Sakhalin and Kamchatka, yes, they were interesting. . . .'

'You can grow potatoes and cabbages, but that's it for this area.' His father jabbed a thumb at the abandoned fields. 'The frosts get down to −47°F.'

' . . . but my boat was laid off half the year, so I worked on shore in . . . restaurants, and the fishing-fleet shrank and I was . . . well, they couldn't keep me.' His talk sank to a litany of failure, purposeless, as if he couldn't stop himself. His slack mouth seemed to taste every grievance. 'And I worked at whatever came up, in restaurants . . . and now I don't have anything. Maybe I'll find something in Blagoveshchensk. I've been out of work two years now. . . .'

'Three!' said his father. The car skidded, straightened itself. He beamed. 'Don't worry. Me and this car are both pensioners! I bought it eighteen years ago! It cost only 15,000 roubles then. And what do you pay now? Three million!' He banged the dashboard. 'What can a poor person do? Just stay at home and sleep! While those parliamentary deputies earn eleven million roubles a month! Then they stash the money in Switzerland, and get baby-doll mistresses!' His face danced with resentment and vicarious dissipation. He accelerated over sheet ice. I clamped my eyes shut again.

His son said: 'The only work round here is at the military station upriver, or in the lumber-camp.'

'You!' His father guffawed. 'Lumber!'

I asked: 'What about fishing?'

'Twenty years ago you could pull up sturgeon by the dozen,' the old man said. 'Now you hardly catch anything. It's those Chinese. They've got big, close-mesh nets, I've seen them. And they're polluting the river from factories. . . .'

His son was staring at his boots with bowed head. He was starting to go bald. 'We can't even get our own ecology right,' he said. 'Look at Baikal. We're polluting as much as they are. Everybody's polluting.'

I began to feel sorry for him. He had longed to become one of those New Russians who people Moscow restaurants with their ornamental mistresses and mobile phones. But now he would not even become a waiter there. Printed with the deepening defeat I saw on many urban faces, I imagined him returning again and again to the peasant family which so embittered and sustained him.

'You can grow water melons,' his father said. 'There's always water melons.'

We were weaving among the scattered cottages of Albazin now, and suddenly the Amur was beneath us. It coiled in a steely flood out of its desolation, dividing China from Russia with an unearthly peace. Making for the Pacific a thousand sinuous miles away, it already measured a third of a mile across, and curved below in a dark mirror, stained with the tannin of fallen trees.

We stopped by the earthwork of the Cossack fort above it. The old man wished me well; his son smiled and took my picture. Then they vanished in a cloud of black exhaust into the white land.

Snow barely dusted the ramparts which crested the bluff in a rectangle of grassy earth. In the mid-seventeenth century this redoubt had marked the south-eastern reach of the Russian dominions as they touched the northern limit of the Manchu, and here the two empires clashed in mutual ignorance. Founded by Cossack renegades, Albazin became the spearhead of Russian colonisation on the lower Amur; but by 1685, after the Manchu resurgence, it was the last bastion left. Its commander, Aleksei Tolbuzin, hopelessly outnumbered, was forced to surrender, and with foolish magnanimity the Manchu granted his forces unmolested retreat, razed the fort and fell back to the south.

As soon as they had gone the Russians returned with over 800 men and twelve cannon, and rebuilt Albazin more formidably. They crowned the bulwarks where I walked with a log palisade, buttressed by corner-towers, and skirted it with a deep ditch and pits concealing sharpened stakes. A raised gun-turret turned their cannon in any direction, and the breastworks were lined with baskets of resin to illumine night attacks.

But in July 1686 the Manchu returned, angry and in force. I crossed the rumpled ground where they had dug in their long-range cannon and locked the fort in a triple tier of earthworks. Their gun-boats sealed off the river. On the island opposite, their headquarters now lay sunk in sand and shrubs, among the ruins of a flooded fishing-village. For over a year they rained down cannon-balls and incendiary arrows on the fort, charged it with leather-coated siege-engines and fired its battlements with resin and straw. Once, the starved garrison mockingly sent out a 50-pound meat pie to the Manchu commander, to persuade him they were well provisioned. He asked for more. By the time Moscow sued for peace and the siege was lifted, Tolbuzin was dead along with all but sixty-six of his men.

In the Treaty of Nerchinsk which followed, Russia retreated from the Amur altogether, and Albazin was demolished. In China the Cossack prisoners-of-war became a company in the bodyguard of the Manchu emperor; their descendants intermarried with the Chinese and lost their Russian looks and language. Yet until the Communist Revolution a few still attended their church in north-east Peking, and lifted their lidless eyes to pray before the leftover icons of Albazin.

It was more than a century and a half after the stronghold's fall before the Russians returned under Muraviev-Amursky, thrusting down the river with a convoy of seventy-five military barges. As the site of the fortress hove into view, the soldiers fell silent, the band struck up hymns and the governor-general landed to pray beneath the overgrown ruins.

He had breached the Nerchinsk pact, of course, as China weakened. Thereafter its text would be unpicked and reinterpreted: the Chinese bitter at the Russian reconquest, the Russians – as recently as the 1960s – claiming that the treaty was exacted under duress. For hundreds of miles a wall of electrified barbed wire immunised the Soviet Union against China. It straggled eastward still intact, but had disintegrated in a rusty tangle across the bluffs where I went, and nobody had bothered to repair it. The hills of China lifted empty beyond. From a watch-tower a blank-faced sentry gazed across the river, his Kalashnikov on his back. Any communication with the Chinese was forbidden here, but to the east the barriers were down, and traders were crossing the border points almost at will.

I dropped down earthworks into the redoubt of the fort. Here and there the ground rippled where a church or a barracks had stood. A few dead, recovered years later, lay in a common grave under a black cross. Otherwise nothing showed but bare earth. An icy wind was scything across the river. Inside the scarp, the earth walls still showed a trace of reinforcing stones. Their layers were the compacted history of Albazin. I probed them with frozen fingers. A queasy wonder overcame me. A foot beneath the surface a one-inch smear of ash wavered in a black artery, and grains of burnt wood fell out at my touch. Among them, where it had missed its mark over three centuries before, a tiny, corroded musket-ball trickled into my hands.

The house no longer matters to her. Its duckboards meander through derelict outbuildings to an earth closet and a smashed greenhouse. Two red stars over the gate, each bordered in black, commemorate two family members killed in the war. Agrippina Doroskova sits in a back room, writing. She is close to ninety. Beneath her cheekbones the flesh has caved fiercely in, and her mouth is thin and withheld. Yet until recently she walked half a mile every day through the snow to the Albazin museum which she started with her own funds: a collection of locally gathered weapons and fishing tackle, updated with gramophones, samovars and a Singer sewing-machine.

All day she labours at her four-volume history of Albazin. Her family is Old Siberian, seven generations back. She has finished writing the nineteenth century and is grappling with the twentieth. It is very hard. Because only after Lenin's death, she believes, did the system go wrong. Her face has withered round two dark-rimmed eyes, which gleam out bird-like.

'Even here, in the thirties, they arrested sixty people. Decent, ordinary folk. Tractor-machinists, and others. Some were my friends. But people informed on them to the secret police, and the police had to fulfil their quota.'

Yet she cannot bring herself to indict Stalin. The red stars on

her gate commemorate her brother and sister, all she had, killed
in the war Stalin won. Her fragility is deceptive. She has been a
schoolteacher all her life, and wields a didactic energy. 'Stalin may
have been wrong sometimes, with all those arrests. But even those
are exaggerated. I've read Solzhenitsyn and I'm not impressed. He
could only write about what he knew, and that was limited. It
gives him no authority to guess at numbers. Sixty million dead!
Now the archives are opening, you'll find the numbers are less,
far less than he says. . . .'

I frown at her, and don't answer. I have not inhabited these
horrors as she has. It is those who have inhabited them who may
measure, mitigate, even excuse them. Twenty million dead, to
Agrippina Doroskova, is far more forgivable than sixty million.
To me both figures bulge towards the unimaginable. She pulls out
yellowed heaps of manuscript. Her Stalin is still Lenin's heir. All
the Soviet history she is penning seems to her like a long, tragic
falling-off from a pure Socialism which she cannot quite locate in
time.

'Until look what we've got now!' A downward flicker of her
hand consigns the government to oblivion. 'I've already written
it, about that Yeltsin. I've said everything I think.'

'In Stalin's day you'd have been shot.'

'No! I spoke as I pleased then! And I wrote what I pleased! I
always have!' I look away from her. Has she already forgotten?
'By 1938 the Soviet Union was cleaned up! Everything was all
right! It may have been bad for some people, but for most it was
fine. But who do we have to protect us now? Here in Siberia
we're rich in wood, in gold. And the Americans and British, they
wish we weren't here, so they could grab them. That's what
they want!' She has forgotten, or never known, that I am British.
Her eyes are angry. Her chin wavers forward. 'In time our stupid
young people will understand what I'm saying. In the West they're
building up weapons, while ours are declining. What we need is
a new Revolution. But we're afraid of the West invading. If we
change politically, the Americans will send in an army and take
power, and we'll become slaves. . . .'

I listen numbly. The span of her experience is so far outside mine, her language of power and slavery too strange. I recoil from her, from the whole world which haunts her. I feel glad she is so old, so past. And a little ashamed of my gladness. I notice how incongruous her hands are: hands that had belonged to an earlier, bigger woman, and been left behind on her lap.

'But our people always overcome hardship!' Her voice is edged with hysteria. 'Russia will be victorious! Simple people will take power into their hands anyway. Russia dies, then rises again!'

*   *   *

Leaning from my train window in the early morning, I saw a different country. All night we had pushed east towards Khabarovsk and the ocean, and now the forest had receded, and level snow-fields gleamed to the horizon. The whitewashed cottages of early Ukrainian settlers dissolved into this starker whiteness, and isolated larches made a frosty beauty in the sun, and the pines were silvered Christmas trees.

Beneath my berth the cubicle was humming with exercise. Six times a minute the sweaty deltoids of the man below emerged level with my head as he grunted through his pull-ups on the bunk-rail, and the burly youth opposite sat up and was rotating his shoulder-blades. Everybody seemed to be in training. Their pectorals quivered under T-shirts inscribed 'Top Fit' and 'Bulls'. A team of athletes, I thought – or perhaps a circus troupe – had boarded the train in the night.

Then I climbed down, and the fantasy dissolved. The man whom I'd imagined a shot-putter turned out to be an engineer on his way to Belogorsk, and the youth with the shoulder-blades was attending technical college. The lanky fellow in the bunk below (I'd made him a marathon runner) was out of work, and the nymphet who looked like a gymnast was the daughter of the man who wasn't a shot-putter.

Around noon they got off at different stations, leaving behind a whiff of illusory prowess, and my carriage filled up with others. The farther east we went, the more packed and boisterous it grew. A crowd of youths roamed the passages to argue, show off, pry, flirt; and gangs of shaven-headed sailors were drinking their way to the Pacific. In my cubicle three Moldovan gypsies – fierce-looking teetotallers – were doing undiscoverable business between Belgium, Turkey and Vladivostok, and a full-skirted Old Believer was commuting between her fourteen children. Threading their way through the carriage, a pair of drunks preyed on all the rest. Their eyes tried to meet ours, build a moment's camaraderie, then they wheedled for cigarettes. Two railway police marched down the corridors and took one away.

What had he done? Nobody knew.

Beside me a young Tajik chemist, seeking work in the Russian Far East, asked me questions with delicate insistence. His eyes shone out of fine-boned darkness. He seemed gently troubled by me. Why was I alone, he asked? Wasn't I afraid? Why did I learn Russian when English was the language of the future? Siberia was meaningless, wasn't it? Why did I go to places whose history was over? Why . . . ?

Only a madwoman stopped him. She wedged herself between us, ranting. She had the desolating thinness of the self-tortured, with beautiful, web-frail hands. But her language was angry gibberish. With her cropped hair and knee-length cardigan, she looked as if she had just escaped an institution.

The man opposite us, a balding giant, pushed her in the ribs and shouted at her: 'I don't understand your lingo. So I'll tell you in Russian, fuck off!'

Then her exhausted face fell silent, as if she'd found the peace she wanted. She went slack against my shoulder.

The giant was an old-style nationalist. He went on to deride the government in bursts of virulent sarcasm which rang through the carriage eliciting gales of laughter and concord. Even old people, to whom such words had once imported death or prison, roused themselves to smile or argue, and our carriage became a chaotic parliament. 'Remember my words.' The giant had already singled me out. 'The Soviet Union will come back! It will coalesce again. Everything will be better only when that happens. And it will! The people want it. Zhirinovsky's the man. What do people think of him in the West? Are they afraid?'

He wanted me to say the West was afraid. He wanted fear, as Stalin had been feared.

But the buffoonish reactionary Zhirinovsky touched me only with distant apprehension. I said: 'In the West we think Zhirinovsky's a joke.'

He was silent a second. Then: 'So Yeltsin's your man? But his crew have just evolved out of the taiga!' He dragged his fingernails over his chest. 'Apes!' A ripple of laughter went up. 'They're all agents of America! Puppets of the CIA! They're all in league. When the time comes, we'll kick them over the border, since they love the West so much, and leave Russia to the proper Russians. The people want reunion . . .'

'How do you know what the people want?' I was getting sick of this.

He wagged his passport at me, fixing me with small, lashless eyes which were not stupid. 'I've travelled all over the Soviet Union, that's how I know.' I wondered vaguely what his job was. 'If you go to Tajikstan or the Ukraine or anywhere from the old Union, they say: How are things with you? How are things? They all feel like brothers who've been split apart. Borders should be demolished! The people don't want them.'

I said: 'Some people do. Badly.' I appealed to the Tajik. 'Don't you?'

But he only looked sweetly astringent, and the giant barged in: 'They've had war there. In the old days they never had a war. . . .'

On the bunk above him, oblivious, a small Uzbek girl was cradling a cosmetics case. Methodically she was ringing her eyes and thickening her eyelashes with kohl, and her frown of concentration drew them together.

But the giant was in full spate now, gripped by an incontinent patriotism that could not believe itself unloved. 'We don't want to live like you in the West. We don't want a world where everybody's just for himself, where a man says: This is *my* house, that is *your* house! *Your* car, *my* car! We're a people who share and who open our doors. We're close, we're brothers!'

Everybody nodded at this, especially a drunk slouched opposite. They were staring at me for a reply; but I only found myself muttering 'Fine . . . that's fine. . . .' I was trapped in his sentimentalist's Russia. I denied it at my peril. All down the corridor it had turned smiling to listen: housewives, sailors, the old, the unemployed. Only the madwoman stirred and spat.

The man rushed on: 'Our people have always been together! Russia! The Baltic! Central Asia! Georgia!' With each name he hacked the air in a karate-chop. 'All through the Great Patriotic War! We fought side by side. We were brothers!'

I said dourly: 'You think they wanted your Union?'

But at once I saw myself in the passengers' eyes, and regretted it. They found the West shoddily triumphant now, and I, perhaps, its emissary. And their pride, their last pride, lay in the war. So I blundered out the West's debt to them, afraid that only half of them were listening. Their expressions softened, but I had only made confusion. The Tajik patted my knee.

Above us, her hair glossily pleated and ribboned and her eyes wide with kohl, the Uzbek girl was gazing at herself in a mirror, and secretly smiled. Outside the snow was falling like some universal blessing or accident, laying the land to sleep.

I clambered out into a quiet station. All around Birobidzhan the marshy plains were smoothed to snow-fields and sheet-ice under wooded hills. I glanced up through drifting flakes under the station gateway, to see the town's name inscribed there in Hebrew.

But I emerged into a conventional Siberian settlement, into the muted classicism of buff and pale green apartment blocks, a drift of cottages and prefabricated suburbs. Ice and snow were heaped along the pavements, and choked the gutters. Nothing reaffirmed the promise of those hallucinatory Hebrew letters that here, in this land of persecuted and sheltering minorities, there had grown the bizarre dream of a Jewish homeland.

What happened was grotesque. The pogroms and chaos of the Civil War, and the breakup of the Pale that had confined most of Russia's Jews since the time of Catherine the Great, created a 'Jewish problem' in the 1920s, which eluded quick solution. It was a time when subject peoples of the Soviet Union were being graced with nominal autonomy, the first step on their ascent towards a perfect, unifying Communism. Both Ukraine and the Crimea were mooted as suitable Jewish homelands, but their local people resisted. So in 1928 the Jews were allocated this wilderness along the borders of China. Larger than Palestine, it was conceived as a propaganda counter-blow to Zionism. It would attract Jewish finance from the West, while populating the Soviet East against Japanese expansion. Above all, it would instate the jobless or unskilled Jews of European Russia as farmers in a conventional Soviet cast, insulated from their Orthodox elders, building the Socialist future.

But the promises of a rich and waiting land drew only a trickle of settlers. Religious and integrated Jews alike distrusted it. Ilya Ehrenburg openly castigated it as another ghetto. In its first ten years 43,000 settlers arrived, including idealistic groups from America, Europe, the Argentine, even Palestine. They found a derelict land of mosquito-plagued marsh, wild forest and mud tracks. Often nothing was prepared for them: no implements, no barns, no livestock. Many immigrants were urban artisans with no experience of planting crops or draining soil. Their scant loans and allowances soon gave out. More than half of them returned, or took up their old occupations in Siberian cities, where Jews had been prospering for a century.

But little by little those who persisted founded a city. In 1934 their province became the Jewish Autonomous Region of Birobidzhan, and the thrust for agriculture was being redirected into industry. By now the population was overwhelmingly Russian – Jews numbered 23 per cent – but textile factories grew up, furniture artels, Jewish newspapers and schools. It was a hesitant beginning.

Yet I wandered a town of Slavic quiet. I saw no more signs in Hebrew, heard no Yiddish. In the museum its post-war Jewish history faded away. The receptionist in my hotel – standing on Sholom Aleichem Street – said there were no Jews left. I wore myself out trudging the suburbs. Half their alleys dribbled into scrubland where the hills stood grim and withdrawn, splashed with leafless forest. Only outside the concert hall a sculptured musical clef was shaped like a Jewish menorah; but its neon lights were broken and the ensemble inside was billed to play 'Far East Russian style'.

Nowhere seemed farther from that other promised land. The market was monopolised by Chinese traders arrived across the border near Khabarovsk. Walking between their stalls of track-suits and sequined cardigans, I understood why the Russians feared them. They were watchful and needle-hard. They lived on nearly nothing, crammed noodles into their mouths where they worked, camped all together in cheap tenements. They spoke a harsh, slurred Mandarin. Their Russian competitors, by contrast, were comfortable and slow. I searched in vain among them for a Jewish face. Even the older street façades showed no trace of the early immigrants. That vision had died away into the ice, the concrete, the unsanctified spaces.

After 1936, in the purges which swept the whole Soviet Union, the leaders of Birobidzhan and the committees supporting it were liquidated. The post-war years saw a fleeting revival, after 10,000 Jews arrived from the ravaged Ukraine, but persecutions let loose in 1948 dashed the region's hopes for ever. One by one its leading figures disappeared, accused of obscure conspiracies. All Jewish institutes, schools, theatre, newspapers closed down. The only Jews who reached the region now were penal exiles, and only Stalin's death prevented it from becoming a zone of mass deportation, even mass murder.

The province had run on Leninist principles, of course, not on religious ones – the first settlers held their prayer-meetings in secret – and its tentative synagogue had burnt down in 1956. Afterwards, with no rabbi, the depleted faithful rented a little house where on the Sabbath they might raise a quorum. By 1990, during emigration to Israel and America, the Jews dwindled to fewer than 10,000, just 6 per cent of the inhabitants, and Yiddish vanished from the streets. I did not know what had happened since. Perhaps they had been subsumed in the Slavic majority. Perhaps they had all gone.

But next morning, on a nondescript street, somebody directed me to a painted cottage where chrysanthemums were poking through the snow. I peered inside. The shutters were drawn back from a flood of winter light. A pretty girl brushed past me in woollen stockings and ankle-length skirts. Inside, all the walls and benches were painted mud-brown in the Russian way, but the tables were heaped with Hebrew prayer-books. On the lectern a Torah lay open. Cupboards were piled with scrolls wrapped in crimson velvet, and the walls shone with mementoes: a framed photograph of Jerusalem, a map of Israel whose boundaries enclosed the Palestinian West Bank, pennants carrying the Star of David, the Lion of Judah.

In an alcove a small, bent man was trying to comfort a weeping woman. Some spinal deformity had stooped him forward from the waist, but in the white dust of his hair and beard a steep forehead and tranquil eyes lent him dual authority. As I sat at a bench the woman detached herself and he limped over to me. 'Who are you?' He wore blue dungarees and built-up shoes.

'I was looking for the rabbi here.'

'There's no rabbi here. I'm just a caretaker.' His voice was high, courteously inflected. He sat beside me. 'For years there's been no rabbi.'

'But this is your synagogue?' It appeared domestically simple.

'It's scarcely a synagogue, just a prayer-house.' He was staring hard at me. 'We don't have ten men to form a quorum now.'

I looked for his sadness, but found none. 'Then you can't hold services?'

'We have our books. We read books.'

I gazed at them, piled before empty seats. 'Too many people have left?'

'Yes, everyone's going. And it's a good thing. They're going to Israel, and some to Germany and America. More than 9,000, I think, have gone already, and most of the rest will follow.'

'You too?'

'Yes.' He pointed to the map on the wall beside us, to a village near Beersheba. 'There. My brother and sister are already there. You see it?' He stood up to touch it. That reaffirmed its existence. 'It's a Russian-speaking village. Metevot. It's already more my home than here. Next year . . .'

'So you've been to Israel already?'

'No.' He smiled at the idea. 'Have you?'

'Yes.' I tried to describe to him the glittering clarity of the land, so alien from here, the sound of the sea he had never heard, the bitter beauty of Jerusalem, while his lips quivered in their beard, and his fingers noted points to remember. It occurred to me that he wanted above all to die there. But what would happen back in Birobidzhan, I asked, after the last Jews had gone?

'Here, I don't know, I can't tell. A few families are staying, because they're ignorant. And there are the very old, or the sick, those who can't stand up. . . . They'll die here.'

'And your things?' I gestured at the stacked cupboards.

'All our valuable scrolls were stolen. Somebody smashed through the windows at night. People from Moscow. Jews.'

'How do you know who they were?' Perhaps some fear lingered, of accusing the Gentile Russians.

'We just know. Only Jews would realise their resale value. But the police never found them, of course, they didn't try.'

The woman had remained standing with her back to the door. From beneath her headscarf her hair gushed in hennaed curls and her mouth was a confusion of gold teeth and black gaps. She cried out: 'We can't stay any longer here! Everyone wants to go to Israel! Thirty years I've been working here, and now I've been made redundant, and what can I do? It's very hard, life for me now. My husband's dead, and I'm – '

'Calm down, Clara,' the man said, as if hysteria were her habit. He turned to me. 'Jewish life here is over. We used to have newspapers in Yiddish, but now there's scarcely a page. The editors are all Russians. The radio too . . .'

'And your Musical Chamber Theatre?' I asked. Once it had been the cultural flagship of Birobidzhan, with forty singers and dancers.

Clara hooted with mirth. The man looked angry: 'They never lived here, those people. It was just propaganda. They all lived in Moscow. Maybe they toured here once every few years. They just took our name. Many of them weren't even Jews.' He opened the prayer-book in his hands. 'Pure Jews here are very few now. Some have intermarried with Russians and their children never learn a

Jewish prayer. With intermarriage, everything's changed with us, and our religion's been lost. There's no Jewish district in this city. Even our dead are mixed in with the Russians.'

Clara burst in: 'We must all pray to God!'

He went on: 'Of course there are Jews here doing well in business, so why should they leave, except for Moscow? They're rich. We call them Chinese Jews.' He laughed tightly. 'It's a tiny percentage, but it exists. So only the very poor and the very rich remain. And the poor are being helped to go. If you have "Jew" in your passport, Israel will help you. But in the past, Jews who were afraid of anti-Semitism got "Russian" substituted, and now it's hard for them. Everybody's trying to get "Jew" in his passport now! We're multiplying!'

The desertion of Birobidzhan, for some reason, made me sadder than it made him. Its sacrifices were leaving no trace. 'Are there Jews out in the farms?'

'Not any more, almost none. There was one collective called "The Will of Lenin", which was managed and run by Jews. But they've all left for Israel. They're working on kibbutzim.' His laughter came easily now, musical. 'The Will of Lenin has gone to Israel.'

I was standing in the snow at the head of the street, when Clara came by, lugging two carrier-bags. Her headscarf was wound round her neck under her spray of disordered hair, and she looked fraught.

'My children are hungry at home,' she said, 'always hungry. I don't know what to do.' Although she looked too old to have young children, her complaint sounded like an accustomed lament. I accompanied her into the nearby shop, where she bought a little rice and flour, and I found myself wanting to give her something. I bought her a chicken, but she grew ashamed and tried to give it back. Then she asked me to eat it with them. 'Join us, join us. My children are fine children, they believe in God. Aleksei will be there too. He has a wife and children but he spends his time with me.' She talked in a fever of catchwords and distress-signals. 'We are going to Israel next year, leaving here. And Aleksei too, he will leave. But it's hard for him. . . .'

As we approached a heartless, white-brick tenement, she hesitated and stopped. 'You must pardon us. We live very poor. And Aleksei is often ill. He's, well . . . he's my lover. . . . We love one another, but it's difficult. We're far apart in age. He is only thirty-three, while I'm forty-seven.' I had thought her older, but I saw now that her slackened neck and concave cheeks were less those of age than of malnutrition and worry. Her smile resurrected a face which had once been pretty. 'He does not believe in God, and that is the great trouble between us. However much I talk to him, tell him how foolish he is, he still does not believe. He has a difficult mind.'

They lived in two rooms on the top storey, furnished by iron beds and scraps of broken furniture. The panels had fallen from the rooms' doors, leaving them to swing on gaping frames, and wherever people had converged or habitually stood, the brown-painted floors were scuffed bare, so that the family movements could be traced from bed-head to window to kitchen sink. A cuckoo-clock without a cuckoo ticked in a cupboard. The walls were green with damp, and snakes of new cement traced the passage of electric wires.

As we entered, Aleksei hovered to his feet from the bed where he had been smoking. On the floor beside him an ashtray was heaped with stubs. He looked as a sick hare might, whose delicate scaffold of bones could break at any time. His cheeks were brushed by stubble, and – at thirty-three – quite grey: so that for a second I imagined him elderly. He wavered towards me and extended a soft, bony hand.

Clara said, as if explaining him in his absence: 'Aleksei thinks only about the Afghan war. He's obsessed by the war.'

He asked: 'What does she say?'

'About the Afghan war.'

He came close against my ear. 'I was just a teenager, a conscript. . . .'

Then Clara's daughter Yulia got up from the bed opposite. At barely sixteen, she was a sultry beauty. 'Do we have to listen to all that again?' Her black hair curled on to her cheeks in two inverted horns, but out of this protection she fixed me with a saturnine attention: sensuous, rebellious eyes, which did not waver or deflect. She barely greeted me. Clara tried to pinch her cheek, but she glowered back.

Aleksei said: 'I'm going. I have to go now.'

'You can't go,' Clara said. 'Colin's bought us a chicken.'

'I have to leave.'

Yulia said: 'The war haunts him,' as if again he were not there, and followed her mother into the kitchen, through whose splintered door the noise of argument instantly erupted.

Aleksei picked up his cap, scrunched it in his hands. But he seemed unable to leave now. 'You see, I was taken prisoner by the Afghans. I was imprisoned in Pakistan, with forty-five others. I was there half a year. We weren't treated as humans. Just as animals. We were their animals. . . . Sometimes I thought they would shoot us.' I held his shoulder. It was shaking. 'Then we were exchanged for Afghan prisoners, for *dushmuni*, bandits. Four Russian soldiers for four bandits.'

Clara charged back into the room. 'He was hit by a bomb,' she said. 'Shell-shocked. He dreams of the war all the time in his sleep. He has nightmares. War! War! How people died, how he killed them.' She blundered out again.

'Look, look,' Aleksei bleated. He reached into a cupboard and pulled out his army tunic, fingered its five medals. 'I was awarded the Order of the Red Star posthumously. It was given to my family. My father received a letter from the regional commandant of Birobidzhan, saying I was dead, a hero, and this Order. Dreadful . . . dreadful. . . . It said I had died in the performance of my patriotic duty, defending the Democratic Republic of Afghanistan. I think those people who let loose this war should be interned . . . it's horrible. . . .' His voice had dropped to trembling obsession.

I asked: 'What happened when you returned?'

'For a long time my family could not take it in. My father just said to me: "You're a dead man among the living." Only that.' His eyes wandered over me. It had become true, I thought. He had never returned. He said: 'Then I saw a list of living soldiers come back to be presented with medals, and I wasn't on it. Only later I was given the Order of the Struggle of the Red Flag. And as a former prisoner-of-war I receive privileges, money. Not only for a flat, but for a pension, for social services. I'm a war veteran. Look. . . .' The medals clinked under his fondling. One was inscribed in Russian and Arabic: 'With the gratitude of the Afghan people'. But no irony touched him. 'So you see, you see. . . . I have a document that I'm an army veteran and it's stamped "Veteran of Afghanistan". I'm . . . I'm . . .'

Clara returned, with Yulia in pursuit, but their fracas stopped at the broken door, as at some psychic frontier.

Aleksei squashed his cap over his head. 'I have to go.'

I had imagined their union platonic, but he moved behind Clara like a young lover and kissed her half-turned lips. 'I'm coming back. I'm coming back this afternoon.' He cupped her averted cheek in his hand and forced her mouth to his. Then he left.

She sighed and laughed. He had lit a gypsy charm in her; her long, pinched face and dark eyes turned gay. 'He wants to come to Israel,' she said. 'We've already decided to marry. But I'm afraid of his wife and children. I don't know what the future holds. You see, he's young, Colin. But then I think age doesn't matter. "All years submit to love." Isn't that right?'

I gave a cowardly mumble.

'Maybe he will reach God through me. In Afghanistan he saw too much. He lost God there.'

With the earthy comfort of her body, she cherished the role of saviour. But the cruel thought surfaced that she might be Aleksei's ticket out of here: if he married a Jew, Israel would accept him. She repeated like a litany: 'He wants to leave with us.'

But Yulia half shouted: 'He doesn't believe in God! He's not a Jew! Nobody knows what Aleksei will become!'

Clara said sadly: 'It's true he doesn't believe. But perhaps a miracle will happen.'

'He just thinks about the war.' Yulia's voice was surly, older than her mother's. 'And it's already nothing. It's over. Over.'

Clara opened her arms helplessly. 'As soon as the debt on this flat is paid, we'll go to Israel. All my relatives have left already.

We're the last ones here. I've no idea when we'll go, but my brother and sister are in Hebron.' She did not know that this was a Jewish island in an Arab sea. 'We are studying Hebrew now, and my son Igor's learning Yiddish. There's still a little institute here.'

The door opened on a clear-faced boy. He was clutching his Yiddish text-books, and grinning at some leftover school joke. Igor was fourteen, but looked years younger. Whatever demons were harvesting his sister, had passed him by. His eyes were blue in an eager face.

Clara cried out: 'These are my fine children! We're all believers!' She pushed him forward. She laughed in a glare of cavities and gold, as if her world were complete. 'Look what wonderful children the Lord gave me!' Then she steered me into the second room. 'When I was four my mother took me to a synagogue for the first time, and I received God into my heart. Look! Look!' The room was as stark as the first. But a Torah lay on a stool, and on the wall hung a sentimental picture of the Madonna. Clara's Judaism had strayed innocently into Christianity, nurtured by Russia's isolation and her own incontinent emotion. A calendar of Jewish prayers hung above Yulia's bed beside a picture of Christ on a donkey.

Then Clara went to stew the chicken, and to the unrelenting battle with Yulia, while I was left alone with Igor. From the kitchen Yulia yelled in a heartless cannonade: 'Can't you take anything in? I can't repeat myself again . . . the directions on the packet are plain. . . . Read them yourself. I'm sick of it. . . .' Then Clara, explosively: 'What are you doing with the *kasha*? Haven't you seen buckwheat before? What . . . ?' Occasionally they would break off to wrangle over something else. The patching of Yulia's jeans, or the sticking of a plaster on her mother's neck, produced gales of complication and mutual fury.

Igor only grinned at me. 'Always noise.' He seemed miraculously unscathed. 'Just noise.'

Sometimes Clara would clump breathlessly into the room in her elaborately buckled boots – the only luxury she seemed to possess – then storm out again, switching off the lights, forgetting anyone was there. More often, after some tempestuous exchange, she would re-enter as if nothing had happened, all rage evaporated. 'These are my children! Isn't Yulia beautiful? Isn't she? She was sixteen on the twenty-fifth. . . . And Igor so fine! And they believe in God. Both of them. We are all believers!'

Igor hunted the flat to show me things. With a guileless certainty of my interest, he opened over my knees two frayed albums filled with photographs from factories and institutes where his father and grandmother had worked. It was these two ancestors who peopled his mind, and who began to occupy mine as we pored over their frozen lives. Several snapshots showed them standing rather formally in parks or on street corners, in the 1940s. The boy wore a black suit, his mother a flower-printed dress.

They had come from Belorussia in 1933 to build the promised city in the marshes of Birobidzhan, and the young woman had run its first kindergarten. To Igor they inhabited a place of grim glamour, long ago. But in photo after photo the woman looked overcast by some inner melancholy, and her son became a lost stare among the group portraits of state schools.

'That's her in the carpet,' Igor said. He pointed to the wall above Aleksei's bed, where a hanging rug made the only colour in the room. In these mass-produced carpets you could have your portrait woven into prefabricated scenery, and the kindergarten teacher had chosen to be transferred to the nineteenth century, sitting in a landscape garden by a chocolate-box lake. A white sash caught in her long dress at the waist, and her blank prettiness was shaded by a wide-brimmed hat, to which one slender arm lifted in genteel languor.

'Isn't she beautiful!' Igor exclaimed.

It was an unsettling glimpse into her heart. Even as she had laboured in Stalin's Siberia, uplifting the masses, the schoolmistress had wanted to be an English lady picnicking by a lake.

But Igor's father had grown into a tortured casualty. He had worked at the pioneer Dalselmash factory turning out tractors, and there was a photo of a young mechanics' brigade earlier than his own: Jewish workers unsmiling in peaked caps and frogged jackets. I wondered what had happened to them. The flail of Stalin's last years had yet to come down; but retrospect tinged their expressions with foreboding, as if they must have known. 'That factory's gone downhill now,' Igor said. 'Once it was the best.'

As the photos of his father followed one another into the sepia years of Brezhnev, the man's face fell out of true. If the camera lied, then it did so again and again. At first he appeared like the young Pasternak: the same long, carved features and full lips. (His face was reborn in Yulia.) Then he started to be gnawed away. He postured cynically before the lens, but his eyes were on fire. 'That's my father,' Igor kept saying, locating a new portrait, 'and that's my father again. He was tall like you.' He had died at forty-two. 'Something went wrong in his head. My mother doesn't know what.' The last photograph showed a man with bruised eye-sockets and a look of unconcern for anything.

Then a howl came from the kitchen. Yulia flounced in to snap on her cassette-player, and pop songs started up. Igor grimaced. 'Next year we'll be in Israel!' he said. 'Everything will be all right in Israel!'

I began to feel it would, at least for him.

Somebody was thrumming a tattoo on the door. He jumped to his feet. 'That's my friend Sasha! My great friend!' He threw open the door. 'My greatest friend!'

Sasha was Igor's age but he seemed light-years older: a solemn youth with a dust of adolescent moustache and a look of waiting for something. His family had already received their papers for emigration to Israel, and would leave next month. He sat down on a broken stool, while Igor told him jokes and Yulia snuggled to his side. He responded to her with a brooding shyness. Anything he said was enough to detonate the sunburst of her smile over him, and to leave Igor isolated. At such moments, while his sister and his friend receded from him, he looked bewildered. He tugged at Sasha's sleeve and sometimes hit his back to no avail, while the youth languished under Yulia's smile. From time to time Sasha would shake Igor off; but he did so gently, apologetically, as if remembering older, clearer feelings, unconfused by this perturbation, while the music blared from her cassette.

I don't need another you. . . .

Yulia stood up and writhed to the rhythm, gazing down at him. She had touched in some blusher along her cheekbones and over her eyelids, and when she smiled I imagined all her mother's lost teeth migrated to her mouth in a blaze of near-laughter. But Sasha only stared at his shoes. 'I've got lots of songs!' she yelled. 'American ones! English ones!' Her hips turned in quickening abandon. 'Lots!'

I don't need another you
Not another you. . . .

But Sasha was retreating into his earlier self, into boyhood, and Igor. They began to shadow-box together. Then they arm-wrestled. Yulia's dancing grew more violent. Her hair oscillated across her face in black scythes.

'Oh, look at my daughter!' Clara arrived in the doorway with a colander of rice and charred chicken. 'Isn't she wonderful? She's such a daughter to me!'

Yulia stopped and dumped herself on a bed. Sasha was showing Igor his Chinese digital watch, which played a tinny march.

'I love dancing too.' Clara gazed at me. 'But do I look very bad?' Her mouth opened on vanished teeth. She did look rather bad. But she went out and returned in a mask of rouge and lipstick, and plucked me from my stool. We began to waltz. My squeaky boots and her clashing buckles made a ghastly duet over the scuffed floor. She was solid, but light on her feet, her face suffused by the pleasure of it, while Yulia watched her with stormy eyes. Her cassette went on playing all the current Russian favourites – 'My Love', 'I'm Guilty' – and Clara's words scattered and drowned under the din. 'He's divorced, you understand . . . Aleksei . . . suddenly . . . to reunite with his wife. . . . I don't know . . . he loves me. . . . He wants to go to Israel. . . .'

By the time we assembled round the chicken it was cold. And now it was Igor who rebelled. We had waited too long for Aleksei, he said, and Aleksei hadn't come. So he refused to eat. Perhaps the photographs had resurrected some distress in him, I could not tell. 'Aleksei just does what he likes,' he said, and turned his back.

But Clara folded her hands before the chicken and *kasha*. 'And now Yulia will say the prayer.'

'If you want it, you say it!' Yulia shouted. 'Stop getting me to do things!'

So Clara began stoically: 'Lord, we thank you . . .'

* * *

In the railway ticket offices they ask the price of a fare: sturdy old women, headscarved and slippered and so alike, superficially, that it is easy to discount them. The office barks a reply, and they consider the cost in disbelief. Then they consult together, return and ask: 'Just for *one* ticket?'

Bark.

They sit down, weary-faced, wondering about other means of transport. Next they enquire about concessions. Bark.

You long to help them. But their pride, or your sense of it, prevents this. You know that the West has won the Cold War, that its values appear to have prevailed. The old are more easily hurt now, because their world is slipping away, all that they fought for. The war veterans seem to wear their medals with a last-ditch defiance. So I let the old women trail away. I never did help one of them.

This is a passage of shame.

* * *

It was almost November, and the Baikal–Amur Railway had carried me north along the river valley to within a hundred and fifty miles of the Pacific, to Komsomolsk-na-Amur. Hooded and quilted against the cold, I tramped down streets carved out for the heavy traffic of a future which never came. Komsomolsk was

Stalin's 'City of the Dawn', founded by young Communist pioneers in 1932 far from the Trans-Siberian and the eyes of foreigners: a galaxy of warplane factories, submarine yards and concentration camps, cradled in xenophobia.

I had expected a place of worn ugliness. Instead, austere streets lined by façades of dull gold radiated away in a faintly forbidding classicism. The replication of their stuccoed brick lent them a muted theatre. In their stately shabbiness, they looked older than they were. The snow was falling along their avenues in wet, heavy flakes so that little infidelities of style (gauche friezes, useless *colonnettes*), the crumbling corbels and collapsing balconies, faded down long vistas of puritan uniformity, almost beautiful.

On the banks of the Amur, swollen a mile wide, a granite boulder marked the landfall of the first Komsomol volunteers. They had arrived on two steamers, the *Columbus* and the *Comintern*, in May 1932, and began to build their city in virgin taiga, spending the first winter in tents. The Soviet press turned them into a legend of young heroism, and the local museum was still reverent with their leftover mess-tins and paraffin-lamps, while diaries and letters recorded the hardships of dwindling supplies or an early scurvy victim ('the first grave in our future city').

The town's buildings are still blazoned with old pieties: corn-sheafs and banners and Lenin heads, and with the city's motif of a Komsomol cadet rising from the sea. The First Builders Avenue runs for seeming miles towards a sheaf of defunct smokestacks, and a monument raised to these pioneers portrays them climbing ashore in a windblown vanguard beside the Amur. Yet they march out of another moral world, whose paeans to metallurgical plants and blast furnaces, always on the brink of overtaking America, evoke easy cynicism. It has so quickly, cruelly, gone. When I inspected the memorial I saw – instead of the stock musclemen of Socialist Realism – a rather incompetent-looking and naive gang of youths. Beyond them, for hundreds of yards, the start of the First Builders Avenue had disintegrated to a track of weed-sown concrete dribbling through scrubland.

For it went through an old concentration camp. In fact the whole city was haunted by these sites. The 'First Builders' had barely formed a bridgehead before 100,000 political and criminal prisoners were herded in to build, and were soon to be followed by thousands of Japanese prisoners-of-war. Unmarked mass graves still scatter the city, with Japanese memorials to their dead. Komsomolsk's older inhabitants say their home town was not built by Komsomols at all, but by convict labour.

And now the city was emptying, its rationale faded. Its secretive distance from any industrial centre turned it illogical. Some of its arms factories were closing down, or exporting their submarines to India, or flying-boats to China, or converting to the manufacture of gliders, trawlers and yachts. All the same, I was not sure if I was permitted here. Nothing near Komsomolsk was on my visa. But the women managing my hotel, immured in one of the blocks built by Japanese prisoners, explored my passport in fascination, and did not register me. I settled in a room with a splintered door-lock, a communal basin and some stained blankets. But the stout radiators blazed with heat, and for three nights I slept in the silence of the deepening snow outside.

During the day I wandered the city in the anonymity of falling whiteness, hoping for something to happen. A waning populace of rough-faced men and boisterous women in vinyl coats and bobble hats made muffled processions over the pavements. I was back in Brezhnev's Russia. Every cafe I tried was closed or in desultory repair. The clerks, the shop-assistants, the restaurant waitresses seemed trapped in Soviet cliche: unsmiling, gross, bawling, dyed blonde or ginger. My arrival was always a hostile intrusion. Shops existed for those who worked in them: customers chanced along afterwards, like bad luck.

On my city map the once-secret industrial suburbs were whited out. I walked down alleys whose dinosaur factories were sloughing tiles and glass. Some had been abandoned in dereliction, their overhead railcars ground to a blackened sleep, their compounds splashed with murals glorifying work or a long-past anniversary. But most still panted smoke and steam, and the air stank of lead and coal tar. I stopped in the pouring snow to re-examine my airbrushed map. In this congested power-house it showed only a furniture factory and a centre for 'experimental mechanics'.

Boris understood secrecy. For years it had been his business. He lived with his wife in a flat near the city centre, from which he visited its prison three times a week to hold services. He was a chaplain in the resurgent Baptist Church, and he accepted me as the emissary of a Baptist penfriend in England, whom he had never met.

'You might imagine that prison hopeless,' he said. 'Beyond God.'

'I did.' By chance I had prowled round it that morning: a lavatory-brick hulk, half of whose 1,200 occupants, I was told, were crowded in underground cells.

'Many of its inmates have been criminals for years. Some reoffend and return after a few weeks of freedom, others are quite *happy* in prison – just as if it was here!' He opened his arms on his narrow sitting-room, cleaned by his absent wife; it was intimate with stained furniture, books, cassettes. I had brought him inhalers from England for his asthmatic daughter, and he left them standing on the table between us like symbols of trust. 'But most prisoners are just ordinary fellows, and they come to me one here, one there, for counselling. I exploit the loudspeaker system to relay prayers and songs which get to every cell, every room.'

But his evangelism was sober, grounded. At fifty-seven, he did not hope easily. I found him reassuring. The droop of his moustaches to a trimly barbered beard turned him faintly lugubrious, and he spoke in one of those resonant, half-swallowed voices which fill the bass roles in Russian opera and the Orthodox Church. But the songs he relayed over the prison tannoy came from Baptist America. His favourite cassette was titled 'He's Still in Business', sung by a wholesome couple from the Midwest.

Boris was guiding inmates through Bible courses too, coping with a mound of exam papers. I leafed through them. They were question-and-answer tests from 'The Source of Light School' in America. I read: 'What is the greatest sin which a person can commit? Choose between the following: a) Murder b) Disbelief in Jesus c) Adultery.' The ex-robber Viktor had duly ticked b) and got full marks. Now he had triumphantly completed the 'New Life in Christ Course One'.

I tried to imagine what this might mean to a man festering in Komsomolsk prison: the sense of some other authority, some graspable goal.

'A few prisoners convert to it deeply,' Boris said. 'They've even converted their guards. With others, it's hard to know. A while ago I had to counsel a young murderer. He'd gunned down seven men, I don't know why. He was sentenced to death. I told him of the two thieves crucified on either side of Jesus: the one repentant, the other not. And he said he understood. Soon after, he was taken away and shot.' His melancholy had deepened. He had a face of cautious, conditional kindness. I liked him.

'I thought there was no death penalty in Russia,' I said.

'It ended that year.' He looked grim. 'Perhaps he was the last.' Then he handed me the snapshot of a bearded young man with ambivalent eyes, standing between Boris and another pastor. 'But here's a success story! I converted this one in labour camp. The moment he left he came straight to the church!'

I asked: 'What had he done?'

'I can't tell you. When we are converted, the past is wiped clean.' His hand swept the air with a sombre authority. 'He has become a new man in Christ. Whatever he did is best forgotten. It is no longer he who did it.'

I looked down at the photograph, touched by doubts. Christ had not wiped away his look of hunted cunning. I said: 'So you visit labour camps too?' The words still carried a muffled shock. I knew the camps still existed, but their last political prisoners had left in 1992, after the fall of Gorbachev. Now they were peopled only by reputed criminals; but the image of virtual death-camps lingered in me.

'I've visited them all over our Far East,' Boris said. 'There are three in this area alone. They still house convicts in barracks – a hundred to a room sometimes, but sometimes forty or six or one, it depends. Prisoners have lavatories now, and the barracks are made of brick. But their bedding and clothes are still atrocious.'

I thought of the lethal corvées of the Gulag, men worn to bones. 'What about work?'

'There isn't any. They should be working in factories, but everything's closed down in the last five years. The convicts just sleep and eat – and the food's less and worse than five years ago, and they fight. It would be better if they were working. It would be more dignified. And you find boys as young as fourteen quartered with the rest, just sleeping on the opposite side of the barracks. So you can imagine. . . .'

I began: 'But you've gained entry to these camps. . . .'

'Well, I haven't always been a chaplain. How could I? I followed my father into the army.' He went to a cupboard and pulled out his military uniform. I watched him without surprise. Half the Siberians seemed to keep their Soviet identity closeted away like this, as if they might need it again. But Boris's tunic was formidable: a dark turquoise dress-uniform, tiered and spattered with medals. On the right breast I saw two decorations hanging separately and I noticed, with only a slight tremor – as if something already known had slid into place – the embossed sword-and-shield of the KGB.

'Yes,' he said. 'I worked for them.' He was smiling. 'I worked for seven years in counter-intelligence, then eleven years in camp administration for the Interior Ministry.' He turned abruptly and hung the jacket in its cupboard again. I stared at his back, his trim head, wondering what they had done. But he believed in the power of conversion, of course. He must have undergone it. *'Whatever he did is best forgotten. It is no longer he who did it.'*

When he turned round he was still smiling, at ease. The KGB did not mean to him what it stirred in me. He said: 'My duty was principally to cleanse the army of spies – like Americans and British.' He touched my forearm. 'But we never found one!' He was looking at me with an expression of quaint caring. He had already marvelled that I had travelled so far unscathed. I must have reached him through the grace of God, he said. He was used to recognising a higher bureaucracy. He repeated: 'No, we never caught one,' with a wondering relief, focusing me, imagining.

'In the end it was an accident that brought me to God. My unit was transporting lumber in the taiga – the army does those kinds of things – when my lorry crashed and I was knocked unconscious. I was six months in a hospital in Khabarovsk, stretched out immobile. I lay thinking of my past life, and of the future. And that's when it struck my heart. It was because of this' – he picked up a solar pocket radio. 'I already knew the religious programmes, because I'd worked for six years listening in on foreign wavelengths. We had very sophisticated equipment, and anyone could pick up the American network FEBC from the Philippines.'

'You weren't overheard by your chief?'

'Nobody could tell what we were listening to. We wore earphones.' He shifted upright in his chair, as if back on duty. 'In hospital I asked my wife to bring me a radio. It wasn't difficult to find the Philippines station. So I would lie there in the dark, listening to hymns. Sometimes I wondered how I'd survived the accident, and why. Then God entered my soul.'

As the Soviet Union started to tear apart, he had exchanged the failing certainty of Communism for this less earthbound promise. He had already been conditioned to a world in which dreams shrouded facts, and now he passed without cynicism from secular to divine revelation. 'I joined the Orthodox Church at first. But it gave nothing to my heart. So in 1990 I became a Baptist. And my search was over. I'd been invalided out of the army with one leg four centimetres shorter than the other. Look.' He tossed off his socks and shoes and extended uneven legs. 'But I still had to work. A pastor's wage isn't anything. So I got a job as a security guard. I go around checking windows at night. You've seen how all windows in Russia are barred. We still live in a prison!' Then he looked at me sharply. 'So how have you found our people? It must seem we're in great darkness. You know Siberia was once a better place, more honest than Russia to the west. Are people turning to God?'

I struggled to answer. His God was not mine. Siberia had been simpler to define before I travelled there. People were finding different consolations, I said – as they did in the West – or finding none. Perhaps Russia, at last, was entering the age of post-belief, or minority belief. The collective was splitting into private plots.

Boris frowned. Pluralism made him uneasy. It was too inchoate, would not be policed. He kept touching his fingers together fastidiously. 'It's become chaotic,' he said. 'Do you know how many churches there are in Komsomolsk alone?' He counted them off. 'Two Baptist, two Seventh Day Adventist, five Pentecostal, one Charismatic, two Korean Methodist.' Then he smiled. 'But we Baptists have churches all along the BAM. We've secured every big station.'

'And what about the Orthodox?'

'They have two churches and are building a third. But they prefer anyone to Protestants!'

I said: 'I read about a new law restricting Protestant missionaries.' To me, at least, it had smelt of Orthodox prompting.

But Boris shrugged the law away. 'I think it's just a law. Nobody understands it, or how it should be implemented, or even what it means. It's already washed out. President Clinton, you know, is a Baptist, so I doubt if we'll be pressured.' He laced his hands over his stomach. I imagined them, for some reason, interlaced like this on his desk at the Ministry of the Interior. Then his face grew bemused. 'But he's a strange Baptist, allowing homosexuals into the army, and so on. In Sweden I've read they can even get married in church – and by a female bishop! She says animals have souls, so dogs and ants are welcome at her services. Well, we have two cats which are good mousers, but when they start running among the pews I lock them in the chapel kitchen.'

But he brooded a little about the new law. 'Ours is not a government to love,' he said. 'It is only the government we deserve.' He reached for the Bible beside him, and read out Romans 13.1–2. ' *"The powers that be are ordained of God. Whosoever therefore resisteth the power, resisteth the ordinance of God: and they that resist shall receive to themselves damnation."* ' His cavernous bass wreathed the words in divinity. 'We believe that. And I think we Russians suffer the government we do because we rejected God in 1917. This is our punishment.

This present age. Only after we become a believing people again, after we return, will we have rulers worthy of us.'

A ferry crosses the Amur to the village of Pivan. The granite cliffs above the far bank loom in and out of blizzard, and for an unblurred moment I glimpse the railway tunnel high up in their face. By the time we reach the landing-stage the wind is lashing the snow from the shore in a frozen dust. The passengers squash their fur hats lower over their ears and muscle forward laughing into its blast. Their skin shines raw, their eyes narrow. They look as if it has been blowing in their faces for years. Soon we are wading through shin-deep drifts. The visibility drops to 50 yards, the snow falling so thick. A comical dog appears and bounds alongside with an expression of ridicule, its snout and whiskers pickled in snow. After a while a village of smothered dachas turns up. I ask the way before the final stragglers scatter into nothing, and am at last alone.

The tunnel was started in 1939 to link Komsomolsk over a giant bridge with a railtrack to the Pacific. Hundreds of convicts died in its blasting. But the war aborted it and afterwards the route was deflected upriver. I reach the tunnel down an abandoned cutting, unsure why I am exploring it. Its concrete ceiling runs through the mountain like the segmented intestines of a worm. The only rails inside it belong to the excavators' vanished trucks; they surface and sink under a litter of stones.

A hundred yards inside, where a vagrant has made his summer home and gone, a barricade of rocks had been raised to bar the way. Beyond, supposedly, it is dangerous. I crawl over the boulders, and drop into darkness. Behind me the outer world, ringed in the tunnel's semicircle, disappears. My torch-light flickers over pure granite. At first I hear the drip of water, then silence. In front, for more than half a mile, a jagged road pushes through the crystalline mountain. Sometimes, when the tunnel ceiling lifts, the trains come whistling and thundering through in my head; more often the track rears up in a stony mass which has never been blasted clear, and razor-edged rock glints close above.

Charred beams lie crashed across the way, or sunk in iron-stained puddles. Every few yards, I realise, an anonymous labourer died.

A pinprick of light hangs ahead. It seems quite near. But it is almost an hour before I am worming on hands and knees out of the last, shrunken tunnel. Then I clutch its walls in vertigo. I am 300 feet up on a cliffside. The blizzard is still raging. A flock of startled redwings whirrs up from the shrubs under my hands. Beneath me the water is lisping on powdered black rock. Beyond I imagine the unbuilt bridge over the grey running sea of the Amur, carrying its trains for over a mile and a half from the tunnel of wasted dead and into whiteness.

I trudged through the snow with the KGB major turned Baptist minister, to a chapel built with American dollars in Communism's City of the Dawn. Siberia was growing surreal. Although Boris himself walked with a stick, he felt a fastidious concern for me, as if I could not move without his help. 'Watch out for the ice . . . don't hurry. . . . The snow's deeper here. . . .'

Four pastors were waiting for us in the chapel kitchen. Their faces had converged into a childlike seriousness above their matching suits and ties. They looked glad to see me. My foreignness carried the aura of a far-flung Church. They were so trustful, so expectant, I felt ill at ease. My boots were still mewing and my Orthodox prayer-belt squeezed my waist like a heresy – but so worn that it resembled blue rope. When I pulled off my anorak I saw that its friction had drawn out a film of downy feathers from the quilted jacket below. Boris looked worried. 'I think they're chicken feathers,' he said. I was afraid I was letting him down. As we processed into the church, he marched behind me, picking the feathers from my back, murmuring 'Chicken . . . chicken. . . .'

We trooped in before a congregation of 200. Among the sea of old women were some young office workers, a knot of students, three soldiers. The chapel was new and airy. There was no altar. The pastors and choir faced the congregation from a ramp of simple pews, backed by a fresco of Golgotha. Then the service began in a surge of prayers and hymns to the lilt of a harmonium.

Everyone participated. Impromptu supplications welled up, one old woman's plea rising to a tearful music, and two children sang a duet. There was a personal testimony which I could not follow. And a nervous woman was inducted formally among the faithful, clutching her handkerchief.

Nothing seemed further from the liturgy of the Orthodox, with its esoteric signs and hierarchies, and the mystical presence of all its sanctified and tortured past in the massed icons of saints and martyrs. In place of these mysteries, the chapel exuded democratic energy. Man was foremost. God dwelt, above all, in man. A moral force was abroad. The pastors studded the carefully orchestrated devotions with four sermons. First came a shy, youthful homily; then a hectoring bombardment from a visiting preacher; then an august elder bestowed homely prestige. Spontaneous questions rose from the congregation: somebody felt confused about divine grace, somebody else wanted to know how much drinking was a sin. And finally the chapel's pastor – a spirited optimist swirled in black hair – resolved all the rest in a plea that our hearts open, and that Christ march in.

Then, to my alarm, he announced the advent of an English writer amongst them. Boris nudged me to stand up and say something. I scrabbled in my head for the right thoughts, the right words. The chapel had gone silent. I got to my squeaking feet. In a rush of warmth and bad grammar, I stumbled out my gratitude and pleasure at being among them. But in the pew beside me Boris started cautiously picking at my back. 'Chicken . . . chicken. . . .' I realised my legs were shaking. I imagined myself feathered like Papageno. I hoped my prayer-belt with its distracting verses ('He shall cover thee with his feathers' etc.) was undetectable. 'Chicken. . . .' But the sea of worshippers beneath me – old women and young men – went on smiling as I told them I would hold them in my heart after I had left, and would wish them well.

Before dawn the bus clatters to the railway station through awakening suburbs. Its seats are filled with workers, with punch-drunk faces under black caps. Outside I see mud and snow and fitful lamps. The banked lights of tenements go on and off in the dark like a dingy quiz-show. On either side the undrained streets blacken to ice-rinks, or have turned to slush.

Maybe because I am leaving here – and leaving Siberia soon – I watch the passengers with a new attention, and an ache of ignorance. Who are they? I feel as if they have slipped from my grasp.

Perhaps it is my concentration which turns them to such strangers. Sometimes an individual brightens into sharper focus, yet remains alien. Who, for instance, is the youth with the pockmarked face and retrousse nose? Or the bigger man with a boxer's punished features? I don't know. I feel light-years from knowing. Ivan is here, of course, slouched in the seat beside me, and asks for a cigarette. He has grown older, greyer. And what of the theatrically pallid young woman, black-shawled like a widow in mourning, but chewing gum? Who is the child beside her with the blank face?

The train-wheels carry me away to Khabarovsk. I don't know . . . I don't know . . . I don't know. . . .

9

The Planet

The city of Khabarovsk trickles along three ridges where the Amur and Ussuri rivers unite and the border with China veers south. It was founded in 1858 by the belligerent governor Muraviev-Amursky during his push to the east, and was named after his distant predecessor, the merchant-adventurer Khabarov, who had savaged his way down the Amur two centuries before.

Flanked by boulevards running through valleys of silver birch and apple trees, Muraviev-Amursky Street courses along the central ridge to the river. As it goes west the skyline quivers into life: onion domes sprout up, with spiked finials, Russian gables, brick pediments, turreted windows, cupolas like Tartar helmets. The city accrues a spurious look of age. Transverse streets, scored with tramlines, dip and swing over the valleys. The people and the shops have dressed up a little. The concert hall is featuring Masha Rasputin, pop star. Among the gasping Ladas and Zhigulis the streets are scattered with Toyotas and Nissans: Japan is only three hundred miles away.

Yet I idled here with a sense of being in Europe, strolling west along the capricious street. I ate in the gilt cubicle of an 1890s cafe, where workers were furtively downing *pelmeni* among a fledgling *beau monde*. In the Geological Museum I gazed through a microscope at fragments of moon-rock scooped up by Luna 16: globules of accreted crystal and basalt, four and a half million years old.

Amursky Street ends at a square of broken grace. On one side a derelict gateway opens on the site of a vanished cathedral. On the other you descend through parklands to where the river wraps itself round the western city. On its far bank some thin suburbs puff smoke, and a white circumference of mountains rises. A few steamships are plying the water. Beside you, sculptured high on a plinth above the headland, Muraviev-Amursky readies his map and telescope, looking towards Japan. His statue was installed in 1891 – passing Russians would take off their hats to it – and although the Revolution toppled it, its moulds were by chance preserved, and in 1992 a plaster Lenin was ousted and a bronze Muraviev came back.

You reach the tower on the headland where a cafe enjoys a view of the Amur, and a pretty waitress in high-blocked shoes serves you ice-cream and coffee. A glacial wind blows across the river-sea. As you go out you look up and see from an inscription that sixteen Austro-Hungarian bandsmen prisoners-of-war were butchered here in September 1918. They had refused to play the czarist national anthem.

Suddenly I wanted peace. I rented a flat from a lugubrious tout outside the Hotel Sapporo, and settled down for three days. The dust had congealed over its two rooms, and inky water dribbled from its tap. Then I became prey to the telephone – calls are still free within Russian cities. It started late in the evening. I said to the blithe female voice: 'I think you must have the wrong number.'

'Why, it's you, isn't it?'

'Yes, it's me . . . but I don't live here, I'm just – '

'You're alone, aren't you? Are you Japanese?'

'No. Who are you?'

'I'm Therese. I'll come along now. That's okay, isn't it?'

I was very slow. But now I told her I was happy with my girlfriend.

'Oh,' she said, 'that's all right. I'm sorry.' She sounded, for the first time, attractive.

I hung up.

Khabarovsk is a city of 600,000, but it sprawls as wide as St

Petersburg. I took a bus five miles into the suburbs to the chief market: a grid-town of corrugated iron. It was swarming with Chinese vendors. They had arrived overland or by river-boat from Harbin, pounding tensely ashore under massive loads. Down aisle upon aisle of canopied tin stalls they had settled – men and women together – into alert waiting. Their money-bags swelled like paunches under their pullovers. Cheap black and brown vinyl jackets festooned every booth, with artificial fur and sham sheepswool coats, and T-shirts stamped with the faces of *Dallas* starlets. They were selling all the consumer goods at which the Russians were so inept. Chinese had even reproduced the generous Russian bras. A shadowland of pirated logos and yearned-for cities pervaded their wares: New York, Paris, Milan. Fake Reebok and Adidas shamelessly abounded, alongside 'London Fog', 'New Trend' and misspelt enigmas 'Aotive Sperts Line' and 'CN Spcts'. Korean overcoats were stamped 'Made in Italy', but nobody insisted it was true. The suggestion itself bestowed cachet. Towards evening the traders wheeled their goods away and locked them in steel sheds.

This alien presence was nothing new. By the end of the nineteenth century every town in south-east Siberia had a burgeoning Chinese quarter. They worked as builders, retailers, railway workers, and as dockers in Vladivostok where they outnumbered the civilian Russians. There were 200,000 Chinese farming rented land east of the Ussuri, and ruthless hordes of poachers. Only after the Civil War did the numbers start to decline, and in 1937–8 they suddenly withered away in an obscure and brutal purge.

But since 1989 the flood-gates have opened all along the border, awaking old Russian fears of a Yellow Peril. Siberians say there may be a million Chinese living illegally among them, including many criminals, and that a purposeful population shift is under way. Chinese poachers have returned to hunt out rare animals for traditional medicine, and traders to exploit a region which Moscow appears to have half abandoned.

China overtook Japan in 1992 as the leading economic partner here. Japanese tastes are flattered by special shopping complexes and restaurants. They occupy, even own, the more expensive hotels. But the Chinese, it is feared, infiltrate and settle down. In return for their consumer goods and sometimes illicit labour, Beijing imports Russian arms, trucks, fertiliser and machine tools. There is a notion that the Russian Far East – perhaps all Siberia – might turn away from the west altogether and integrate with the Pacific rim: a future in which Russian raw materials, Chinese labour and Japanese expertise will spur the region to economic life. A Union of Sovereign Northern Republics has been fancifully mooted, minting a Pacific crown, with its capital tactfully located on the Tartar Straits, away from the old rivals Khabarovsk and Vladivostok. But a contrasting, reactionary fear imagines such a land despoiled of its riches in the service of Asia: a Siberia tainted by Chinese and Korean immigrants, polluted, lost to itself.

Yet the volatile Russian economy, along with managerial incompetence and corruption, creates a precarious ambience for exploitation. Even a century ago people were speaking of Siberia as the land of the future, but despite its vast western oil and gas deposits, and the mineral and lumber riches of its east, Siberia has proved too harsh, too guarded, too inaccessible, to comply.

Everybody wants to be blonde. In the street-side kiosks labelled 'Olga' or 'Katya' (but usually staffed by a Masha or Valentina), selling identical preserves, chocolates, contraceptives and fruit juice, half the dozing heads wear low-carat gold bouffants. Office clerks with peroxide chignons are betrayed by dark complexions, black eyebrows, black body hair, but at least for the moment, they feel, they are blondes. Blondeness turns its back on Asia. It is classically Slav (tinged, perhaps, by California). It is even ousting the traditional ginger henna of the middle-aged, or invading it in a red-gold compromise. Everyone seems to be mimicking the lustrous inhabitants of *Lisa* magazine or *Him plus Her* or *She*. The children's dolls are all blonde.

But Natasha was darkly herself: a handsome woman in middle age, black hair swept back from proud, rather delicate features. She was sipping coffee beside me in the Art Nouveau cafe. She joked that this was a luxury for a teacher with a husband who hadn't been paid for six months. Talking with a stranger, I think, was a relief. 'You know, all my younger life I never thought it would be like this. I just thought of my work and didn't consider the future. But now . . . now I'm afraid.'

The word struck a sudden chill. She looked capable, even stern. But she said: 'I don't know how we'll live when I retire. My mother saved 6,000 roubles for her retirement – in her day that would have paid for a car. But now, after inflation and the Yeltsin years, it'll buy two loaves. Pensioners' savings were swept away overnight like that. So I've taken my mother in to live with us. I've even tried to save, myself, bought a few shares. But I call it funeral money.' She did not laugh. She was typical, she said, of all her middle-aged generation. 'When Gorbachev came to power we were overwhelmed with hope. Then slowly we realised that it was only talk, talk, and that everything was running out of control. Then when Yeltsin took over we cautiously hoped again, but that only lasted a few months, and now. . . . I don't think it will get better in my lifetime.'

I glanced at her still-dark hair, her eyes and mouth barely pinched by lines. I found nothing to say.

'Even the Japanese are withdrawing from Khabarovsk,' she said. 'It's too risky investing here, too corrupt. And there's no help from Moscow. In fact whatever happens in Moscow happens very thinly all over Siberia. So there are just a few rich in Khabarovsk, all mercenary. But Moscow!' She made as if to spit. 'If I was God the Father I would erase it from the earth!'

I ordered us more coffee, hoping it would not seem like charity. 'And it's typical of my generation', Natasha quipped, 'to be leaving things to God! That's Orthodoxy for you. For centuries it's inculcated obedience, always obedience. We're always on our knees. "Forgive me, forgive me!" we cry. What for, I ask? What for? For working thirty-five years and then getting no pension? You know, people still go into the factories and offices to work, even though nobody pays them. Why? Why do they do it? It's just habit, obedience. My husband still goes to work – and for over six months he hasn't been paid. Last year half his salary was just forgotten. And this spring he was paid in *glass*. Can you imagine it? Some customers had paid the firm in sheet glass, so it was just passed on to the employees. I was furious. "Can we eat glass?" I asked. "Can we wear glass?" But my husband just accepted it. We're too patient, we Russians. It's our national failing. Any other country would be in revolt. But us? No. We just sit and hope. We get used to having less. People survive by reverting to their dachas and vegetable plots, or they go into the woods and pick berries and mushrooms. Old people are near death. After my mother paid her rent, she had enough left only for bread. And now you see them in the streets, these old women, begging. Men in Russia have a life expectation of fifty-seven, and that's just as well. But women go on to seventy, seventy-two. That's why they're out there, in the streets, when it would be better to be dead. I will be dead rather than beg.' She lifted her hands and shut her eyelids with their fingertips. 'Better.'

I asked hesitantly, because she had not mentioned children: 'What about relatives?'

'Ah, that younger generation. My daughter's twenty, and do you know what she did? She went somewhere in Khabarovsk and bought herself an e-mail connection. So now she gets information from abroad. *E-mail!* When I was twenty I barely dared buy a stamp! Nobody moved or did anything without permission. But she and her friends simply see and feel things differently.'

They were the first generation without fear, I thought, the children of Gorbachev. 'They may make a new Russia.' Yet it seemed far away.

'I hope so, I hope so. But if things don't change fast enough, they'll lose heart, just as my generation lost heart in *perestroika*. They'll sink into bitterness or drink . . . or they'll go abroad. Our children are happier abroad than we are. I was once in Germany, and whenever I saw a silver birch – our national tree – I used to stroke it and ask "What are you doing so far from home?" Even our old songs, I love them. But my daughter's generation isn't sentimental like us. They may love Russia, but they can leave it.' She frowned at me, as if wondering for the first time why I was here, so far from my country. 'Can you understand that?'

Yes, I said, they would leave it because it wasn't the future. The future was geographical, and it had moved westward from under their feet.

She went on: 'If my daughter stays here, she may not find a job. But if she goes abroad she will lose her Russian ways altogether. She'll lose them and forget us.'

Abruptly she finished her coffee, wanting to go, afraid where these thoughts led: a faraway daughter, a husband dead at fifty-seven, and those old women multiplying in the streets. She shook back her hair. 'Let's go now.'

The prostitute Therese – or somebody like her – knocks on my door towards midnight. I slide back its spy-hole and see a blonde primping up her curls on the dimness of the landing. Then I realise she has a companion. He has flattened himself beside the door, but the shadow of his head is thrown forward on to the wall. The woman simpers in the circle of my vision, opening her coat on her breast. While he waits.

I return to my kitchen but for some reason I am unable to ignore them, and I pick up a heavy bottle. Later I hear that these night visits are a frequent ploy. Someone opens his door to the promise of a girl, then regains consciousness to find his flat robbed. But when I throw the door open, Therese and her shadow have gone. I hear only footsteps – light and heavy – hurrying down the stairs and away.

*   *   *

A native legend tells that above the Khor river, fifty miles south of Khabarovsk, two sacred birds flying from the north and south collided and dropped their gifts of seeds. So in the Primoriye, the Maritime Province, the flora of temperate rain forest intermingles with Nordic pines and birches. Vines and lianas wriggle over conifers, and maple, acacia, walnut and a host of other broad-leaved trees start up, with jasmine and the aralia palm. In these misty hills the giant Ussuri tiger, endangered, roams among Himalayan black bears. Siberia fades away. Many geographers, who dispute its boundaries even along the Urals, designate the whole Pacific littoral a separate land. Siberia, it seems, cannot exist alongside grapes and roses.

So I turned away from this semi-tropical province, where the Pacific Fleet was rotting in the harbour of Vladivostok, and flew north a thousand miles into a country inaccessible to foreigners until a few years ago. The Sakha republic is as huge as India, but peopled by barely a million inhabitants. Its coast fringes the Arctic for two thousand miles. At its heart Cossacks in 1632 established a fort which later became a roistering tangle of bars and brothels serving gold-rush miners in the Lena valley, and is now the Sakha capital of Yakutsk.

I landed in a town of ice and twilight. All its buildings were raised above the permafrost a regulation four feet on concrete stilts. The air was frozen still. The apartment blocks hovered in yellow cliffs above the whiteness, and seemed recessed coldly into the sky. The marshes and inlets of the Lena were frozen under seamless snow. Snow turned everything else black. People trailed along the streets in black overcoats and black hats, like loosed shadows. By day the sun barely winched itself into the sky above the white hills.

Between the tenements long streets of cottages dip and sway over the unstable earth. As their weight softens the permafrost, one side or another starts to sink, until their walls loosen to a wave of unaligned shutters. The permafrost may go down 1,300 feet. In the end its unseen stresses warp and split the planks until the houses shake apart.

The Yakut people who inhabit this republic almost equal the Russian populace, and are multiplying. You hear their clipped tongue everywhere in the streets, see their trim physiques and neat, Turkic features which turn the Russians' gross. A millennium ago some catastrophe pushed them northward from Lake Baikal into the barren middle Lena, and their language is still shadowed by the region and life they lost. It retains words for 'write' and 'read' from a time of interrupted literacy, perhaps, and remembers beasts and landscapes which the people themselves have forgotten. Its epics are roamed by tigers and eagles, and sing of a lush land where the white cranes never fly away.

As the Yakuts migrated north they lost their sheep and camels, but their cattle and shaggy ponies adapted to the cold, and gave them the advantage over the scattered peoples round them. In time, like all others, these 'horse people' fell under the Cossack whip, but instead of being decimated by smallpox and syphilis, their enterprise and resourcefulness grew. Alone among Siberians they understood the making of pottery, and knew how to smelt iron. They intermarried with the Russians, sometimes absorbed them. Their leaders had aspirations to enter the czarist nobility. In nineteenth-century Yakutsk, Russian buildings in wood and stone intermingled with Yakut cow-dung cottages windowed in mica, ice or translucent cattle bladder. Their women rode oxen in the streets. Typically, in 1922, they were the first Siberian people to declare their region a republic, and for a heady moment they even raised the green-and-white banner of Siberian autonomy. In 1990 they declared their independence within Russia, announcing the sovereignty of their own laws over federal ones.

The Yakuts are the iron men of Russia's north. In the past, their old people might ask to be killed beside their graves. They could survive on slabs of frozen milk and on the underbark of larch trees boiled with curd. They supplied the hardiest shock-troops of the Second World War, and lost nearly a quarter of their soldiers, and many women. In Yakutsk they inhabit a bitterly salinated earth, yet in the brief, nightless summer they grow vegetables. They live in a land of diamonds and gold – Sakha is the second greatest diamond producer in the world, with reserves vaster than South Africa's – but they see almost none of it.

At night, before I go out, the Russian concierge in my crumbling hotel tries to prevent me. 'No! No, you mustn't go!'

I say: 'But it's not cold.' It is only −20°F, which is not cold for here, and there's no wind. Besides, I'm dressed in reinforced thermal underwear, two mountaineering fleeces and a wadded down jacket. I take up twice the space I used to, and find myself edging crab-wise through doors and waddling about knocking into things.

'Of course it's not cold!' the woman cries. 'But it's Saturday night! There are drunks everywhere! You know the Yakuts – they only have to sip a mouthful and they're blind drunk. Don't you go.' Her voice dies after me in the dark. 'Don't. . . . Don't. . . .'

Over the half-lit pavements, compacted with snow and ice, discarded vodka bottles gleam. Dogs descend out of the shadows and flit across the snow like wolves. But when I reach Lenin Street, I find it lamp-lit and shining. Yakut girls are walking arm in arm, laughing and chattering under mountainous fur hats with silver fox-tails dangling saucily behind. They look absurdly pretty – their complexions clear and matt in the wan light. Everyone seems happy. A young couple have scraped the snow from a park bench and are kissing in the tree-shadow. In Lenin Square the leftover statue, its arm upraised in wooden largesse, is glazed in silver dust, its pate and moustaches glistening avuncular white. The only drunks are harmlessly crooning to themselves in the near-silence. No car or footfall makes a sound. A restaurant that somebody recommended is closed. The Yakut Drama Theatre is closed. The Russian Theatre is closed. Yet in the streets the faint, carnival atmosphere persists, like part of the thin air. A few worshippers are trickling out of a church reconsecrated after housing the Party archives. All around, the houses taper into darkness on their stilts like a range of phantom cupboards. This is Saturday night in Yakutsk. And the temperature is still falling.

I wondered where the focus of Yakut identity lay, the selfhood of a people driven in czarist times from an ancient paganism to a superficial Christianity, then converted to evangelical Communism, then stranded in wilderness. I could not imagine an easy haven for them. Yet in Yakutsk the House of Folk Creativity was rumoured less the museum and folklore centre it appeared than the powerhouse of a pagan revival. Several people had heard of it, but nobody seemed to know where it was. Only after tramping the streets for hours did I meet a woman who took me there.

Tania was a sturdy Yakut. The folklore centre would be as strange to her as to me, she said. She followed me in. A silent official unlocked a door for us, and we found ourselves wandering ceremonial rooms. The first was frescoed with yurts and horses in pastel pigment, scattering an idyllic valley, the birthplace of some legendary ancestor. Along its walls the benches were strewn with animal skins and overhung by horse-tails and carved horse-heads, while across the double doors a painted shamaness surged towards the sun in a blaze of sanctity and flowers. The place reproduced a shrine under the open sky. But its windows were boarded over, excluding the real sun, and painted with tulips. It looked like a nursery school. In one corner two roundels of stone ground corn for ritual meals, and from their noise, said the man beside me, you could predict the future.

He was a slight, aesthetic-looking scholar, elusive from the first: a student of 'paganism', he said. He worked here. 'In this room we hold ceremonies. And in this one too. . . .' We walked into a hall whose fireplace held a witch-hat chimney above a crude mural of flames. I heard distant singing. The offices above us were creaking into life, but here were only two languid cleaners, chain-smoking, and Tania shadowing us in silence.

'What are these ceremonies?'

'The ritual changes. Every month holds a different meaning for us.' The man motioned Tania and me to some painted chairs, pulled out a sheet of paper and started to draw. 'Our year starts in June, the month of the horse. . . .'

He inscribed a cartwheel of months: for the harvesting of grapes, for the lakes, for the god of women. Tania had composed her face into a patient blank; behind their thick glasses her eyes settled on him unreadably.

He explained gently, conscientiously. A wraith-like beard completed his fragility, and his greying hair fell over an eggshell forehead. The revival of paganism, he said, had started ten years ago with the work of a Yakut philologist. Out of the prolixity of surviving lore, nine moral precepts had evolved, and a neo-pagan calendar. They were already being taught in secondary schools. 'With us there are nine gods above the earth in different skies. All through the year we pray to these gods, even in winter when the dark regions are closer. In summer we walk clockwise as we pray. But in winter we walk against the sun. . . .'

From under his hands an elaborate diagram was unfurling, like the backbone of a fish. From God the Creator at its head it plummeted through many skies to an underground seething with demons, hitting bottom where the 'Terrible Fire Man' dwelt. A side-ladder was full of evil white spirits which could be evoked to attack or divert the subterranean black ones. It was complicated.

From time to time the scholar's face would peer round to meet mine, yet seemed preoccupied, distant even from his own words. I had read of early Yakut beliefs, I said, in which the universe was horizontal. The Creator sat in the farthest west, with his gods and spirits spread before him; evil dwelt in the east.

But the scholar only said: 'That also is true,' and went fastidiously on. Every month another god demanded a different ceremony. January belonged to the spirits who swarmed up through holes in the ice where hunters fished. February was dedicated to the god who decided the future, March to the birth of ponies. The only constant was fire. 'It is through fire that all the gods and spirits are reached. First there must be fire.'

My gaze swung bleakly to the muralled fireplace. Tania recalled how her parents used to feed the fire-god. 'They would chuck something into the oven before meals,' she announced. 'Vodka, I think.'

'In May,' the man went on, 'we celebrate the individual soul.' He drew a fresh diagram. The Yakut soul looked elaborate, vulnerable. There was the physical *kut* and the psychic *sur*, and *tym*, the principle of breath. 'God gives them to man,' he said, 'and man gives them to woman.'

'How?' I asked. 'How can a man give a woman her soul?' Women had always been viewed harshly by indigenous Siberians. No female Buryat could ever enter a holy place or attend a sacrifice; the Yakuts had denied women inheritance; to the Samoyed, death itself was a woman.

'The man gives the woman her soul at conception,' the scholar said levelly. 'Through the gift of his seed.'

Tania watched him like a black stone.

I asked: 'Do you take this teaching into the taiga?'

'Yes, to the villages. But in many places they know nothing of their past. Old people sometimes talk about it – they remember, but they don't do anything. There's no worship, no rites. We are the true activists.' He sighed. 'But we are very few.'

The villagers were sick of being told things, I supposed, they wanted food. Against that once spirit-crowded country, against the richness of Sakha's oral epics, out of the diversity of their polytheism, this tidied religion would seem bloodless. Next door the singing rose in lonely chorus: elderly voices chanting the traditional *toyuk* songs, formal with quavers and glottal stops.

Four years ago, the scholar said, after the republic wrenched new freedoms from Moscow, the neo-pagans' hopes had run high. But that early euphoria had soured with economic misery. The republic's half-Russian president was striving for unity, and pleas for a symbolic pagan tree and temple in the town's heart had been refused. Neo-pagans accused the president of having a hole where his *kut* should be.

'Those were hopeful times,' the scholar said in parting. 'But they'll come again. And the temple will come. And the sacred tree will come.'

Tania and I stood outside under a sky mauve with coming snow. She closed the fur hood back over her face; her spectacles shone from it like the eyes of a bush baby. We began circling the imitation yurt in the courtyard. She said: 'I don't see the need for this new religion. There are enough religions around already. I didn't like that man. He's very closed. And so many gods! As a child we called half of them spirits, but now they've been promoted. I heard about those goblins that come up through the ice, when I was a girl. There was meant to be a swarm of them, very small. And now they're gods!'

Her cynicism came as an earthy relief. But disillusion had marked her early, I think. At twenty-eight, she was out of work, and single. As we emerged into the street, I asked her outright: 'Do your people want real independence?'

But she snorted. 'What's the use? There are less than half a million of us, and the Russians still outnumber us here. If we can get cheaper food imports and a better deal on our minerals, that'll be enough. Nobody sane imagines separation. We'd be alone. There've been riots in the past, I know, and when Russian workers don't respect our traditions, people resent them. But half our so-called nationalists aren't that at all. They're self-seekers. And now most people are too poor, too crushed, to care very much anyway. As for this . . . this paganism, it can never be a state religion.'

Of course not, I thought. It was too rooted in secrecy, in rural isolation. You could not publicly teach it, put it on state display. All the same, I asked: 'Why not?'

She laughed. 'Because there are too many people like me!' But after a minute her lips quivered with faint self-reproach. 'Nevertheless, it's . . . rather touching.'

In the Museum of History and Culture one of the most perfect mammoth skeletons in the world comes lumbering towards you. The tiny sockets in its skull, together with the rib-cage like broken sticks and the delicately splayed bones of the feet, lend it a melancholy vulnerability. It might have got lost in one of the corridors. Its enormous tusks curl inwards before it, as if to embrace something, and have to be separately supported on rods from the ground. It looks hopelessly incompetent. Its tank-like front tapers away to the tentative tread of stilt-like hind legs and a short, rather ludicrous tail. A stubble of skin and wool still dribbles about the skull.

This is *Mammuthus primigenius*, the ancient denizen of Siberia. Some 20,000 years ago, during the last Ice Age, when the land bridge swelled between Asia and Alaska, vast herds of woolly mammoth trampled the northern hemisphere. They left their bones in the valleys of the Mississippi and the Thames, on the shores of the Atlantic and in the gravel terraces of Mexico. Then, as the ice receded, they mysteriously vanished, to be washed free in their thousands wherever the alluvial soil of Siberian coasts and rivers thawed and unsettled.

Posthumously, the mammoths sowed confusion. In Siberia natives believed they survived deep under the earth, or lurked in mountain fissures and feasted on the dead. The Chinese imagined them a species of earth-shaking mole, which died when it surfaced to the light. Their fossils in Europe were rumoured to be those of giants or unicorns, and sometimes rested in the reliquaries of the great monastic houses. An outsize molar was revered at Valence as a relic of St Christopher, and the miracle-working thigh-bone of St Vincent, exhibited by monks in 1781, was a well-preserved mammoth femur.

In Russia a rare trade started up. As long ago as the ninth century, it seems, the Caliph Haroun al-Rashid sent Charlemagne a mammoth tusk which remained for years in the Crown Treasury at Rheims. The Khan of the Golden Horde sat on a mammoth-ivory throne. By the end of the nineteenth century the tusks of some 45,000 mammoths – each weighing up to 200 pounds – had been traded out of Siberia and converted into caskets, powder-horns, knife handles and necklaces. One Russian official planned to distil the bone marrow and market it as the perfume *Pommade a Mammouth*. But his fortune melted away when he carried his cache of fossils into an overheated house.

By now mammoths had been found emerging from the perma-frost with their flesh and hair intact, although gnawed by wolves and often dismembered by natives. In 1900, on the Berezovka river, a specimen was discovered which had crashed into a crevasse and died embalmed in ice. By the time scientists found it, wild animals had torn out its heart, lungs and liver, and eaten its trunk; but its frame was all but perfect. Traces of herbage were still stuck in the creature's jaws, and when the scientists entered the walls of its stomach they found 30 pounds of grasses, thyme, poppies, gentians and buttercups from twenty millennia before. With winter approaching, they built a hut over the carcass and thawed it out, labouring for six weeks in the ammoniacal stench of its decaying fat, dismembered it, then packed it back in pieces to St Petersburg.

I looked for other mammoths in Yakutsk's Permafrost Institute – now declining for lack of funds – but there were none. They had mostly ended up in the Zoological Museum of the czarist capital, a converted warehouse on the Neva where I had seen them that summer. They parade through its gloom in a queue of helmet-like skulls and spatular feet and crazily twirling tusks. Harmless, obsolete herbivores, their bones are blackened by age and frost. They stand over 10 feet tall. But behind, as with the

Yakutsk mammoth, their rib-cages narrow like the frames of inverted ships, dwindling to stiff-looking hind legs and wispy tails.

The Berezovka mammoth is here too, framed in its hide and hair, just as it was found. It squats on the ground with both hind legs thrust forward beneath it, broken, its forelegs groping at the earth it could not scale. It looks oddly domestic, as if performing a party trick. Its flanks and legs are still fringed with reddish hair. One of its eyelids is intact. So is its tongue, and its lower lip, edged with black bristles.

On its piecemeal arrival in St Petersburg, the skeleton was recomposed and put on display. A week afterwards, Czar Nicholas II and his young empress paid it a state visit. But in the steam-heated hall the stench was so powerful that the Czarina stood with her handkerchief crushed to her face. Nauseous and very bored, she begged to be taken 'as far away from this as possible'.

The new concierge in my hotel bellows at me in the hall: 'Go to the OVIR police! All foreigners have to register! Register now!'

I trudge off, out of interest, to the hideous Victory Square, where a tank squats on a plinth, and enter the half-burnt-out naval college where the OVIR offices are meant to be. For fifteen thousand miles now, faced by the jumbled rules which have succeeded Soviet law, I have avoided all officialdom, delegating my registration to boarding-houses which did not bother, or to nobody, then moving on. Somebody tells me the OVIR offices are five storeys up. There are no signs anywhere. I climb past the dank rooms of a half-abandoned hostel. The police office is littered with rats' droppings. The only official working is a Russian woman who orders me to come back tomorrow, then continues thumbing through documents. I never return.

Marfa and Sergei were circus artists: he a juggler and musician, she a dancer and throat-singer. They had come from Yakut villages deep in the taiga. A few years ago they petitioned the president to build a national circus, but the money had run out, leaving a ghostly circle of concrete foundations near their flat in October Street, and a shortfall of twenty million dollars. They had even bought two bear-cubs, which were now grown-up and fierce. Marfa asked: 'Do you know anybody who'd like two bears, very nice?'

She and Sergei were now in their forties, but they kept the adolescent brightness of the circus. Their apartment was hung with souvenirs from tours abroad, and their dressers piled with photographs, toys and trophies collected over twenty years. They had no children. Marfa's auburn hair jostled round a face of rebellious prettiness. 'The circus is our child,' she said.

They showed me photographs of their homeless troupe on tour – in Nice, in Moscow, in Alaska. Here was Sergei writhing to the rhythm of his drum, in a costume dripping with shamanic ornaments, and Marfa like a page-boy in striped culottes, throat-singing – black eyes and red lips in a moon face. One sequence of snapshots showed them all posed above a wintry estuary of the Lena, as if celebrating something earlier, purer. But a closer look disclosed the hectic antics of the strong man bending nails, and Sergei in a shaman's headband from which a pair of plastic antlers sprung.

It was, I supposed, a marketable version of the culture they had lost. Perhaps this was the only way they knew to preserve it: by this, and by the ancient magic of her singing – the half-involuntary sounds of wandering herdsmen and hunters.

I had never heard throat-singing before. In Tuva the voice can accompany its own melody with a flute-like continuum, as if two – even three – people were chanting at once. The physiology of this singing is still imperfectly understood; but the tongue, touching the palate, separates the throat and mouth into two resonating chambers, to produce a monody of eerie pureness. These songs transformed Marfa. They closed her eyes in a suddenly powerful face. All sense of the hybrid circus vanished.

At first her lament sounded odd to me. The notes travelled in long lines of steel, without tremolo, which would then suddenly, tragically, break. They sounded like some unknown instrument. Sergei had closed his eyes too. This was, after all, other than art: it was an expression of lost nation, a little holy. The song elicited a lonely spareness in her. She had entered the shrine of her voice.

*

'My parents never taught me Yakut things. I only remember there was fear around the places where shamans had been buried. People still remembered those sites, and avoided them.'

Tania is sitting in the Yakut restaurant in Lenin Square. She has dolled herself up. Beneath a glossy black fringe her eyes are cavernous with mascara, and her lips crimson. A grinning Yakut waiter lingers round us. The menu is treacherous with local dishes. Elk is off, he says. So is pine-flavoured reindeer-horn jelly.

'I don't remember Yakut cooking,' says Tania. 'My parents were professional people, they loved Russian things. Only sometimes I'd hear my father singing when he was happy, and his songs were those strange, old ones.'

I scan the menu, but decide against horse-blood sausages or boiled reindeer. I play for time by ordering a jug of *koumiz*, the fermented mares' milk of the steppes, then I opt half-heartedly for pony in a cream mushroom sauce, while Tania orders sauteed horse intestines.

I say: 'But Yakut culture is returning, isn't it? Yakut language in government, Yakut festivals.'

'The festivals are synthetic, they don't mean a thing. A while ago somebody like that museum scholar decided we should revive the summer solstice ceremony, led by a white shaman. I'd never even heard of it. So now everybody celebrates it idiotically in the streets.'

'Where did they find the shaman?'

'Oh, he's not a shaman. He's an actor. The shamans are all dead.'

My pony meat is light and pleasant. I feel vaguely guilty. But Tania doesn't. Yakuts love their horses, she says, but they breed some for eating. Her goldfish lips are smacking a little, and she has ordered a side-dish of *tongber* – raw, frozen pony liver. It lurks by my elbow. Around us, Yakuts and Russians are gluttonously mingled.

Later I joke with her a little. 'Then is nothing left of paganism? Nothing a bit sacred?'

'Only odds and ends.' The currant wine is going to her head. She giggles. It tastes like a sweet port. 'I remember childhood stories about the white Siberian cranes, which are special to us Yakuts – sacred, in a way. I heard that if you went deep into the forest, and saw the cranes dancing, you would be happy for ever.' She pops more pony liver into her mouth. 'I'm getting drunk. . . . But later of course I realised that white cranes were an endangered species, and that you'd have to be a hunter and go far, far up north to find them, and that even then they might not be dancing.'

Since long before the Academician praised the work of Yuri Mochanov, I had wanted to meet the isolated archaeologist who believed that civilisation started in Siberia. In Russia he was a lonely giant. In the West he was almost unknown. In his institute at the Yakutsk Academy of Sciences I awaited him for hours, while scrutinising the dark red quartzites from his excavations. They lay on sorting trays, like blood-clots. At last, nervously, a young assistant guided me to his apartment.

In its doorway I saw a robust man with a handsome, open face. A gush of raven hair turned him younger than he was, and his Brezhnev eyebrows invested him with a look of forceful enquiry. In his broad-checked shirt he looked more like a lumberjack than a scientist. His hands came out in welcome, as if he already knew me.

'From England! Come in! There's just me and Paula here. But come in!'

His flat was crowded with bric-a-brac, and walled in books and journals. Paula was a German shepherd dog, lavishly greedy. Her bowls of meat and biscuits dotted the landing, the hall, the kitchen. Everything was misted in dust. Ashtrays scattered the chairs, the desk, the lavatory floor. The study was a cell of smoke.

Every room betrayed the long absence of a wife. 'She's very ill. She's with our children in Kiev. Something has gone wrong with the glands of her neck.' In the harsh light of the kitchen he looked paler. 'I think she's been through too many expeditions with me. We've worked together for thirty-five seasons, always. And like me she doesn't stop smoking.' He lit another cigarette. 'I won't be happy until she's back. When she's back I'll start to work again.'

We sat in his cramped kitchen in the old Russian way, the way I remembered among Moscow and Leningrad dissidents twenty years ago, talking in heady abstracts, drinking vodka or coffee out of chipped cups. In Yakutsk, time had stopped.

It was hard being alone here, he said. He had just finished his last season's excavations after sixteen years at Diring Yuriakh, the site on the Lena which had made his name. He did not want to go on. He was already sixty-five. His workers had grown old alongside him, become fathers and grandfathers. Money was short. 'I want to document it all now.'

He had uncovered 4,000 artefacts above the old bedrock of the river – mostly quartzite choppers and scrapers – and he believed they belonged to a civilisation over two million years old. To anthropologists, the claim was astonishing, almost unthinkable. It turned human evolution on its head. Earliest man was stirring not only in the Rift Valley, Mochanov maintained, but in the wastes of Siberia.

He showed me many charts and photographs. He sounded angrily bewildered. 'Western archaeologists refuse to believe my work. I don't know why. They've come from everywhere – France, America, Britain, Germany, Sweden. They slap my back and we get drunk together, and they're like friends. But when they see the work they simply say: "This cannot be!" And they go quiet. I say: "Tell me, if you can't believe it, why not? Where have I gone wrong?" The artefacts, the stone tools, they're beyond dispute. It's the stratum that's in debate. Yet it's the oldest stratum above the Lena bedrock. Geologists have confirmed this. So the geology is right, the archaeology is right – but still they don't believe me! And this civilisation could go back two and a half million years! Older than African man – or maybe the same age.'

I asked: 'But who were they? Where did they come from?'

'I don't know. Nobody knows.' He became peevishly vague. 'Who can know the age of man on Earth? Only God knows, or maybe doesn't. Maybe these civilisations were caused by something out of the cosmos.'

With misgiving I mentioned the Academician.

'Yes, he's a friend. A very intelligent man ... he has these

theories . . . and it is hard to understand the world without them.'
A silence fell, filled with his frustration and my scepticism. Then
he said: 'I was astonished when I started the dig in 1982. I hadn't
anticipated anything like this. I thought I was going mad. I kept
saying: "No, this can't be. Something will happen. We'll uncover
something to disprove this." But in 1983, it was more of the
same: tools at bedrock level. And in 1984 we found beautiful
stratigraphy. And then I believed it. I believed it.'

He burnt with a thwarted energy. He was a field archaeologist
in his bones. But now he wanted time to read, to think. In this
isolated town, his scholarship was long out of date. Often his
reading had come to him by chance. He talked of Teilhard de
Chardin. . . . 'And the work of Moritz Wagner, a contemporary
of Darwin, saved me from madness at that time. He explored the
possibility of man's origins in a cold environment instead of a
tropical one, and he valued stone implements – rather than bones
– like I do.'

But stone, I thought cruelly, did not submit to radio-carbon
dating. You could dream around it.

'Some people say Diring Yuriakh may be as old as three million
years. Yet others' – he gazed down, and I sensed that these others
were the vital ones, the heavyweights of the West – 'well,
others say it is 500,000 years old. Or less, even less.' Paula thrust
her muzzle into his hand. He seemed to be caressing her loyalty.
'Do you want to see the excavation video?'

We went into his sitting-room; it was crowded with kitsch, as
the Academician's had been: Chinese seals, mammoths carved in
mammoth ivory, cheap Buddhas, a bust of Peter the Great. He
closed out the light, and the video flickered on. 'It's a beautiful
place,' he said.

It poised 120 metres above the east bank of the Lena, and
looked like a sandy beach. His bulldozers had ploughed its terrace
two kilometres square, but the permafrost began only six metres
down, he said, and the work had been back-breaking. 'But we
dropped shafts to 40 metres, and still we found the same things.
There was no doubt. You see the clusters there?'

I saw oval groupings of stones: an anvil, hammer-stones, flakes, axes. 'We found them again and again. They seem to form little workshops. The place was a town, certainly, a kind of town. In its day it was level with the Lena. And look, there's my dog!' Paula was often in the picture, cantering across the dunes. Then the camera strayed back over the circles of precious stones, while the bulldozers puttered behind. Down the excavation shafts the permafrost enclosed smears of red sand, like undried blood splashed against the walls. 'It's beautiful,' he said, 'and it's already falling in, vanishing. This was our last day.'

Workmen were wending down from the abandoned terrace, while he watched them beside me, in silence, in his slippers. Sometimes his camera wobbled off, beguiled by the watery mud-flats of the Lena's west bank, by an elk swimming the river, by its hills at sunset. He was afraid of forgetting. At last he said: 'Now that it's all over, I want to convene a world conference. Because what can be more important than the arrival of man on earth? How did it happen? Man is not an animal.' He stroked Paula apologetically. 'Darwin was a fine scientist who knew about physiology, but the movements of peoples were not his field. That is what we need to discuss now. The origins of man.'

He was not a Russian chauvinist, I sensed, only fatally cut off from his peers. I promised to send him some articles he requested from Britain: on excavations in Pakistan which seemed to parallel his own. I was also to send him, with a heavy heart, the findings of American geoarchaeologists who had tested Diring Yuriakh. They had used the new technique of thermoluminescence, which can estimate how long quartzite has been buried by measuring the electrons trapped in its crystals, and they had come up with a site date around 300,000 BC. Perhaps Mochanov already knew of this, and could not bear it. He did not write back.

Yet the site was unique in its way. Mochanov's findings pushed back habitation of the Arctic edge to a time far more remote than had been supposed. Here, it seemed, some unknown people had slipped through a crack in the Great Ice Age, and made a fleeting life.

Before I left, Mochanov quaintly took my photograph and gave me his interim report on Diring Yuriakh, published in 1992. He lingered in his doorway. With Russia's economy in the state it was, he knew his conference on the origins of man was a pipe-dream. But there was one thing he wanted to do, he said, while he still could. He wanted to fly to Kenya with his wife – 'we always used to fly together' – and to look down, at last, on the Rift Valley.

* * *

The only other passengers in my twin-engine Antonov were three soldiers wrapped in overcoats against the cold, with caps clamped over their ears. Beneath us the Lena, freezing over from shore to shore, still trickled steel-grey through its ice. But all its tributaries had frozen solid, and the floes drifting on its current were sticking on snow-blurred islands. I had hoped to find a truck going east to Magadan and the Pacific, but the single road was impassable, ruptured by permafrost, and this battered Antonov was the only way out. As it banked over Yakutsk, the wrecked collage of thousands upon thousands of snow-drowned cottages showed in pencil-line walls and the dark tracks around them. Once I thought I could make out the empty site of Sergei and Marfa's circus; then came the toy figure of Lenin in his square; then the chessboard of tenements where Tania waited for a future and Mochanov laboured over the advent of man. At last the clouds closed over them and we were heading east under a darkening sky.

The faint, continual vibration of the aeroplane kept me awake, vaguely alarmed. From time to time, when the clouds parted, a frozen desolation of mountains glimmered below, with no sign of life. And this wilderness continued for six hundred miles. Seventy years ago, along its single track, a few traders from Yakutsk brought brick tea and contraband vodka to depleted tribes, and returned with mammoth ivory, furs and a few girls to the brothels of Yakutsk, sold by their clans for the price of a poor reindeer each.

Below us now the valleys were black with stunted larches, where the rivers lay inert. Soon we seemed to be flying over pure glacier, knotted with peaks and clefts. Its icy stillness filled our cabin. The soldiers were muffled asleep, and I gazing down, numbed.

Within living memory this emptiness had become a continent of death-camps. In 1931, a few years after huge gold deposits were discovered, a region embracing all north-east Siberia beyond the Lena – a land vaster than Mexico – fell under the agency named Dalstroy, which soon became a branch of the Ministry of the Interior and the secret police. Dalstroy was a law unto itself. In its zone the Soviet constitution did not hold. It ruled a waking nightmare.

This country of Kolyma was fed every year by sea with tens of thousands of prisoners, mostly innocent. Where they landed, they built a port, then the city of Magadan, then the road inland to the mines where they perished. At first the convicts were peasant kulaks and criminals, then – as Stalin's paranoia heightened – imagined saboteurs and counter-revolutionaries from every class: Party officials, soldiers, scientists, doctors, teachers, artists.

They died in miners' tunnels from falling rocks and snapped lift cables, from ammonal fumes and silicosis, scurvy and high blood pressure, spitting up blood and lung tissue. In winter, when steam-hoses melted the gold-bearing sand, they wheeled its slag from the hot panning-sheds into temperatures as low as −60°F, and were dead of pneumonia or meningitis within a month. In less than ten years Kolyma was producing one third of the world's gold. Every kilogram, it has been computed, cost a human life. But the numbers of dead are in fact unknown. They have been guessed at over two million.

It was night by the time we landed fifty miles from the Pacific, at Sokol, where I slept in an empty rest-house. Two long-distance buses, I heard, still travelled into the hinterland when snowfall allowed, and by these – and some wary hitch-hiking – I went back into the Kolyma hills.

They had the monotony of the everlasting. They circled the road like echoes or reflections of one another, rounded like old tumuli. Sometimes the wind had dusted their summits to pates of brown rock. The whole land looked unformed, withdrawn into some other geological age. And it was only half-lit. The sun struggled up a quarter of the sky, fell again.

The road I travelled past silent villages had at first connected Magadan for three hundred miles with an archipelago of gold-camps. People still call it the 'Road of Bones'. Thousands of prisoners were hurled into its building at the start, but mud engulfed it, then frost tore it up. One mile of it alone consumed 80,000 wooden beams. By the onset of the first snows in 1932 the convicts were still living in tents and brushwood huts. It was one of the most savage winters in memory. Blizzards raged for weeks on end. Whole camps were frozen alive – prisoners, guards, even dogs. Out of many thousand workers, barely one in a hundred returned to Magadan next spring.

Dalstroy's first chiefs were shot as spies in 1937. Then a purer cruelty set in. The prisoners' fur clothes and boots were exchanged for canvas shoes and wadded jackets, which soon hung in tatters. The intention was now to kill them. Their diet was reduced to famine level: 800 grams of bread, with occasional scraps of salted fish or brined cabbage. They took to consuming animal carcasses, reindeer moss, wheelbarrow grease. Their work-day extended to fourteen hours, their sentences to twenty-five years. Their end was hastened by the setting of unreachable quotas. Work brigades laboured frenziedly to meet them, but their starved bodies could not hold up. As their output fell, their food was reduced in punishment, and they entered a fatal spiral of decline. Every evening and morning lists were read out of those to be executed or those who had already been shot, while the officer dusted the hoarfrost from his papers and after each speech a band of criminals played a little fanfare. The mines broke a man's health after three weeks, and killed him within a few months. Sometimes whole brigades were taken from the work-face and shot out of hand. The criminals among them were appointed overseers, armed with clubs, and murdered the politicals with impunity. (They executed a man, typically, by lifting him up and smashing him to the ground until his already decalcified bones were broken.) But mostly people faded unnoticed into death. Only a few command-ants relished their task, and would empty their revolvers into the paraded workers with shouts of joy. There were camps where nobody survived at all.

You lose your own eyes here, and start to imagine through those of the dead. You have no right to this country. It belongs to them. Is it sometimes beautiful? You cannot say. You only see signposts to atrocious places: Shturmovoi, Urchan, Oimyakon. The camps along the road have been pilfered away. Only a few barracks are being reused as warehouses, or have rotted to heaps ringed by stray concrete stakes. The watch-towers have fallen. Man-made mounds and trenches heave and wrinkle under the snow, the colourless shrubbery.

In the dark my bus stops among the floodlit tenements of Orotukuan: sixty years before, it was a snail-pace interrogation centre, littered with the frozen corpses of those who had waited too long. A girl sells you fruit-juice from an unlit kiosk. Forty miles beyond, a side-valley leads to Elgen, the women's camp where the newcomer Yevgenia Ginzburg joined a herd of robots with brick-red faces, and wept at what she would become. Even the camp overseers disdained to rape them.

At Yagodnoe I ran into a quartet of genial mafia who drove me around town in a Nissan jeep. 'English! Not really? Then why here? Here is shit. Are you doing some kind of business? Then why, why?' It was past midnight and they were hunting prostitutes; but the place looked dead. They found me a bed in a workers' dormitory, paid the porter – 'Russian gift!' – and vanished into the dark.

I woke to a cold dawn and mountains shining under a porcelain sky. It was, yes, bitterly beautiful. In this half-deserted town my arrival had been noticed. Nobody sane came to Yagodnoe. Two local journalists drove me along the Horse river and south to Serpentinka. The road was lacquered with black ice, and the Kolyma tributaries sordid with the hummocks of old waste-heaps which followed them like the detritus of a mole. The vaster hummocks of mountains repeated them in the sky. Abandoned dredgers littered their banks. The convicts had gone forty years before, and prospectors had taken their place. But during the past few years half of these had drifted away, the journalists said. Here and there a gutted settlement overlooked our route, or the shell of a factory or brick kiln.

On a spur above the road snaking down to the river, we came to Serpentinka. Pavlov and Garanin, the new lords of Dalstroy, had built it as a torture and execution centre. It was the black heart of Kolyma. In an overhang beside the isolation cells, two tractors would rev up their engines to drown the shots and screams of execution. In 1938, 26,000 prisoners died here, hundreds by Garanin's own hand. Their bodies were dragged behind its hill on tractor-sledges, or else they were led, alive and blindfolded, to trenches there, and shot in the head. Then, in line with Stalin's occasional policy of liquidating those in state security, Garanin was shot and all the personnel of Serpentinka with him, and the place razed to the ground.

We crunched through its void of snow. Our voices were too loud in its silence. A granite block, bound with barbed wire and a strand of plastic flowers, was engraved to the memory of the 'tens of thousands' murdered by the state. It glistened with ice. Beyond it, a trail of mounds and dead-looking shrubs followed the ghost of a track into nowhere.

You gaze with their dead eyes, and see no hope. Nobody escaped. They called Kolyma 'the Planet', detached from all future, all reality beyond its own. Desperate to escape into hospital, the prisoners injected kerosene under their skin, rubbed acid in their eyelids, hacked off their fingers, feigned madness. But bit by bit they were reduced to savages, famished and broken. They became the animals that the authorities had decreed them to be, so their death left no conscience. They descended into the walking dead, who lingered about camp on depleted rations, then slipped into oblivion. Frail from a characteristic high blood pressure, they longed only to see their families before they died. Their only forced labour was to bury one another. Sometimes nobody knew whose corpses these were. Young men became old within a few months. Their tooth-fillings might yield more gold than they had mined in life. They were tossed into mass graves.

Not far west of where I slept next night is the coldest inhabited place on earth. At Oimyakon a temperature has been recorded of −97.8°F. In far lesser cold, steel splits, tyres explode and larch trees shower sparks at the touch of an axe. As the thermometer drops, your breath freezes into crystals, and tinkles to the ground with a noise they call 'the whispering of the stars'.

Among the native peoples a myth exists that in the extremest cold words themselves freeze and fall to earth. In spring they stir again and start to speak, and suddenly the air fills with out-of-date gossip, unheard jokes, cries of forgotten pain, words of long-disowned love.

The cries that might rise from this earth do not bear thinking on.

In a rare passage of despair, the poet Mandelstam, who died on his way to Kolyma in a transit camp near Vladivostok, imagined his meanings draining away in the deafness of Russia. No future would hear them.

At ten paces, our speech has no sound. . . .

But the words returned – Mandelstam, Shalamov, Ginzburg, Babel: they came back to haunt and undermine the frozen empire, even after those who had spoken them had gone.

As my bus descended before dawn to Magadan, the capital of sorrow, it flooded up in a constellation of lights against the unseen Pacific, and I realised with disgust that it was handsome. Squeezed between sea and hills, its main street dipped and climbed through façades of golden stucco and stone, before it dropped out of sight to the harbour.

After locating a hotel and wrangling about my visa, I marched out into a smarting wind. Everything here was in place, or nearly. The banners in Lenin Square were rasping on their poles, frozen stiff, and Lenin himself (who stood, hands in pockets, giving nothing) stared across with demonic authority to where gold-mining offices had supplanted the Dalstroy building. The tallest edifice in the city – the aborted headquarters of the old Communist

Party – had been stopped in mid-construction ten years before, and gaped behind him. The wind howled through its apertures.

Along the main street the high-pedimented, high-columned offices and tenements looked built to stamp out the earth and its memories for ever, stuccoed with flags and hammers. Alongside, the classical blocks built by Japanese POWs loomed in façades of plastered honey. The whole city core was convict-built. The old telegraph office remained; so did the theatre (now a market) where condemned divas and ballerinas sang and danced for their persecutors.

In those years prisoners who endured to the end would be assigned work in this limbo of Magadan. It was full of strange meetings and deranging memories. The survivors, wrote Ginzburg, had the omniscient look of snakes. And fear remained. They knew that the next political earthquake might see them all rearrested. Nobody trusted, nobody confided. It was overwhelmingly male. The scarcity of women turned wives faithless, men said, and attracted prostitutes. 'Kolyma is the land where the sun is without warmth, the flowers without scent, and the women without hearts.' In the 1980s Magadan was still the divorce capital of Russia.

Now the populace was less than 150,000, and falling. Many workers had come temporarily to earn the 'long rouble' of high pay in eastern Siberia, and were returning west. The mines and fisheries were in decline. In the shifting cold, almost no one was about. The wind was slicing snow off the hills. I followed Transport Road where the columns of prisoners had climbed up from the port. It was grimly ordinary. A few people were clearing snow from their doors. A pack of dogs scavenged in the wastes. To the north, long ridges were pressing on the suburbs, and factory chimneys smoking beyond, as if a steamer was sailing just behind the hills. Below me the circling mountains and promontories of the bay threw a snow-capped palisade over the sea. The water was slate-blue, and so calm that it still showed the passage of a vanished ship.

I was descending the road which prisoners had hewn out round the headland from the quay. Along its crest a few huts threw down rickety stairs. It was shored up with concrete slabs, and the road was rutted concrete. Nobody was on it. Only in my mind they were marching up to meet me.

I dipped my hand in the water beyond its fringe of ice. I felt an odd, transient elation. Everything that had happened here seemed immeasurably past. It could never (could it?) happen again. The shore was littered with iron and cables, burst concrete, old ropes, unhewn stones. A few cargo boats were anchored offshore. Then my head began filling with other ships: the 'death-ships of the Okhost Sea', Sakharov called them, carrying their human cargo of 8,000 or 12,000 slaves caged in their holds. As they passed Japan the hatches were battened and they moved unlit through the night. In 1939 the SS *Indigirka* went to the bottom with her freight trapped inside. In 1933 the SS *Dzhurma* mistimed her sailing and was locked in pack-ice for nine months while her 12,000 prisoners all froze to death, and half the crew went insane.

When ships docked, the sick and the dead were laid together on the quayside where I stood. Yevgenia Ginzburg was one. She was saved by a woman doctor, who nursed her back to life, and who was trying to atone, perhaps, for her husband's atrocities as a police interrogator. Ginzburg understood. In Kolyma, she said, the most unendurable thing was the memory of those you loved.

Perhaps because Fedor was a Russian Jew, he had grown obsessed by the labour camps. His apartment was full of political journals and old *samizdat*. His mirrors hung by string. The kitchen was littered with empty Moldovan wine bottles, and mountaineering and caving equipment blocked the hall. His beard, I think, had grown by default, and the study of persecution, or perhaps something else, touched him with melancholy.

It was he who knew that in this city whose darker past had been casually destroyed, one of the chief transit camps survived as the barracks of security police. 'They abandoned it five months ago. It'll probably be bulldozed soon. Everything gets bulldozed here. Now it's walled up of course.' His soft eyes assessed me. 'But I know a way in.'

So we returned to Transport Road where it dipped over a

stream towards the northern mines. In a silent compound, ringed by cement walls and barbed wire, Fedor had found a crumbling hole. We squeezed through. On the far side, the snow showed no tracks. For a second we stood and stared, covered with cement dust. I wanted time to write down things, to remember. I was the first outsider to see this, he said, and would be the last. But we started furtively to run. Now when I scrutinise my dashed-off notes – their words jagged with cold – the place returns in violent snapshots.

I remember the canteen (we crawled in under barred windows) which prisoners had painted with naive scenes in pastel tints: a dream of rural peace. Its floor sagged in a storm of crashed timber.

I remember the dormitories, and the rooms where the prisoners (I imagined) had been issued their bombazine coats and wadded jackets.

Then I remember Fedor pointing to the three-storeyed block in front. Where a door opened on stone steps, he tugged from his satchel some waders and some helmets strapped with lights, and we lowered outselves into a fetid darkness. Unfrozen water brimmed to our knees. Our words echoed and whispered. 'This was the punishment block.'

We waded down its passageways as down a sewer. I lost count of the iron doors awash with stench, the grilles giving on to blackness. Each dungeon was still fixed with twin wooden plat-forms bound in iron, and might have held forty prisoners. There were twenty such chambers in the basement alone. Their walls were sheathed in ice. Prisoners here, said Fedor (he had known one), used to press the bodies of the dead against the walls to insulate themselves from the cold. In the stone they had scratched weakly, illegibly, with their spoons. 'Ser . . . olenko . . . 1952 . . . Pant . . .' Our lights faded over them. In these hopeless caverns, he said, most people died. His friend had survived because he had been young.

'What had he done?' I asked.

'He didn't know,' Fedor said. 'He lost his memory.'

You lost your memory easily in Kolyma, Shalamov wrote. It

was more expendable than lungs or hands. In fact you did not need it at all.

An hour before dawn I go back into the hills for the last time. A young geologist, Yuri, says he knows the track to Butugychag, and that his twin-axle van can reach there. But it is no place to linger. The native Evenk called it 'the Place where Reindeer Sicken', and their herdsmen sensed something was wrong there. Its earth is filled with radioactive uranium.

The moment we enter the mountains, the snow hits us in a blinding curtain. It swirls like ground-mist over the road, concealing crevices and black ice together, while our engine coughs and roars. Yuri goes quiet as the flakes thicken. The beam of our fog-lamp sucks them towards us down a funnel of silver light. Towards dawn we grind to a halt on a pass, while the blizzard tears the surface from the mountain above us in a howling dust. We wait as a wan morning breaks and Arctic hares shelter against our wheels.

Yuri just says: 'It'll pass.' He has a slow, open face. He never smiles. His yellow hair and moustache, and his lemon skin, are pure Russian. After a while he eases us down into a valley in the breaking dawn, while the falling snow thins and withdraws. Ahead we glimpse distant mountains, no longer rounded but fragile and one-dimensional, like the veins of giant leaves swept against the sky. Slag-heaps are hunched along the river, and sometimes a gold-panners' settlement starts up neat and white-walled, until we see its windows gaping. Beneath us the dead streams make translucent estuaries over the waste.

'This region's emptying. Its workers leave for Magadan.' Yuri is still employed, but there is no work for him, and his salary is ten months in arrears. He does not know what he will do. He is nearly thirty. 'And from Magadan the workers go west.'

Suddenly he tilts off the road on to a half-visible track. In front of us the falling snow sends wavering columns over the mountains. He says: 'This was the worst place, Butugychag. It didn't get worse than this. There were 25,000 prisoners working the mines, politicals and criminals together. They didn't know about radiation. Even the guards didn't know.'

Already we are axle-deep in drifts, butting and plunging as if our chassis were elastic. The tracks of a hunter's Land Rover are filling with snow in front. 'If he can make it, so can we.' Once we crash through the ice of a stream, its released waters slapping at our doors, but we lumber out and up the far bank. 'That's what these machines are made for! Russian roads!'

For ten more miles we blunder in and out of drifts, over the half-wrecked bridges of the miners, along a sunken stream. A flurry of white ptarmigans gets up under our wheels, their black-tipped wings dipping like fighter-planes over the scrub. The tracks of the hunter's Land Rover disappear now, and soon we are climbing into a valley where even the larches thin away. Mountains circle and close it off, dropping their ridges in steep blades out of the white sky. As we go higher, the land becomes scarred and unnatural. The black embrasures of mineheads open in the summits, and cableways stagger high up across the snow-fields, then descend in a relay of broken gibbets to the valley floor. Under the mineheads the waste has tumbled down and powdered the slopes smooth. And the air around us has changed. The snow hangs in a luminous haze, filling the valley with its unearthly shining, and a smeared sun has risen.

To our right, behind a broken barbed-wire fence, the ruin of a three-storey factory rears white walls above the white stream. It was the flotation plant for uranium, Yuri says, dangerous to enter still, where a work-shift could be dead after a few months. He accelerates grimly, and the walls drop behind us. 'Even after they'd left, they died of it.'

A mile later the van flounders against impassable banks, and we walk up through a bright, cold silence. Sometimes the snow surges above our knees. Yuri tramps ahead, indifferent, with his hat tugged down to his neck. I follow in his footsteps, my heart-beat quickening, as if we are entering a cathedral or a morgue. Instead we reach a huddle of administrative buildings in yellow stone. They are all ruined, their roofs caved in, their doors unhinged or rotted away. The window-frames are snow-silvered rectangles of nothing. Steps lead up to a veranda and through a door to a 20-foot drop.

The poet Anatoly Zhigulin, who survived this camp in the 1950s, described brutal maimings, accidents, internecine murders, desperate strikes. A prisoner had no name, no self. He could be addressed only by his number. Some were in chains. They climbed four miles before they reached the mines; and from their camp on the far side of the mountain, a squad of women convicts trudged eight miles every day to carry home cold rations.

The iron frame of the camp gates stands redundant in the debris of its towers. Beneath the snow our feet snag on objects we only guess at, and drag up barbed wire. Rusted machinery pokes above the surface. Beyond, we stumble through the wrecks of barracks and prison cells. In the roofless rooms the guards' benches are still in place, with a range of hooks for their coats. The snow lies on their platform beds in hard, crystalline piles. A pair of boots is discarded by a stove. Everything emits a hand-to-mouth rusticity and squalor. Skeletal iron doors still swing on isolation cells a few feet square. The slots survive where the prisoners' gruel was pushed through, and the barred windows remain intact, and the stove in the guards' sauna.

The air seems thin. But Yuri's cheeks are pink and burnished. He is kicking the snow from around a grid of notched stumps to uncover wood foundations. 'That's where the tents were,' he says. 'That's where they slept.'

It was the same through much of Kolyma. The prisoners lived and died in tents. Despairingly they pressed insulating moss and peat between the twin layers of canvas, sprinkled them with sawdust, and stacked boards outside. Inside was a single cast-iron stove.

And now gently, insistently, the snow is falling. It drifts over the low stumps and covers the buildings with its pale indifference. It floats through the roofless passages, the guard chambers, the rooms of administration, of neglect, of boredom. It fills the valley with a sick translucence.

Yuri goes on kicking at the tent foundations, then looks up at me. 'You know, my grandfather was a village postman, who spent years in the camps for making a joke about Stalin.'

'A joke?'

'Yes. He was in charge of the village telephone, and one day he told somebody in passing: "By the way, Stalin's on the phone to you!" So he ended up in the camps for five years. My parents must have suffered for that.' He presses a wooden slat back with his boot. 'People grew up in their parents' silence.'

We climb to where he remembers the cemetery lay, but it is lost under snow. The opalescent light has intensified over the valley. Around us the trees and shrubs are laden and heavy, as if bearing white fruit. They shiver with tiny wagtails. I pick some dwarf-cedar needles, which prisoners used to boil in the futile hope of deflecting scurvy.

I say: 'Whatever it's like now, things are better than they were then.'

Yuri does not answer at first. Everything with him takes a long time. He has a slight stutter. He says: 'Those were religious times, in a way. People believed things.' He seems to envy that.

So suffering came down from the sky, as natural as rain or hail. There was no one to accuse. No one was near enough, embodied enough. Stalin's empire, like Hitler's Reich, was meant to last through all imaginable time. The past had been reorganised for ever, the future preordained.

I say, not knowing: 'You'll never go back to that.'

Yuri says: 'We're not the same as you in the West. Maybe we're more like you were centuries ago. We're late with our history here. With us, time still goes in circles.'

I don't want to hear this, not here in the heart of darkness. I want him to call this place an atrocious mystery. I want him not to understand it. With his blond moustache and Tartar cheekbones, I have cast him as the quintessential Russian, the litmus test for the future. The mountain air has gone to my head.

But his hand, which was tracing a circle, now tentatively lifts. 'Maybe we spiral a little,' he says, 'a little upwards.' He looks across to where the cableways limp in ghastly procession over the heights. 'I wish my grandfather had lived on. He loved a good joke, and people can joke about anything now. We've still got that. Jokes.'

I clasp his shoulder, but we are too fat in our quilted coats, and my hand slips from him. He smiles for the first time, on a mouthful of discoloured teeth, before turning back along the track.

And on that frozen hillside he starts to sing.

Index